PRIVILEGE

ROSS GREGORY DOUTHAT

PRIVILEGE

Harvard and the Education *of* the Ruling Class

HYPERION   NEW YORK

Copyright © 2005 Ross Gregory Douthat

Library of Congress Cataloging-in-Publication Data

Douthat, Ross Gregory
    Privilege : Harvard and the education of the ruling class / Ross Gregory Douthat.—1st ed.
        p.   cm.
    ISBN 1-4013-0112-6
    1. Harvard University—Students.   2. Douthat, Ross Gregory.
I. Title.

LD2160.D68   2005
378.744'4—dc22

                                        2004052367

FIRST EDITION

10 9 8 7 6 5 4 3 2 1

For My Classmates

Acknowledgments

First and foremost, my father, my mother, and my sister—for everything and then some.

Many, many thanks also to Josh, Alex, Praveen, Allen, Brian, and Tuttle (for all our adventures); Bridge (for friendship and understanding); Sugi (for making it happen) and Sara Jo (for making it more interesting). Also Bronwen, Bolek, Hugh, Roman, Vicky (thesis!), Theresa, Jaime, Steve M., Nirosha, and Tiffany, everyone at the *Atlantic,* and (did you ever doubt it?) Mike.

Deep thanks as well to Rafe, my marvelous agent, for seeing potential, and to Ben and everyone at Hyperion for help bringing it to fruition.

Finally, Abby, without whom the book would never have been begun, and without whom it wouldn't have ended nearly as well as it did.

Contents

The image of Time brought thoughts of mortality:
of human beings, facing outward like the Seasons, moving
hand in hand in intricate measure: stepping slowly,
methodically, sometimes a trifle awkwardly, in evolutions
that take recognizable shape. . . . Classical associations
made me think, too, of days at school, where so many forces,
hitherto unfamiliar, had become in due course
uncompromisingly clear.

—ANTHONY POWELL,
A Question of Upbringing

Meritocracy is a parody of democracy.

—CHRISTOPHER LASCH

PRIVILEGE

Prologue

I T NEVER RAINS ON a Harvard commencement, the myth-makers say, but it rained on ours. The early-June skies had glowered and spat for days, but it was only after the sheriff of Middlesex County bellowed the proceedings open and the band struck up "Ten Thousand Men of Harvard" that the heavens split and the downpour began.

At first, the forty thousand attendees—graduates, parents, grandparents, and guests, overflowing the green sweep of Harvard Yard—opened umbrellas, draped themselves with special commencement editions of *The Harvard Crimson*, and waited patiently for the rain to subside, while the pomp and circumstance continued on the canopied steps of Memorial Church. But as the ceremony wound its way through the various schools, the exodus began: Law students clutching stuffed sharks and Divinity School grads in tinfoil halos scrambled out of their chairs and sloshed their way homeward, trailed by sodden relations and well-wishers.

Only my lot, the undergraduates, the Harvard Class of 2002, stuck it out till the end. *You only graduate from college once,* everyone kept saying, and though many of us were headed for years of further schooling, it seemed like cowardice to abandon the field, leaving our deans and orators pontificating to an empty, rain-swept Yard. So we shivered under newspapers that bled ink across our hands and faces, while our graduation robes, rented for the occasion from the school's Coop, ran pink and purple, streaking neatly pressed shirts and sundresses and clinging coldly to our skin.

Eventually some sensible soul scrambled out and bought a handle of Bacardi, which was passed around, easing our collective hangover, until an air of genial rowdiness held sway. We sent up Bronx cheers for each of the twelve recipients of honorary degrees, whose parade across the stage occupied at least thirty drenching minutes; we hooted madly when Neil Rudenstine, Harvard's ex-president, made an unmemorable appearance; we shouted to one another across the muddy greensward; we fairly roared as the pompous set piece neared its end.

From his perch on the dais, Larry Summers, the current university president, shot dirty looks in our general direction. It was his first commencement, and perhaps our chants and catcalls crossed some nebulous line of preferred graduation conduct. But Summers was dry, bedecked in black and purple, and spilling comfortably out of Harvard's presidential seat, while we were packed sardinelike into rows of folding chairs whose scooped bottoms filled with water whenever we rose to applaud. Also, there would be ten or fifteen or twenty more commencements for him to preside over, most of which would take place amid high-skied June brilliance. This rain-ruined farce was our only one, the sole commencement that our four madcap years had earned, and if we wanted to heckle Daniel Patrick Moynihan ("D.P.! D.P.!" my classmates bellowed), then by God we would.

So we stood and shouted until the ceremony limped to a close and the Reverend Peter Gomes, the university chaplain, mounted the dais to deliver the benediction. Gomes was a rotund, self-consciously pompous figure, a well-regarded biblical scholar and a famously eloquent public speaker. As he leaned up to the microphone, we fell silent, settling back into our seats and bracing ourselves for a final flood of lofty rhetoric.

Gomes surveyed the field for a moment, then grinned mischievously. "God bless you and keep you dry!" he cried, and dismissed us into the rain.

Back at Quincy House, the upperclass residence where I had lived since sophomore year, everything was worse. Quincy is a long brick-and-concrete monstrosity, erected in the 1950s and married uneasily to a neighboring Georgian building, and in its ample shadow a great crowd of parents and siblings and godparents and half-remembered uncles milled, piling their plates with cold cuts and searching for children lost during the walk back from the Yard. A picnic had been scheduled for the Quincy courtyard, but the rain had ruined those plans, and now the long rows of tables stood forlornly in the downpour, shrouded in dripping checkercloth. Some had been overturned by the wind, and the red-and-white cloths carried off into distant corners of the courtyard, where they lay rumpled and forgotten, streaks of crimson marring the greenery.

Within the building, disarray had made a mockery of the careful move-out plans posted weeks in advance on bulletin boards and kiosks. The doors to our rooms stood open, disgorging heaps of furniture that were carted away to cars and vans by parents eager to escape the madhouse. The detritus of college life spilled out in the hallways—microwaves and coffeemakers, bookcases and blenders, sticky, half-finished bottles of rum. A thick, pungent odor filled the air, a strange mixture of beer and sweat, fabric softener and cleaning fluids, with a dash of marijuana. Little sisters lugged laptops, obscure cousins rifled through bags of clothes, fathers and mothers screamed themselves hoarse—and the students, we chosen few for whom this was, ostensibly, one of life's finer moments, exchanged shell-shocked stares or collapsed, sleep-deprived by a week of celebration, on ratty futons and ripe-smelling armchairs.

Through Quincy's rain-streaked windows you could see the endless lines of yuppie cars—Jettas and Audis, Lexus SUVs and Volvo station wagons—fighting their way down the narrow streets of Cambridge. Beyond the campus, the Charles River churned gray and angry; the scullers and sailors stayed safely indoors. Picturesque, postcard-ready Cambridge was vanquished by mud-ridden, rain-spattered New England, and we shivered and peered miserably into the endless cameras that clicked and clattered and whirred, preserving forever the dreary ending of our Harvard education.

But perhaps it was better that we were drenched—that we were baptized by the June downpour, then humbled by the mud and squalor, and embarrassed by the chill, low-rent banquet that Quincy House had prepared for our parents. Commencement's misery killed euphoria and smothered optimism. It reminded us that whatever the speeches and promotional literature might insist, this day was not for good cheer and new beginnings but for endings and sadness and gloom, a day in which the whole of college—all the frantic four years—was being gathered up and put away forever. *We'll never be in college again*, people moaned, falling into each other's arms as Harvard diminished, somehow, into the rain, and then into the past.

I thought at the time, and still think now, that Harvard is a terrible mess of a place—an incubator for an American ruling class that is smug, stratified, self-congratulatory, and intellectually adrift.

But it is also a place that I loved, and the rains fell and I wept along with everyone else.

❖

I had arrived in Cambridge four years earlier with the highest of expectations, clutching an idealized conception of college life that was common—nearly universal, even—among incoming freshmen. Like most newly minted Harvardians, I envisioned college as a magical place, a paradise where the difficulties of my teenage years would be sloughed off and quickly forgotten.

The adolescence I left behind was spent in New Haven, in the shadow of Yale, where my mother had been part of the first class of women. My father was a Stanford graduate, so together my parents had the whole meritocratic pedigree—but they both dropped off the Ivy fast track in fine late-1970s style, bounced around Berkeley for several years, and then migrated east with their newborn son, landing in southern Connecticut half by accident. They both hoped to be writers during these early years of marriage. But my mother was chronically ill with strange and inexplicable allergies by the time I was born, and my father—who had drifted through law school before meeting her—took the Connecticut bar and began to practice law, which he continues to do, successfully and unhappily, to the present day.

So we became superficially bourgeois, taking the form of a thousand similar families: an attorney father, a stay-at-home mother, two kids (my sister, Jeanne, was born when I was nine), and a pair of sturdy Volvos in the driveway. The reality was somewhat different, as my mother's ailments, impervious to conventional medicine, drove us to seek unorthodox cures. We drifted through various diets—first vegetarianism, and then the super-vegan philosophy known as macrobiotics—and alternative medicines, such as homeopathy and acupuncture. My sister was a home birth, delivered by two lesbian midwives and breast-fed until she was two, and neither of us was given the usual round of vaccinations, since my mother was convinced—rightly, I tend to think—that their side effects were worse than the faint risk of whooping cough. In the summers we went to health-food camps in Vermont, where I gagged my way through endless meals of brown rice and seaweed. We were religious wanderers, too, in the strange and ecstatic world of American Pentecostalism, before we finally came to rest, late in my adolescence, in the arms of the Roman Catholic Church.

But superficially, as I said, we were normal, and so I attended a normal upper-middle-class high school in a leafy New Haven suburb. It was called Hamden Hall Country Day, and it was, as its self-conscious name suggests, an aspirant prep school that existed in the long shadow of Choate Rosemary Hall, two towns away. Choate was where the really smart (or really rich) kids went, but my parents deemed it too snobby, so I settled in at Hamden Hall, excelled academically, and cultivated a resentful disdain for my more popular classmates. I was skinny and scholarly, with a concave chest, a romantic streak, and an awful sense of social inferiority. Everyone else seemed to be more athletic, more attractive, and more sexually active than I was, or could ever hope to be.

Looking back, I think Hamden Hall was a good school, and I was far from unhappy there, at least by the standards of American high school misery. But at the time, I wanted nothing more than to get away from the nouveau riche pretensions, the thoughtless prejudices, and the gleaming parentally provided SUVs of my classmates. I wanted to be with more people like my best friend, an equally skinny loudmouth named Michael Barbaro, with whom I read *The New York Times* every day in the library, arguing politics while the inanity of high school swirled around us. We were debate team partners, Mike and I, and we ran the school newspaper and also an underground newspaper that launched anonymous attacks on Hamden Hall's athlete-friendly admissions policy. They weren't quite anonymous enough: One Halloween, the soccer team organized a full-scale egging of Mike's house. But the occasional prank was a small price to pay for our sense of superiority, our smug assurance that we were on our way to somewhere higher and better, somewhere populated exclusively with people like us.

Mike, who loved New Haven, wanted Yale; I wanted Harvard. I had always wanted it, even before I understood what wanting Harvard meant—before the ERBs and the PSATs, the SATs and the SAT IIs, before I realized the earth-shattering importance of *U.S. News & World Report*'s rankings. From my earliest childhood, I associated Harvard not with excellence or achievement but with Boston, which was in turn associated with the ongoing tragedy of the Red Sox, a dolorous saga whose accidents and intrigues dominated my summers deep into adolescence.

As my high school years slouched to an end, though, Harvard shed its old identity as a college offering easy access to Fenway Park and became a beacon of hope to my semi-alienated teenage mind. Once I reached Harvard, I told myself, I would never again have to endure the sneers of the high school jockocracy, the dismissive glances of the in crowd. At Harvard, athleticism and good looks and popularity would count far less than the things that really mattered: native brilliance, and intellectual curiosity, and academic achievement. At Harvard I would be happy. At Harvard I would be cool.

❖

I was right about my happiness, eventually. But Harvard was not what I had expected: It was not a refuge of genius and a sanctuary of intellect. Instead, it was something darker and more complex, more alienating and more interesting. I was educated there, and perhaps even educated well, but what Harvard taught me was not what I thought I had gone there to learn.

As all the world knows, the Iviest of the Ivy League schools boasts tremendously high admission standards, and countless dorks and nerds and grinds from America's high schools are welcomed with open arms. Amid this great welter of intellect, one can easily find students and professors devoted to the ideals of a liberal education, who cultivate the life of the mind and treat Harvard as a scholarly island, a place in the world but not of it, like the monasteries whose power and dignity universities long ago usurped.

But in the wider, institutional culture of Harvard, such academic idealism is regarded as a quaint curiosity at best. It's all very well for the drones and the bookworms and the people who want to be professors themselves, the attitude goes, but for the rest of us, there's no reason to let such noble pursuits get in the way of the *real* business of Harvard, which is understood to be the pursuit of success, and the personal connections from which such success has always flowed. At its crudest, a Harvard education is a four-year scramble to ingratiate oneself—with professors who write recommendations; with employers who offer internships and lucrative post-college positions; and with the pundits and poets and politicians who flock to Harvard to speak and debate and hobnob with students.

In the long run, though, the best connections are forged with one's fellow students, themselves future members of the American elite—if they aren't members already. And most of them are. In spite of all the bright talk about meritocracy, about plucking the best and the brightest from every two-bit high school and one-horse town in America, Harvard students are a wildly privileged lot, culled from the country's upwardly mobile enclaves and blessed with deep, parentally funded pockets. Officially, my alma mater admits anyone who qualifies, so there is a smattering of poor students, of immigrant kids and working-class brainiacs. But the vast majority are the children of urban apartments and leafy suburbs, those blessed with parents who were pushy and involved, who paid for SAT tutors and private schools, who ferried their sons and daughters to soccer games and debate tournaments and flew them around the country, sometimes the world, to shop for the perfect college. Meritocracy is the ideological veneer, but social and economic stratification is the reality.

In a sense, this is nothing new. At the beginning of this century, when the clubby Anglo-Saxon establishment that dominated the West had not yet suffered the fatal shocks of world war and revolution, the university was the intellectual handmaiden to the rising American versions of Rudyard Kipling's cheerfully burdened White Man. In a way, Harvard *was* the establishment, complete with a pedigree stretching back to the Puritan seventeenth century, and an alumni list studded with the republic's Protestant patricians.

On Harvard's campus, reminders of that vanished era are everywhere: in the residential houses, named for Eliot and Lowell, Dunster and Kirkland, with chimneyed roofs and clock towers that seem suited to a sweetly dreaming English college in the days before Verdun and Passchendaele; in the paintings of forbidding, white-haired men in fin de siècle dress that fill the common rooms and lounges; in the inscriptions, on the bridges and over the gates, that offer exhortations redolent with late-Victorian themes of honor and chivalry, patriotism and piety. ENTER TO GROW IN WISDOM, Dexter Gate tells those who pass through, and DEPART TO BETTER SERVE THY COUNTRY AND THY KIND. No one speaks like this anymore—not at Harvard, and rarely in the world. Only the words linger, etched in martial letters that fade gradually with the seasons and the years.

But while the old establishment, with its romantic conception of the world and its comfortable bigotry (there are precious few blacks and Jews and Catholics among the portraits on Harvard's walls), was destroyed, or at least dismissed into the dusty, haunted corridors of anachronism, Harvard has gone through transition into triumph, shedding its outmoded nineteenth-century skin and becoming, in a way, a twenty-first-century university before that century even began.

A popular illusion exists that Harvard, and the elite colleges in general, lack the influence that they possessed in the WASP heyday. This is tied to the conceit, particularly common in conservative circles, that Harvard is out of touch with the American public—that "Harvard Hates America," as the title of one book put it, and that America hates us back.

There is truth in both notions, but they are ultimately beside the point. Harvard's "hard power" may have diminished slightly: The halls of government ring with fewer ex–Ivy League voices than they did in the days of Acheson and Dulles. But the university's "soft power" is greater than ever, extending over the vast web of doctors and diplomats, bankers and filmmakers, journalists and lawyers, that makes up the modern overclass. And the wealth and might of the new American empire is far greater than that of the old American republic, so the power of our elites is exponentially greater as well, and exercised on a global scale.

While Americans may not love their finest, most famous university—indeed, while they may look askance at Harvard graduates and treat us as they would visitors from an alien world—they still want *in,* for themselves or more likely for their children. Promotional literature to the contrary, they do not aspire to be worthy of Harvard because they hope their kids will be well educated or intellectually fulfilled, but because Harvard occupies the most prominent place in the meritocratic imagination, merging a mythology and a grandeur surpassed only by Oxford with an unmatched social cachet. People send their children to Harvard, above all, because they want them to *succeed*—because they want them to be part of the ruling class, and Harvard is the easiest, best-known ticket.

In this sense, most Americans understand the nature of Harvard better than Harvard does itself.

❖

So my famous university taught me, during four eventful undergraduate years, about the nature of the American ruling class, and how to move easily, even effortlessly, within its moneyed, ambitious confines. I entered wide-eyed and naive, expecting to be surrounded by intellectual ferment and immersed in what Matthew Arnold called the "best that has been thought and said." Instead, I was surrounded by privilege and immersed in the scramble for upward mobility, achievement, success for success's sake.

I gained a cultural education, in other words, and perhaps an important one, since the culture of Harvard and the values it inculcates also predominate in places like Princeton and Yale and Stanford . . . in the Ivy League's smaller imitators, Williams and Swarthmore, Amherst and Haverford . . . in the hordes of liberal arts colleges and universities that aspire to Harvardian stature . . . and everywhere that the next generation of American leaders is culled and cultivated. It is a culture that pays lip service to various earnest ideals—like diversity and public service and tolerance—but in point of fact indoctrinates its students in a religion of success, and seduces them, oh so subtly, with the promise that what they have is theirs by right, the right of talent.

Ruling classes have always believed in their own right to rule, but it once was understood—at least by anyone who cared to think seriously about the matter—that their place in the social order was arbitrary, an accident of birth and breeding, rather than a matter of cosmic justice. Ideals of noblesse oblige grew from just this sense:

the knowledge that God (or blind chance) had given the elite much that was not necessarily deserved.

At today's Harvard, much of that knowledge has been wiped away. The modern elite's rule is regarded not as arbitrary but as just and right and true, at least if one follows the logic of meritocracy to its unspoken conclusion. For today's Harvard students, who have passed test after exam and interview upon interview, there is nothing accidental or random about their position in society. They belong exactly where they are—the standardized tests and the college admissions officers have spoken, and their word is final.

So it is that at Harvard, and at similar schools around the country, a privileged class of talented students sits atop the world, flush with pride in their own accomplishments, secure in the knowledge that they rule because they *deserve* to rule, because they are the *best*.

This is their story—and mine.

CHAPTER ONE

The Fall of Straus B-32

E VERYTHING AT HARVARD BEGINS with the Yard. The college itself was founded there in 1636, on an acre lot enclosed by a wooden fence and planted with apple trees, and named College Yard to distinguish it from the cow yards surrounding it. Nearly four centuries later, the campus still begins with the original acre, then radiates outward in a sprawling wheel: the Law School the northern spoke, Radcliffe stretching to the west, the various museums to the east, and the upperclass houses running southward, down to the Charles River and the Business School beyond. And within the hub, within the Yard, every Harvard career has its beginning, in the freshman dorms that face outward on the noise of Cambridge and inward to the grass and the red brick and the quiet, tree-lined paths.

The Yard's main gate, Johnson Gate, is open to automobile traffic only twice a year, for move-in and move-out. We drove through it on the first day—my parents and my sister and I, my stomach tight and my mother near tears and our Volvo station wagon overflowing, and all around us other cars, other families, other students who were probably as frightened as I to have the long-anticipated moment finally upon them.

As we passed into Harvard, the western half of the Yard opened before me—the Old Yard, enclosed by dormitories with ancient New England names, Hollis and Stoughton and Mower and Weld, and by the gray stone bulk of University Hall, where the administrative offices are housed. Behind University Hall, the eastern half lay hidden—the lawns and paths of Tercentenary Theater, the spire of Memorial Church, and the pillared bulk of Widener Library, named for Harry Elkins Widener, Class of 1911, who went down with the *Titanic* in the icy North Atlantic and whose mother (or so legend has it) made her donation on the condition that the university require a swimming test of all its graduates, to prepare them for unforeseen icebergs. And in the midst of everything, staring sightlessly westward at me on that first September day, stood the brown stone statue of John Harvard, a young scholar of Emmanuel College, Cambridge, who came to America in 1637 and died shortly thereafter, but not before bequeathing half of his property and all of his library to the young college, which was pleased enough with the gift to take his name.

A long white tent was pitched beside the statue, staffed with officious upperclassmen who dispensed keys and crucial forms and sent my family and me off in search of my assigned dorm, Straus Hall. Clutching a map of the Yard, we steered through milling crowds of students, many of them ragged and unshaven and toting immense knapsacks, moving in packs and shouting cheerfully to one another. These were graduates of the Freshman Outdoor Program, which annually sends dozens of students on hiking adventures in the Maine woods before school officially begins. Though I hadn't hiked in years, I suddenly wished I had applied for the program, because they all seemed so happy to be here, so comfortable, with none of the fear that I felt, a fear of the new and unfamiliar that threatened to swamp the euphoria of arrival.

The fear was worse when we reached Straus, which turned out

to be close by, in a pocket of the Yard near Johnson Gate, with bed-room windows overlooking the bustle of Harvard Square. It extended first to the strangers who passed me in the stairwells, and then to the names pinned to every doorway—the Rachels and Nicks, the Danforths and Siddarths and Rabias and Nates, the strangers who would be sharing this strange new life with me, and upon whom so much of my happiness would depend.

They weren't strangers for long, mercifully. There were endless introductions in those early hours, endless handshakes on the lawn with my fellow Strausers and their parents, while people passed in a steady stream, carrying computers and suitcases and endless food-stuffs, vats of pretzels and Twizzlers, ramen-noodle twelve-packs and cereal boxes and granola bars, enough to feed an army for a year, or a college student for a week. Amid this turmoil, my three room-mates appeared: Julian Farrell, raised by a Baltimore single mom and the scion of a notable Liberian family fallen on hard times; and two Kentucky boys, Davis Hendricks from Owensboro and Nate Howe, who was from Lexington by way of a senior-year move to Kansas City. We had down-to-earth matters to attend to then, like the mess that quickly filled Straus B-31, our third-floor room, the boxes every-where and the dust swirling dizzily in the sunlight and the only floor space occupied by Davis's snoring, big-bellied father, who had driven fifteen hours overnight from Kentucky and collapsed on our floor to sleep amid the stereo equipment and heaps of clothes and half-unpacked computers.

With all this to cope with, it was nightfall before my fear returned—after dinner in Boston with my family, after twilight came and they hugged me and drove away, and after I went back to Straus and found that Julian and Davis and Nate had all disappeared to dinners and hotels with their parents. Left alone, I spent several long and unhappy hours trying to set up my computer, listening enviously to sounds outside my window, the whoops and shouts and laughter from which I was excluded for the night. *And maybe for all four years,* I thought with horrible self-pity.

But self-pity carried me only as far as ten o'clock, when I mustered the nerve to go across the hall and meet my new neighbors in Straus B-32. They were friendly enough and invited me out with them, and we wandered the campus and explored various minor dorms, laughing at their Alice-in-Wonderland names (Pennypacker! *Wigglesworth!*) and knocking on random doors to introduce ourselves, searching all the while for a party or at least for alcohol and finding nothing, which would be a common freshman experience, though I didn't realize it then. We made dozens of temporary friends that night and then we wandered through Harvard Square, where a Jesus freak was preaching to a crowd of the Square's tattooed, gothed-up runaways, and finally we went back to our dorm and sprawled downstairs on the couches of the posh common area, talking beneath a portrait of Isidore Straus, a Victorian financial wizard who had gone down with the *Titanic*, like poor Harry Elkins Widener.

Later still, long after midnight, I walked out alone and stood in the Yard, beside the statue of John Harvard, while the sprinklers twisted and spat and the dormitories crouched silently around me. Absently, I touched the statue's buckled foot, stroked smooth by endless lines of tourists (some American, most Japanese), remembering a tour guide telling me, a year before, that rubbing the foot is a student lucky charm, an appeal for help from our academic ancestor.

This is a myth: No student has rubbed the foot in years, though many have pissed on it late on winter nights, fulfilling an undergraduate tradition that goes unmentioned by admissions officers and tour guides. But I didn't know that then, any more than I knew that the statue's face and form really belong to some anonymous 1880s undergrad, because by the time it was commissioned, no likeness of John Harvard survived—and perhaps the truth didn't matter anyway, and the statue's gleaming toe did bring me luck that first and only time I touched it. At the very least, it stripped away the last of my fear and let me savor the moment, the thrill of a new beginning amid the sprinklers and the late-night quiet of the Yard.

I'm here, I told myself, reaching for a thought deep enough to suit the moment, coming up empty.

❖

Straus Hall, my freshman home, was a pretty dorm, even if was cramped and sometimes claustrophobic. It had white shutters and green trim and four narrow concrete stairwells whose doors opened onto a tranquil greensward hedged in between our building and Matthews, a taller dormitory with peaked roofs and linoleum hallways. All year people played Frisbee and football on the grass, until it was trampled into mud and the university put up ropes and threw down a bright turquoise lawn-care cream that produced grass in a hurry, before June came, and commencement.

Our rooms, which opened two abreast as the stairs climbed toward the fourth floor—eight rooms per entryway, as the stairwells were called—were originally intended for two people. There were four of us in each one, stuffed into bunkbeds and swimming in one another's clothes, toiletries, and pathologies. They were good rooms, with sealed-off fireplaces and white molding and dark paneling, and large, pleasant windows to let in the sunshine. But they were also tiny, and as the year wound on, the smells and noise and walls closed in on us, and various people flipped out, or broke down, or just developed a sullen, smoldering antagonism toward their roommates and entryway-mates.

Such difficulties prevail at all colleges, where young people of both sexes are crammed together in small rooms, stripped of parental supervision, and informed that this is, somehow, an academic experience. But Harvard offers an extra turn of the screw to its incoming freshmen, since its student body—unlike that of a state school or a smallish liberal arts college—bills itself as being fantastically diverse, almost to the point of absurdity. This is a major source of pride for the university's mandarins, who like to boast that each year's class represents an increasingly perfect cross-section not only of America but of the wider world. Their self-congratulation is justified—or so it seems at first.

Consider the composition of Straus B, the entryway to which I was assigned by the whims of the housing office. True, the first-floor suite was inhabited by hulking, monochromatic jocks who smoked pot and stacked beer cans in their windows until no one could see in, and seldom made the climb to breathe our rarefied, less muscular air. But on the second floor there was a Sri Lankan girl (by way of Texas); a home-schooled Canadian from a windswept rock somewhere off the coast of Prince Edward Island; a Jewish girl from San Francisco; a half-Jewish, half-Catholic girl from Westchester; a white girl from California; a half-Chinese girl from Rhode Island; and a kerchiefed Muslim girl from Florida named Rabia who insisted that the ancient Egyptians were black, that they built the pyramids using levitation, and that "it's not pronounced Muz-lim, Ross, but Moos-lem. *Moos*-lem."

So it was an entertaining group of females, especially when you threw in the pretty, white girl from Maine, the sober Indian girl (by way of Tennessee), and the petite Taiwanese-American girl who lived on the fourth floor—making, for those keeping score, a grand total of two East Asians, two South Asians, a Canadian, two Jews, one African-American, and two Caucasian-Americans.

But Straus B's showcase when it came to dormitory diversity

was unquestionably B-32, the room across the landing from ours, where I had forged my first-night friendships. Pressed together under one low-ceilinged roof were Danforth "Forth" Shelby, the blond, blue-eyed grandson of a cabinet secretary; Nick Patrikis, a brooding Greco-American who resembled a young and slightly heavier Al Pacino, and who decorated his bedroom with vintage propaganda posters from Soviet Russia and photos of bandanna-clad Zapatista rebels; Siddarth Kapoor, a handsome, brilliant, and faintly neurotic Indian whose immigrant parents had settled first in Connecticut, then Columbus, Ohio; and Damian Foster of Montgomery, Alabama, who was southern and black and relatively poor and carried each of the three qualities as chips, or much heavier objects, on his wide and slumping shoulders.

Forth and Nick, Siddarth and Damian: a rich kid schooled at Groton, two children of immigrants, and a great-great-grandson of slaves. The social engineers in the Freshman Dean's Office must have enjoyed putting together that particular slice of Harvard, we joked, and after a while, there was a dollop of bitterness in the laughter.

❖

The remarkable diversity on display in Straus B-32 was the fruit of a decades-old philosophical tension in American higher education. On the one hand there was the 1950s, post–GI Bill notion of pure meritocracy, with the standardized test as its yardstick; on the other there was the 1960s, post–Great Society desire to integrate campuses that had long been enclaves of WASP dominance. Between these two noble concepts fell a shadow, which was the tendency of white applicants—in the '60s and to a lesser extent today—to score higher than minorities on fill-in-the-bubble exams, which ensured that large-scale integration could not be accomplished by color-blind acceptance policies alone.

One solution to this conundrum would have been for colleges to admit that they were abandoning SAT-driven admissions for the logic of affirmative action, which dictated, in LBJ's famous words, that you could not "take a person who, for years, has been hobbled by chains and liberate him, bring him up to the starting line of a race and then say, *you are free to compete with all the others*, and still justly believe that you have been completely fair." But the backlash against affirmative action began almost immediately, and while the anger of the George Wallace multitudes, and later the Reagan Democrats, and later still the Gingrich revolutionaries, posed little threat to the insulated, moneyed liberals who ran higher education, the discomfort of the Supreme Court did.

So it was that Justice Lewis Powell wrote, in the landmark 1977 case *University of California Regents* v. *Bakke,* that "while the goal of achieving a diverse student body is sufficiently compelling to justify consideration of race in admissions decisions under some circumstances," racial quotas are "unnecessary to the achievement of this compelling goal, and therefore invalid under the Equal Protection Clause." With this edict, a new orthodoxy took over college campuses, in which race was to be merely *considered* in admissions decisions, as one of many factors necessary to creating "a diverse student body."

Private schools like Harvard were officially unaffected by the Supreme Court's ruling, and they could have continued defending affirmative action in terms of redress for past discrimination indefinitely. But they didn't, perhaps because it was important to hang together with Ann Arbor and Madison and Berkeley, lest they all hang separately; or perhaps because the parsings of *Bakke,* and two decades later of Justice Powell's intellectual heir Sandra Day O'Connor, were more appealing than the righteous rhetoric of Lyndon Baines

Johnson's epoch. After all, affirmative action *was* reverse discrimination, however you spun it, and no one really wanted to be associated with discrimination. Far better to smooth the rough edges with Powell's argument that "the atmosphere of 'speculation, experiment and creation'—so essential to the quality of higher education—is widely believed to be promoted by a diverse student body. . . . It is not too much to say that the 'nation's future depends upon leaders trained through wide exposure' to the ideas and mores of students as diverse as this Nation of many peoples."

So the age of "diversity" was born, an age in which few colleges have anything so controversial as quotas, but everyone knows that it's easier to be accepted to a top-flight school if you happen to be Latino or black (or Native American or Pacific Islander, probably), and harder to get in if you happen to be white, and harder still if you are one of those annoyingly overachieving Asians or Jews who do so well on standardized tests. The goal, after all, is ethnic balance—or to put it in Bill Clinton's favored language, a campus that "looks like America."

After a while, though, it was not enough for Harvard (or Yale or Penn or Duke or wherever) to look diverse and leave it at that. The logic of *Bakke* was explicit: Considering race as one of "many factors" in admission was permissible only if the point was to make the campus a better educational environment, and that would happen only if the children of Anglo-Saxony rubbed shoulders with the Other somewhere besides in freshman Expository Writing. Unfortunately, the Others showed an unabashed reluctance to serve as educational aids to their Great White Brothers and Sisters, preferring to found specifically ethnic organizations, religious groups, dance troupes, and what have you, in which they rubbed shoulders exclusively with one another. Segregation was back, but it was self-segregation, and thus a much trickier beast to root out.

Since the importance of "group identity" was one of those 1960s mantras that soon hardened into dogma in academia, there was no question of abolishing race and culture-specific extracurricular groups. Instead, there would be social engineering—integration enforced with a velvet fist.

At Harvard, this meant the end of the old system of residential living. Early in the twentieth century, President Charles Norton Eliot had established a house system for upperclass students, modeled after the college system of Oxford and Cambridge. After spending freshman year in the Yard, Harvard students were assigned to one of thirteen upperclass houses, named for famous Harvardians like Adams and Quincy, Lowell and Mather, where they lived for the remainder of their college years. On a large and impersonal campus, one's house was supposed to be a haven, a local community, a place where like-minded scholars bonded in dining halls and common rooms and intramural athletic events, strenuously pursuing the life of the mind together.

It was with this goal in mind that students were allowed to pick their houses, or at least to rank their choices, and join with "blocking groups" of friends who wanted to be placed in the same house. Over time, each house acquired a distinct identity, which allowed the incoming freshmen to easily decide where they would be most likely to fit; the houses, meanwhile, could tailor their resources and traditions to the tastes and habits of their residents. So Mather House and Kirkland House were known as the jock houses and boasted the best weight rooms on campus; Adams House was the artsy house, well known for its theatrical productions and masquerade ball; Quincy was the Asian house; Eliot the blueblood house; Dunster the political house; and so on.

This sort of parochialism would have been bad enough, from the point of view of the apostles of diversity. But there was an extra twist of the knife. In the 1970s, Harvard absorbed its sister school,

Radcliffe, and in the process gained three new upperclass houses—Cabot, Currier, and North, later renamed Pforzheimer after a donor vain enough to like his awful name. These three former Radcliffe dorms were at least a fifteen-minute walk from the rest of campus, and the Radcliffe Quad quickly acquired a reputation as an upperclass ghetto where freshmen dreaded being assigned. Nobody wanted to live there except for Harvard's African-American students, eager to carve out a room of their own in the still-WASPy confines of the college. So the Quad houses—Currier and Cabot especially—acquired their own identity. They were the black houses.

It took nearly two decades of embarrassment over having black students self-segregating themselves into the upperclass ghetto before Harvard finally decided to do away with the old system. In 1995, three years before my arrival on campus, the powers-that-be announced the randomization of the upperclass houses. Freshmen would still be allowed to form blocking groups of up to sixteen friends with whom they wanted to live (the number was later cut to eight, to better accomplish the work of diversity), but henceforth they would have no voice in *where* they would spend the next three years. Instead, each blocking group would be randomly assigned to a house—by an utterly impartial computer program, we were assured. There would be no more jock houses and preppy houses, and certainly no more black houses. Every house would be a perfectly random mosaic of difference in which undergrads could get on with the pressing business of being exposed to "students as diverse as this Nation of many peoples."

Almost everyone objected to the plan. Students hated having their residential choices taken away, while tradition-minded alums and faculty hated the destruction of the house character they had known and loved. But the most vociferous critics of the new liberal-minded policy were minorities, who regarded randomization as a blatant attempt to break up their enclaves and scatter them around campus, where they would better serve the educational purpose for which—or so one might reasonably infer—they had been admitted to Harvard.

All these objections were in vain, however, and the old system of house identity was swept aside forever. Yet in spite of the social engineers, Harvard upperclassmen are still allowed to pick their blocking groups and roommates—and their friends and extracurricular activities—without any interference from the powers-that-be. This leaves plenty of room for self-segregation, and Harvardians take full advantage of it, as a cursory glance around any campus dining hall (filled with all-white, all-Asian, and all-black tables) attests.

Only during freshman year, when roommates and neighbors are assigned based on a scattering of survey questions and the careful whims of the housing office, is the university free to press true diversity upon its unwilling, stubbornly provincial students. Only there does the Powellian laboratory of democracy work full-time, bubbling with the "speculation, experiment and creation" that is ostensibly "promoted by a diverse student body." Only there do the social engineers have free rein.

The result is rooms like Straus B-32, where unsuspecting eighteen-year-olds are packed together in tiny spaces with people vastly different from anyone they have ever known before, relieved of adult supervision, and asked to learn from one another's differences. The nation's future, Justice Powell would say, depends upon such experiments.

❖

So Forth and Siddarth and Nick and Damian all took up residence together, and for a while, against all odds, B-32 seemed united. Early in college, social life depends on preexisting friendships, so Forth's network of boarding school pals merged temporarily with the people Damian knew from Harvard Summer School, and with the crowd of Siddarth's friends from the Freshman Outdoor Program. Everyone was on their best behavior in those early weeks, determined to transform new roommates into the instant bosom friends that college is supposed to provide.

Damian and Forth in particular were constantly together, going out for pizza and having long political discussions during which Damian spilled out a stark, unhappy view of America as seen from the poorer precincts of Alabama, and Forth marveled at how much he was learning from his newfound friend. They even went to parties together: Forth in khakis and Brooks Brothers shirts, his fair hair swept back by the September wind, and Damian alongside, often all in black, his gaze swinging suspiciously across the Harvard landscape.

But it wasn't just Forth and Damian—they were *all* tight-knit, it seemed, and after that first night I often felt excluded, envying their easy friendships and the aura of cool that emanated from Straus B-32's surprising camaraderie. Among its four inhabitants, with their myriad connections and networks of friends, B-32 always seemed to know where the party was and where the popular people were congregating, which was highly prized information during those early weeks. My roommates and I, by contrast, were decidedly clueless, so we sat in our room night after night, puttering online and arranging furniture, thinking wistfully of the excitement we were missing.

Eventually, though, as we all became friendlier, the connections and social energy of their room came to benefit the entire entryway. I went out with the B-32ers more often, as did my roommates and the girls downstairs, and soon the social life of Straus B was revolving around their room. These were glory days for Nick, who had be-

come the domestic god of B-32, where he held sway with an accom-
modating spirit, organizing furniture and bedrooms, and seizing any
opportunity to showcase his much cultivated Mediterranean cooking
skills. It was Nick who took the lead in organizing an early, illegal
party in their cramped common room, where Damian did the music
and partygoers drank and danced and kept a weather eye out for
spoilsport authority figures.

That party, sweaty and cramped and kept afloat by cheap Cos-
sack vodka, was filled by a rare, never-to-be-repeated blend of Harvard people. There were the entryway kids—my roommates and me,
and the girls from upstairs and down. There were preppies in plaid
and oxford cloth, friends of Forth's from the Groton School, which
had been churning out Harvard men since the time of Roosevelt,
and a few of the bottle-blond, pinched-looking girls who always
seemed to flock around them. There were Damian's friends, and Siddarth's, and there was even a parade of people from Boston College,
ruddy Irish kids who had gone to high school in an all-boys' Catholic
academy with Nick, and who had crossed the river with however
many BC girls they could lay hands on, in search of the Harvard fun
that Nick had happily promised them.

College parties, I later learned, are stinking, sodden affairs in the
best of circumstances, thick with sweat and bad cologne and worse
beer, with the same six songs of the moment blasting from the ceiling and an awful air of heavily made-up desperation clinging to the
people in attendance. Within a year, I was tired of them, tired of
clawing through the crowds in search of warm beer and wretched
screwdrivers, tired of gyrating and grinding and generally pretending to have fun, tired of staggering home on a Saturday night having
searched in vain for a good time.

But all of this was still in the future during that first party, in
Straus B-32 before the fall, and so we danced and drank and sweated,
black and white, WASP and ethnic, crowded together until the walls

shook and the floor turned sticky. There was even some comic-opera drama, when one of the uglier BC girls hauled Nick into a back room and tried to make out with him, only to have Siddarth break in and drunkenly rescue his roommate from a premature deflowering, a feat that quickly became the talk of the entryway.

Afterward, well past midnight, we made a pass at cleaning up, then sat around on beanbag chairs and futons, watching *Austin Powers* and feeling gloriously cool. The very next week, the kids in the entryway next door—Straus C—tried to duplicate our feat and got caught and hauled in front of the freshman dean for underage drinking. And we felt cooler still.

So for that first month, as classes began and autumn settled in, Straus B was a wonderful, tightly knit mosaic of difference—a Harvard administrator's dream.

Then Winston appeared.

His full name, which he inevitably used when introducing himself, was Winston Bell Horn III—not Bellhorn as I erroneously assumed for many months—and he was a mountainous human being, as wide as he was tall, with a gigantic moon face crowning his six-foot-five frame. When he smiled, which was often, his face resembled a benevolent jack-o'-lantern, an effect accentuated by the immense gap that split his two front teeth.

It was a weekend night when I first met him, early in the year, and I was coming back from a typically fruitless search for alcohol, girls, and fun. It was probably Nate and me clambering up the stairs, reaching our landing, and finding it occupied by a huge black man in a crimson baseball cap emblazoned with our school's "H," and a crimson warm-up jacket with "Harvard Law School" printed in capital letters across the back.

"Hello," he announced in a booming singsong. "I am Winston Bell Horn the Third. I am *very* pleased to meet you."

We shook hands warily, and then Siddarth appeared, and Forth, and they explained that Winston went to the Law School, that he had taken summer-school classes with Damian, and that he was twenty-seven years old and more than willing to help us acquire what every eighteen-year-old wants—illicit alcohol.

"In fact," Winston boomed, "I brought you some tonight," and he dipped into a pocket and brought out a handful of miniature plastic bottles—Fleischmann's vodka, if I remember right—which he poured, like doubloons, into our eager hands.

He was, we were told, a former football player (this I could believe) and a graduate of the University of Alabama, where he had played for the practice squad but never cracked the starting team. He hailed from backcountry Georgia and had worked his way up from a sharecropper background to reach Harvard Law, leaving him—he insisted—with a deep-seated contempt for poor blacks who went looking for handouts from white people. So strong was his distaste for welfare and affirmative action that he was actually that great sign of contradiction: a black Republican.

That, at least, was what he told Forth later on that first night. Forth, who then called himself a Democrat but was already drifting rightward, lapped it up. They talked for a long time, with Winston occupying a buckling corner of our futon, and our new law-student friend peddled a straight reactionary line, explaining to a bemused Forth, *You know, I'm black, but I like the KKK. They're just a bunch of real nice boys. It's like a social club—they aren't really racist at all anymore. In Georgia, white and black people get along much better than in the North, anyway.*

Then he showed us his pager, which whistled "Dixie" whenever he received a phone call.

"He's an amazing character," Forth said to me late that night. "Amazing . . . like something out of Faulkner. I hope he comes back. He really had a lot of interesting things to say about life in the

South. It's amazing how wrong some people have got things, don't you think?" He paused. "But God, that stuff he said about the KKK is a little much, isn't it? And that pager—whew."

Winston did come back. I saw him a week later waiting at the door of our entryway for someone to let him in—only students with swipe cards could access the stairwell—his hands laden with plastic bags from Au Bon Pain.

"I brought you all a present," he said, beaming, following me upstairs and then into my room as if he had been coming there for years—as if it were *his* room, I thought, darting a glance across the hall, where the door to Straus B-32 was conspicuously closed.

"I don't think Damian's around," I told him.

He dipped into one of the bags and produced a handful of gigantic, gleaming croissants, all sticky-sweet with hardening syrup. "These are for you, Ross," he told me, his eyebrows dancing with the glee that I later realized was a permanent mood for him. "For all you guys . . . I used to work at ABP, and I know a guy. Every day they make these fresh, so the ones they don't finish, they leave out for the homeless. So I just stop by, and my friend lets me take some." He paused, seeming to consider the matter, then smiled anew. "So I bring them to you guys."

"That's really nice of you, Winston," I told him.

"No, no—we're all going to be great friends here at Harvard. So this is what friends do—give each other presents."

He continued to give them, intermittently, for weeks after that. Again and again he would appear at our door, laden with buns and cakes at first, then cheap plastic bottles of alcohol, then stacks of videos culled from the sale racks at some unknown department store. There was pornography, too, in spite of Forth's vocal protestations—glossy low-rent magazines, *Hustler* and *Swank* and seedier stuff, and films where grainy lesbians panted after potbellied men—until the room across the hall fairly swam with it, spilling out of the drawers where it was stuffed whenever the girls came up to visit. There seemed to be no limit to Winston's largesse.

It was after his third or fourth visit—each one tended to conclude with him sprawled out, snoring, on B-32's beanbag chair, because it was too far to walk back to his apartment—that we began to notice the constancy of his wardrobe. He dressed entirely in Harvard apparel, day in and day out: Harvard hats and Harvard jackets worn with Harvard sweatpants and over Harvard sweatshirts, which on warmer days gave way to Harvard athletic shorts and Harvard T-shirts. If the university had manufactured socks and shoes, he would have worn those, too.

His wardrobe must have caused the confusion that first day, when we all thought Winston was a student at the Law School. Forth and Siddarth were sure that either Winston or Damian had told them so—but no, it couldn't be, it must have been the jacket he was wearing, because after a few weeks, word spread that Winston was an undergrad, a transfer from Alabama, and he was taking a semester off. Or maybe he hadn't even started Harvard yet, and he was just easing himself into Cambridge living, working as a bouncer at a Boston bar, before starting classes in the spring. Or something like that.

It was at this point that I floated a theory about Winston. I suggested maybe he was a con artist, that he was buying his way into our lives with his baguettes and his porn, and that we would all wake up one day and find our computers and expensive electronic equipment cleaned out. I was proud of my theory—it added spice to our lives and made me feel worldly-wise and cynical. It also gave me a reason to complain about Winston's presence without admitting that he intimidated the hell out of me.

Nobody else was buying it.

"Well, there's something *off* about him," Julian allowed during one late-night bull session. "But he's just too innocent—he's got a Forrest Gump quality. He's not smart enough to be a con man."

It was hard to argue with that sentiment. Winston might have been accepted to Harvard and draped himself in crimson apparel, but he seemed more blissful naïf than hardscrabble academic achiever. He was fascinated—more so than even we freshmen were—with the freedom of early college life, and with all its attendant excesses. Staying up until ridiculous hours watching second-rate movies, drinking heavily, stuffing himself with sweets and junk food, and poring gleefully over pictures of naked women: These activities kept him in a constant state of giddy enthusiasm.

"Look at this—look at this," he would shout, his eyes popping as he burst into our common room, and we would be dragged across the hall to see yet another smorgasbord of leftover goodies or the latest bizarre pornographic delight. There was, for example, a *Penthouse* poster that seemed to show a photograph of Bill Clinton's face, until you peered at it closely and his cheeks and nose and hair resolved into hundreds of tiny photographs of frolicking lesbians. Then there was the gigantic peach-and-orange sofa bed that Winston tracked down through some mysterious suburban source and dragged up the stairs to fill the empty floor space in the middle of B-32.

"It was *free*," he boomed, as if it were the most remarkable thing in the world.

And perhaps it was.

Then, unexpectedly, it was November, and events began to conspire against the happy life of Straus B.

It started when Forth and his prep-school friends began going out every night to bars while Damian and Nick and Siddarth were left behind to nurse cheap vodka in their room. The latter two claimed that they would have the necessary fake IDs soon enough (although it would be two years before they did), but Damian took a different tack. He had always maintained a blustery contempt for drinking, which he complained was typical of white people, especially *northern* white people. Whenever we were at a party that he didn't find fun—which was often in those early weeks—he would declaim loudly that this was such a *white-people party,* that black people didn't need alcohol to loosen up and have a good time, and that there was nothing more ridiculous than a bunch of buttoned-up guys downing Jell-O shots to muster the nerve to hit on similarly uptight women.

Once Forth began barhopping, though, Damian's ire narrowed its focus. Suddenly, instead of complaining about *white people,* Damian would complain about *Groton.*

"It's not like the other prep schools," he would tell us at lunch and dinner in Annenberg Hall, the cathedral-like space where Harvard freshmen eat. "I went to summer school at Andover once, and the people there were nothing like these kids, these friends of Forth's . . . they weren't so stuck up, so pretentious. Groton feels like an all-boys' school, even though it isn't. Can you even imagine a Groton *girl?*"

There was a glimmer of truth in what he said. I liked Forth, but when you put him together with his high school friends, a strange and disconcerting synergy emerged, and you were conscious of their unity, their shared world, and your outsider status. It wasn't that they were unfriendly, exactly; other people complained that they were arrogant and aloof, but that wasn't it. It was more of a sense that they had far more in common with one another than with anyone else, and that you moved within their social world on sufferance only—that only they really belonged there.

So it was easy to make fun of Groton, and God knows we all did. "Finally I found it, the Groton connection," people in our entryway would joke, watching Forth troop out to the bars with people like Tyler Sheridan, whose stepfather had founded Staples, or Reardon Leary, whose unkempt WASP hair never seemed to encounter a brush.

We laughed at them, but we envied them as well. As they vanished night after night to drink and carouse and stumble home late from Harvard Square's bars, we could sense the brief harmony of the early fall disappearing. Or at least *I* could sense it, even though Forth always insisted that I should get a fake ID and come out with them. I could have, I suppose—indeed, any of us could have—though how I would have afforded the bar tabs is another question. But I never worked up the nerve to acquire an ID, and after a while Forth stopped asking, and the stratification of B-32 hardened and festered.

In most of us, it festered quietly, and I suppose that plenty of people in Straus B weren't sufficiently shallow to even care that Forth was climbing Harvard's social ladder while we were stuck below. For Damian, though, it became an obsession, as if everything that he despised and feared about northern life, or white life, or Harvard life, had been distilled into a hatred of one particular New England prep school. Under the weight of this animus, his fast-forged friendship with Forth began to buckle.

Then matters grew worse. Damian had become infatuated with Savina, the sober, quietly intelligent South Asian girl who lived upstairs. He was in love with her, he claimed, practically at first sight—a necessity, perhaps, since they hardly ever spoke and certainly never became friends in any meaningful way. Nevertheless, he was convinced that in her, he had found the *one* person who could make him happy.

Such unrequited freshman-year love was a mistake that many of us made, and Savina did her best to let Damian down easily. But then, late in November, she began dating my roommate Julian.

For Damian, this was the ultimate betrayal. Not only had his one true love forsaken him, she had chosen to date the only other black man in the entryway. Up till then, Julian had been his friend, his "brother" amid the alien northern whites—though it was always an imperfect brotherhood, because Julian was private-school-educated and generally more comfortable with the aspects of elite culture that Damian found so disconcerting. Now, though, Julian became his mortal enemy, and while Damian's antipathy toward Forth and Groton had found willing listeners in Straus B, his hatred of Julian and his obsession with Savina began to alienate him from the rest of us. Over the autumn weeks, he became a baleful figure, haunting the entryway and stalking across campus beneath a perpetual cloud. At night he took to walking along the Charles River, walking for miles, I learned when I accompanied him one evening, his shoulders hunched and his warm-up clothes blending into the dark.

"To be stabbed in the back like that," he raged to me. "How could he do that? How could he? In the South, this wouldn't happen. People are different up here, Ross. The weather's different, the people are different."

And then, "I'll never find anyone else. I never found anyone in high school. There were lots of girls who wanted to date me because my father was a minister. They always said, 'Damian, let me be your girlfriend.' Whenever I went to dances, they always played 'Son of a Preacher Man' for me—drove me nuts. Then I came here, and what are the odds? What are the odds that I would find the perfect woman right upstairs from me, and that she wouldn't want me? It's like God's mocking me."

He talked about suicide. He talked about throwing himself off one of the river bridges. He talked about God—did I believe in God? He did—but how could a good God let people suffer? That was always the problem, but he hadn't understood it till now. When atheists talked about suffering, and how it showed that God couldn't be real, he hadn't understood it, but now he did.

"He's mocking me," he said again and again.

Meanwhile, the fabric of B-32 continued to fray. With all the competing personalities and ideologies, there had been political arguments in the entryway from the beginning. As autumn sank into winter, these debates slowly transformed from friendly bullshit sessions into verbal pissing matches in which people screamed themselves hoarse over the consequences of British imperialism, or the fate of the welfare state, or the comparative evil of Stalin and Hitler. The arguments tended to split right-left, usually pitting me and Forth against Nick and Damian, with Siddarth and my own, less combative roommates pleading helplessly for a middle ground. And while Nick and I managed to remain friends amid the carnage, what remained of Forth's friendship with Damian was eroded by Christmas.

They went round and round a hundred times on every conceivable topic, and it always seemed to come back to the relationship between black people and white people—between Africa and Europe—between the West and the rest—between what whites owed to blacks (Damian's case) and what everyone else owed to Europe (Forth's position). Below the surface, though, was an even more fundamental divide that made their arguments a nightmarish tangle. Forth was an intellectual Catholic, a reader of philosophy, a devotee of rigor and logic and cold-blooded reason, and his prep-school education had armed him with an arsenal of pertinent facts to be dropped at will into any argument. He debated clinically and confidently, marshaling arguments with tidy precision, whereas for Damian, an argument seemed less a test of logic than a test of wills. Perhaps it had to be so for him to have any chance, for while Damian was quick-witted and persuasive, his own education had left him ill prepared to take on Forth's vast store of knowledge. So he met his roommate's precision with bluster and bombast and the rhetoric of personal experience, which he always insisted trumped whatever arguments his roommate could muster.

"That's true!" Forth would plead. "Can't you see it?"

"No," Damian would retort, "that's what's true for *you*."

So Forth argued and Damian preached, and their ideological positions slowly swung away from each other, hardening as they went. In the fall, Forth had described himself as a Moynihan Democrat, while Damian had been known to remark that were it not for affirmative action, he would likely vote Republican. By midwinter, after twenty too many arguments about slave reparations, imperialism, police brutality, and similarly high-voltage topics, Forth had flowered from an incipient conservative into a full-throated man of the right, while Damian had developed a withering contempt for what he saw as the elitist and racist underpinnings of Forth's political theories.

Even so, they might have come, like so many roommates, to an uneasy truce, their debating fires banked by the knowledge that in five months or so, they would go their separate ways. But Damian was lonely, and his rages and moodiness often alienated even Siddarth and Nick, who clearly wanted to side with him against Forth. Damian must have sensed that he was losing them, and that soon he would have no friends in Straus B. It was at this point that he started hanging out more with his summer-school pals and joining student groups, like the Black Men's Forum and Kuumba, Harvard's famous gospel a cappella choir.

It was also at this point that Winston—with what seemed to be Damian's enthusiastic blessing—took up semi-permanent residence in Straus B.

In the fall he came by every week or so, but around Christmastime these visits picked up, and by midwinter hardly an evening went by without an appearance—which usually extended into the wee hours of the morning and concluded with him spending the night. Winston never seemed to have any qualms about presuming on our hospitality, even those of us who didn't live in B-32. At some point he discovered the phone number to my room, which spared him having to wait outside for someone to happen along on those nights when Damian wasn't home. I came to dread his calls. The phone would ring in our room, and I would pick up to hear the deep cheerful roll of his voice: "Uh, no one answers in Damian's room . . . can you guys come down and let me in?" And what could I—or any of us—do? If we didn't let him in, someone else would eventually. I was afraid of him and always wanted him gone as soon as he appeared, yet somehow I became used to going downstairs and opening the door to find Winston bouncing giddily on his heels just outside.

The gifts continued; indeed, his generosity spilled over from the confines of B-32 to include the entryway's girls. He bought them posters and stuffed animals, and when one girl celebrated a birthday, he presented her with a pair of gigantic, fluffy pink bunny slippers. Often they shooed him out of their room, insisting that he was disturbing their work, and from then on he liked to pound on their door as he climbed the stairs, shouting "Do your work!" when they opened up, then exploding in thunderous laughter. Sometimes he would even invite them up to watch pornography with him, although only Gabby, the artsy, homeschooled Canadian girl who hung out with cross-dressers and dated a gothish townie, ever took him up on the offer.

It all sounds creepy, and it was, but there was still something innocent about him. Even the porn watching was less perverse than naive. He liked watching naked people simulating sex, and he couldn't imagine anyone else not liking it, even if that someone else was a woman. I remember an appalled Siddarth trying desperately to explain to Winston why one just *couldn't* invite girls up to watch seedy sex tapes, and Winston grinning beatifically and nodding, clearly not following a word.

He was always full of big plans, too, dreams and schemes and bizarre angles. He scanned business magazines and stock pages religiously, and always talked about his investments—or the investments that he would have once he graduated from Harvard and cobbled together some cash. One night he announced that he was going to teach himself Arabic, for reasons that escape me now, and he proceeded to buy the books and spend long afternoons in B-32 painstakingly copying the strange, curving letters onto blank paper. (That fancy lasted about a week, and then the sheets of scrawlings joined the room's steadily growing mounds of trash.) But I think the scope of his ambitions was best expressed near the end of the year, when he wrote a long letter to Siddarth proposing that they found a club, or a secret society, through which they could achieve great wealth and unlimited power—suggesting that at the very least, Winston understood why people went to Harvard.

Gradually, as Winston's presence overwhelmed the room, B-32 was transformed into a wasteland. The trash piled up inexorably, filling bag after bag and then, when no one could be bothered to take it out, spilling over and conquering half the floor. A beanbag chair, mauled and leaking, lay half buried under garbage; posters hung slack from the walls, and heaps of old food—the remnants of Winston's Au Bon Pain raids—were piled, stinking, in the corners. The bathroom smelled fetid, and a horrible odor emanated from somewhere near the refrigerator. (It wasn't until the end of the year that they hauled out the fridge and discovered a four-month-old chicken rotting underneath.) In the middle of the room sprawled the hideous oversize sofa, usually with Winston himself lying in state across it.

As spring inched toward Cambridge, Siddarth decided to rush one of Harvard's underground frats, so he was rarely in the room.

When he had to be home, he sat at his desk in the room's far corner, buried in work and wearing headphones. Nick moved his own desk into the narrow bedroom that he shared with Damian, and worked with the door safely shut; the rest of his time was spent in our room, away from the mounting chaos.

Forth chose exile over torment. He still slept in B-32, and occasionally I saw him in his bedroom, sitting at the window that looked out over Harvard Square, typing furiously on his laptop. But he lived elsewhere, in the libraries and the lecture halls and the rooms of his Groton friends. His home increasingly belonged to Winston.

By the end of winter, Damian's friend—and ours, in theory— was there almost every single night. He ate in B-32, he slept there, and he showered in the narrow, foul-smelling bathroom. Sometimes I would cross the hall early in the morning and find B-32 empty save for Winston, just emerging from the shower, with a towel hanging napkinlike around his massive waist. He would beam and shake his head: *Nobody here but me, Ross.*

Eventually the truth came out. It was late on a Saturday night, and I was working my way through *Godfather III,* when Nick came in and sat down beside me.

"He's homeless," Nick said.

"Who's homeless?" I asked. But I already knew.

"Winston," he said. "He's *homeless.* He doesn't have an apartment."

"You mean he left his apartment? He moved out?"

"No," Nick said. "I mean he never had one."

"But he said . . ."

"Yep, *he said.* He said, he said . . . but he was lying, apparently."

"Where has he been sleeping? He's only been sleeping here for—"

"Yeah, I know. He's been sleeping during the day. Apparently he sleeps in the common areas around campus. In Loker Commons, in the libraries, you name it. He's been showering in the Y—sleeping there, too. And there are other people he knows, people he stays with, I guess. But sometimes he's slept outside, I think."

"So he's not a student? He's not going to be enrolled here?"

"Are you kidding?" Nick shook his head. "Now he claims he's taking expository writing classes at the Extension School."

"How is he paying for it?"

"Oh, no, he has a job," Nick said. "That part is true—he worked at ABP in the fall, and then as a bouncer, and now at a hotel. I mean, he *must*. He keeps coming up with money somehow. And Damian says he has a job. He says he's been to the hotel where he works."

"Oh."

"Right. So he has a job, and he just spends all the money on alcohol and porn and food. And he sleeps here." Nick looked at me sorrowfully. "What the fuck, Ross? What did I do to deserve this?"

There was no good answer, so I just laughed. "You decided to go to Harvard, didn't you?"

In the end, Nick came to terms with it remarkably well. Instead of being outraged, he decided that it was his duty to get Winston on his feet, to help him find an apartment, start saving money, and so forth. If we didn't help him, nobody would, Nick declared, and with that, he began giving Winston miniature classes in adult life.

I would come into their room late at night, when everyone else was toiling over problem sets and papers, to find Nick hunched over his computer, typing up a budget for his permanent houseguest. Or they would be sitting together on the sofa, amid the heaps of trash, and Nick would be explaining to Winston how if he just saved for two months, he could afford *this* apartment (a jab at the classifieds), and how he just needed to stop spending so much money on junk food, and movies, and pornography.

"Did you look for a place this week?" Nick would ask, and Winston would dissemble and say that he had, but then he couldn't say where or when, and finally he would unhappily admit that he was lying, and in fact he hadn't been looking at all.

I thought it was an absurd, futile effort. I told Nick that he was wasting his time, that it wasn't his responsibility. I told him that we needed to make Winston move out—that Nick should talk to the entryway's grad student proctor, Sam Finch, or to some other administrator—that it was stupid, not to mention extremely dangerous, to allow a homeless person to live in his room. We didn't know anything about Winston, I argued, and anything that we thought we knew was probably just another lie.

Nick retorted that most of what we knew about Winston was true. He *was* from Georgia, he *was* from a poor background, he *had* come to the Northeast in order to go to Harvard. He wasn't a liar, exactly; he was too simple to understand that he couldn't enroll in our Harvard, and too naive to see the difference between taking a class at the Extension School and actually attending the college. Coming to Harvard, in this sense, was of a piece with learning Arabic or building up a stock portfolio or founding a secret society.

"He just told us what we wanted to hear," Nick insisted. Besides, he added, wasn't I supposed to be a Catholic? Where was my sense of charity? Winston was harmless—he needed to be helped, not to be turned out into the street.

I couldn't see him like that, though I sometimes tried. I no longer seriously regarded him as a possible con man—he was too simple for that, too genuine. If Winston was taking advantage of us, his methods were totally guileless; he was an idiot savant grifter, at worst. But he still frightened me, in an unpleasant and visceral way, and sharing space with him inspired a constant tension and an equally constant desire to remove myself—or better, him—from the premises. I hated the imposition, the anxiety and discomfort, and the sense that Straus B was somehow not my home; that Winston could shoulder his way in at any moment, oozing unease from the folds of his Harvard parka. And I could never bring myself to care a whit about his eventual fate.

So Winston's presence, then, gave me a dose of self-knowledge. Before that year I thought I was charitable, always willing to help friends in need, happy to drop money in proffered cups, disgusted by naked greed and ambition. Perhaps I was, if charity means an easy, self-indulgent mediocrity of spirit in which one loves friends, smiles at enemies, and assuages the pangs of guilt inspired by the truly unfortunate. But if it means laboring to help those who need it most—the lost and the innocent, and yes, the stupid—even when the labor is hard and possibly fruitless, and even when you get nothing for your pains except a stack of smutty videos . . . well, then charity might be something that I have yet to acquire.

He's not our responsibility, I said again and again, and it was true. But that wasn't the point.

Unsurprisingly, people in Straus B were more likely to back my guilty realism than Nick's charity. Siddarth accepted the news of Winston's homelessness with a strange equanimity, as if nothing could surprise him after six months in B-32, but everyone else was appalled, and there was general agreement in the entryway that our permanent houseguest needed to be expelled. The girls, who already lived in vague, unsettled fear of Winston, were particularly vociferous on this count.

Yet nobody was willing to do anything about it. No one was willing to go to our proctor, or to some higher-up administrator, without first talking to Damian about it, and no one wanted to assume that responsibility. The girls were alienated from Damian by this point, and my roommates and I were tainted by our association with the hated Julian—and I, in particular, by my continuing friendship with Forth, and by my own conservatism. (I began writing for *The Harvard Salient,* the campus's conservative rag, during the spring, and shortly thereafter Damian added the *Salient* to his expanding list of rhetorical targets.) Then, too, there was the faint fear inspired by Winston himself, who was friendly and eager to please, but also loud, peculiar, pushy, huge, tremendously strong, and (did I mention this?) *homeless*. Everyone wanted him gone, but to be the one to push him out seemed fraught with peril.

The irony was that Damian might have been willing to listen to us at that point. For a little while, there was a weary, resigned tone to his voice when he talked about Winston, particularly about Nick's attempts at social work—a tone that made me hope Damian would do what the rest of us were too cowardly to suggest.

But he didn't. And then, finally, Forth got fed up.

It was perfectly understandable. He was living with a roommate who regularly abused him, his friends, and his high school, with increasing disregard for whether Forth was within earshot. That same roommate hosted a generous, friendly, but truly bizarre friend in their room—a friend who had essentially turned their common room into his private suite, sending Forth into a self-imposed exile. And neither Winston nor Damian was exactly small, neither could be ignored, or tuned out, or dealt with in any fashion that didn't involve fleeing the room.

The breaking point was the spring semester's midterms, a time when Forth had to be in the room, to study and to use the Internet. So he approached his roommates and asked if it was possible for Winston to spend a little less time in B-32. Siddarth and Nick referred him to Damian, and while Damian might have been tired of Winston, he detested Forth. So there was no compromise, no agreement, and Forth took the argument upstairs to our proctor, Sam Finch.

Sam was a tremendously nice guy. He was chubby and bespectacled, with two orange cats and an equally chubby fiancée, and he organized fabulous study breaks, with soda and candy and sticky Rice Krispie treats. But the problem of B-32 would have defeated a master diplomat, and Sam Finch, to put it mildly, was no Kissinger.

The simplest thing to do, and probably the right thing, would have been to insist that Straus B was not a way station for vagrants, and to order Damian to limit his peculiar friend's visits. But Damian was bellicose and emotionally unstable, and he and Winston together made an immovable object against which a more unstoppable force than Sam might well have spent itself in vain. Besides, Sam's job, as he saw it, was to smooth feathers, not ruffle them, and to make everybody happy, at least to the best of his abilities. So it was decided that there should be a discussion in which everyone in the room could speak his piece about the problem of Winston Bell Horn.

The summit of Straus B-32 was held at eight-thirty in the morning, to accommodate Sam's class schedule at the Medical School, and that is an ungodly hour by any collegiate standard. Somehow, while the rest of us slept, the four boys dragged themselves out of bed and stumbled upstairs to Sam's room. Once there—or so we heard later, in overlapping accounts from Forth and Nick and Siddarth (but not from Damian, who wasn't talking)—they arrayed themselves around a table with Sam, who said good morning and then announced that since it was Forth whose complaints had provoked this meeting, he should speak first.

Forth was ready. He stood up and said briefly that while Damian had a right to invite anyone he wanted to visit, or even to spend the night occasionally, Straus B-32 was simply too small a room to have a fifth person there constantly, especially one who occupied so much space, figuratively and actually. Forth added that he was especially concerned by Winston's homelessness, and by his seeming presumption that he could make B-32—its couch and bathroom and so on— his rent-free apartment. He concluded by hoping they could compromise; he didn't want Winston banned from the room, he just wanted his presence reduced. That was all. Forth sat down.

Sam turned to Siddarth and Nick and asked them what they

thought about the matter. They were both noncommittal—yes, Winston was there a lot; no, it wasn't that big a problem; yes, sometimes it was an inconvenience; no, they didn't want him gone, necessarily; yes, it would be nice if he were around a little less. Siddarth inclined more to Forth's side, and Nick—still nursing hopes of rehabilitating his homeless guest—leaned toward Damian's, but neither was eager to step out on a limb.

Finally it was Damian's turn. He rose from the table, paused, and then pulled out a lengthy-looking prepared text. "I had to write this down," he said, "because I was afraid that if I came up here and started talking off the cuff, I'd say things that I would regret. So I'm just going to read from this instead."

And read he did. His speech rambled, repeated itself, and doubled back. Even immediately afterward, no one could remember all the bitter points that Damian spilled out across Sam's table. (There was apparently a still-longer version, packed with grievances, racial and otherwise, that Nick had convinced him to edit down.)

Still, the general sense was clear. Damian wanted everyone to know how isolated he felt at Harvard, especially in Straus. Everyone else felt at home, everyone else fit in, everyone else could make friends easily. But he was a stranger. Part of it was being black, but more of it was being from the South. The North, he said, was different from anything he had ever encountered, and he felt completely adrift.

"That's why I like having Winston around," Damian said. "He's like me. He has the same background—he's a southern black man. He and I have experiences in common that I don't have in common with anyone else." In fact, he added, Winston was one of the only people he had met all year to whom he could truly relate.

At the same time, Damian insisted that Forth was exaggerating, that Winston was not around *all* the time—that it was closer to a few days a week. Forth clearly didn't like Winston, Damian noted darkly, so he was using his need to study as an excuse to drive away Damian's only friend in the entryway. But even if Forth was sincere, it didn't matter. Damian needed Winston around, so Forth would have to put up with it.

"Yes, you have had to deal with Winston, Forth," Damian read. "But I have put up with a lot, too. I have put up with your Groton friends and their lifestyles. I've put up with you wearing plaid shirts and blue jeans all the time. I've put up with your music. You're always listening to church music, choral music, and to oldies. I hate those, but I don't complain, I put up with them. So it shouldn't be too hard for you to have to put up with Winston. I tolerate things I don't like about you; I want you to extend the same courtesy to me. And to Winston. That's all."

After this, somehow, a deal was struck, and Winston's presence diminished. He still spent the night sometimes, and I occasionally overheard Nick lecturing him, patiently, on the value of a dollar. But his rule was broken, and he retreated into other haunts—the couches in Harvard's common areas and TV rooms, the showers of the local Y, and (or so it was rumored) the dorm rooms of newer, less-disillusioned friends.

Forth didn't get his room back, though, in those final months of freshman year. It still belonged to Damian, whose hatred of his privileged roommate was now a palpable thing, filling the air of B-32 as strongly as the odor of decaying chicken. Meanwhile, the mess remained and grew worse, as did the stench.

The year died slowly after that, and the diverser-than-diverse inhabitants of Straus B formed themselves into blocking groups and were scattered around campus by the housing lottery. Gabby, the Canadian girl who fancied necking in graveyards and dressing up for *The Rocky Horror Picture Show,* went off with a band of cross-dressers, bisexuals, and men who majored in women's studies; she moved off-campus within a year to live with her shaved-headed sister and smoke to her heart's content. Forth made his flight back to Groton official, joining a blocking group with his high school roommates and an assortment of pedigreed girls whom he barely knew; he was assigned to Dunster House, a salient of Georgian brick that faced the Charles and sprouted chimneys like blades of grass from its steep slate roofs. Rabia, the zealous Muslim girl, declined to join a blocking group, declaring that Allah would guide her; she ended up in the distant Radcliffe Quad, in Pforzheimer House, and was never seen again. And Damian joined up with a largely ethnic crowd placed in Lowell House, where the college's great bell tolled over a rectangle of stately brick and ivy.

The rest of us stayed together, remarkably enough—me and Julian and Nate, Siddarth and Nick, and the girls from upstairs and down. We were assigned to Quincy House, a hybrid of old Harvard and new, with a beautiful courtyard between where people held barbecues and concerts as the weather warmed. While we would drift apart from the girls over the course of upperclass life, we Straus B males were still living together in a Quincy House suite three years later, when graduation claimed our Harvard careers. A Hindu and a Greek, a Connecticut Catholic, a Kansan/Kentuckian, and a Liberian-American, all educated at private schools, but never mind that . . . just *look* at us! How *diverse* we were! How *proud* Harvard must have been!

And they only had to break a few eggs along the way.

I still saw Damian from time to time after freshman year; he slimmed down considerably during the following fall and seemed much happier and much more stable. He had learned to swim in Harvard's waters, I suppose, and his career blossomed: He was hired to work at J. P. Morgan in New York over his junior summer, and loved every minute of it. Then we graduated, and he went to law school at Columbia University. As far as I know, he is still there. I wouldn't want to face him in a courtroom.

In the spring of my senior year, the *Crimson*'s weekend magazine ran a long article dealing with self-segregation on campus. They interviewed Damian, who had just finished a term as the brotherhood chair of the Black Men's Forum.

"When he refers to the Harvard community," the reporter noted, "he says he means black students. 'The community ends at the black community,' he says."

As for Forth, he learned to laugh about his freshman-year trials. We stayed close friends, and in later years, it would become a tale told in bars, or near the end of dinners, when everyone was deep in their cups: the story of Straus B-32 and the homeless man.

"I mean, it was nuts, wasn't it?" Forth would say near the end of the story, when he had reached the early-morning summit and Damian's dramatic speech. "Plaid shirts? Choral music? And for God's sake—*oldies*?"

❖

The irony was that while Damian might have seemed nuts, he wasn't really wrong. Indeed, he had put his finger on something that no one at Harvard—or any elite college, for that matter—would admit: namely, that today's supposedly diverse campuses aren't really diverse at all.

Oh, they are ethnically diverse, with blacks and Jews and Asians and Hispanics jostling for space amid the rhetoric of tolerance, of multiculturalism, of *e pluribus unum*—or, more aptly, *e pluribus pluribus*. But beyond the most superficial form of diversity—the diversity of color—Harvard is a remarkably uniform, *un*diverse place.

When Damian talked about being from the South, and how alienated he felt adrift in a sea of northern kids, it was easy to laugh—except that there were very few people at our school who hailed from below the Mason-Dixon Line. Harvard is a global university, but for its American students, it remains intensely regional.

Consider my class, the class of 2002, which boasted just five students from Damian's Alabama. There was one kid from Mississippi, three from Louisiana, and nine from Kentucky. Arkansas sent five; the Carolinas between them sent sixteen. And it wasn't only the South that was underrepresented: There were seven students in my class from Indiana, five from the Dakotas, seven from Missouri, two from Nebraska, and similarly low numbers from other midwestern and Rocky Mountain states.

By way of comparison, New York and Massachusetts together sent roughly five hundred kids to Harvard in 1998, nearly a third of my sixteen-hundred-person class. New Jersey sent eighty-nine, Connecticut forty-nine, Maryland and the District of Columbia forty-five; California sent a hundred and eighty-one. All told, almost two thirds of the Class of 2002 hailed from a grand total of eight states.

Perhaps "regional" is the wrong way to understand this split. Better, maybe, to understand it in terms of the 2000 election, when the country was famously split into "red" and "blue" states, with the former—the mountain West, the rural plains, and the old Confederacy—going for George W. Bush and the latter—the coastal states, and states boasting large-scale urban centers—going heavily for Al Gore. Harvard, located in the bluest town of one of the bluest states in the Union, is cobalt to the core. It's a school where even the kids from red America—the Indianans and Carolinians, Coloradoans and Texans—tend to hail from blue enclaves, from the Austins and Chapel Hills, Boulders and Bloomingtons, from places where guns are scarce, coffeehouses outnumber churches, and *The New York Times* is the daily bible. Harvard kids arrive at Cambridge from the suburbs, and from the posher urban districts; they rarely come from rural America or from the inner city, the unhappy, glossed-over heart of blue country.

This geographic phenomenon is accentuated when you consider it on a school-by-school basis. In September 2002, *Worth* magazine commissioned a study, "Getting Inside the Ivy Gates," ranking the American high schools, public and private, that did the best job of getting their students into Yale, Harvard, and Princeton over a four-year period. They concluded that although "colleges have increased their emphasis on student diversity" over the last fifty years, "a college feeder system is alive and well in America." Top-flight high schools "cultivate relationships with top colleges" in what *Worth* called an "elaborate dance" in which "counselors actively woo colleges, visiting admissions officers and inviting them to come visit," and "high schools network to get invited to conferences that are hosted—and often paid for—by colleges."

The results are unsurprising. There are 31,700 high schools, public and private, nationwide, but only 930—roughly 3 percent—could claim more than four students in their 1998–2001 graduating classes who matriculated at Yale, Harvard, or Princeton. And *Worth*'s top hundred sent a total of 3,452 kids to the big three during that time, meaning that roughly 22 percent of the "Yarvton" student bodies emerged from fewer than 0.3 percent of America's high schools.

These schools are located overwhelmingly in blue states. Of the top hundred, twenty-eight can be found in New York and New Jersey; Connecticut boasts seven, the greater D.C. area eleven, Pennsylvania six, California eleven, and Massachusetts eleven. (All of the top ten, interestingly, are located in the Bay and Empire states, including number four, Forth's Groton, which sends nearly 20 percent of its senior class to Yarvton every year.) There are three schools on the *Worth* list in Texas, four in Florida, and just three in the rest of the

South combined; the Midwest has only seven, and four of those are in Ohio. There are none in the thousand miles of America that stretch from the Sierra Nevada to Missouri's Pembroke Hill School, where my roommate Nate spent his senior year.

This is no mere matter of geography—it's also a matter of class. Pembroke Hill is located near Johnson County, Kansas, the fifth-richest county in the nation, and the rest of the top hundred are similarly well placed, in Fairfield County and Montgomery County and Manhattan and other areas where the wealthy and well connected cluster. They are exclusive even within these already exclusive communities: Ninety-four of the top hundred are private, many with tuitions running upward of twenty thousand dollars a year. And the few public schools that do well on the *Worth* list are invariably located in hyperaffluent towns like Greenwich and Palo Alto, where wealthy taxpayers ensure that their schools have more in common with private academies than with public schools in poorer districts.

The result is an inevitable economic stratification, extending well beyond Harvard. The Educational Testing Service recently surveyed 146 top colleges and found that the poorest 25 percent of the American population has a 3 percent representation in their student bodies. Indeed, the bottom economic *half* of the nation has just a 10 percent representation in elite schools, while the top economic quarter has a 74 percent representation. This means, effectively, that you're twenty-five times more likely to encounter a wealthy student than a poor student at an Ivy League or Ivy-imitating college.

Straus B, I eventually realized, was a typical Harvard entryway in this regard. We were cosmetically diverse, but skin color aside, we hailed from the same kinds of places (the suburbs) and had attended the same kinds of schools (private ones). Forth was from the East Coast, and Nate was from the Great Plains, but Forth's Chevy Chase, Maryland, and Nate's Johnson County, Kansas, boasted similarly lofty levels of average income. Siddarth and Julian and Nick looked like an odd trio—Indian, black, southern European—but all three had been educated at elite Catholic high schools in their respective cities. The same pattern held among the entryway's girls: They were from upper-crust San Francisco or Westchester County, from suburban Boston or SoCal's exurban sprawl. They were not from rural America or the inner city; nor were they from the Deep South, the Great Plains, or the Midwest.

Not that we Straus B-ers were cookie-cutter personalities—far from it. But we were not nearly as diverse as we seemed at first blush, or as Harvard's promotional literature insisted that we were. Our flesh bore different pigments, and we had been raised in different places, but most of us were creatures of the same comfortable, upwardly mobile slice of the country—a slice that looks like America, but isn't. If our university meant to expose us to the "ideas and mores of students as diverse as this Nation of many peoples," then it failed resoundingly.

Appearances to the contrary, then, Harvard is not some bubbling stew of diversity. It is a place filled with haute bourgeois students from the professional and creative classes, a place where a smattering of strivers from underprivileged backgrounds are asked to become the "seasoning in the rice," as one minority tutor put it bitterly during my freshman year. They are forced to sink or swim in an alien environment, and some of them doubtless integrate without incident into the posh confines of the meritocratic system. But others, like Damian, find themselves drowning and seize on to anything that reminds them of the world they left behind—even if it happens to be a massive, moonfaced homeless man.

I'm not sure I can blame him for it.

CHAPTER TWO

The Old Boys' Club

E VERY HARVARD FALL, THE envelopes arrive, dropped
anonymously into door boxes and pushed through mail
slots. Stamped with foxes or bears, boars or rearing griffins,
they invite a favored group of sophomore boys to cocktail parties,
outings, and dinner parties. The sponsors of these events are the
"President and Members" of clubs that compose a strange bestiary:
the Owl, the Phoenix, the Fly, and the Fox; and, more cryptically,
the A.D., Spee, Porcellian, and Delphic.

Harvard does not have secret societies, as Yale does. There are
no windowless "tombs" littering the Cantabridgian landscape, no
mysterious tapping rituals during senior year, and (alas) no fanciful
movies like *The Skulls* set at suspiciously Yale-like universities. Instead, we have the final clubs: exclusive all-male societies with pedi-
grees stretching back generations, and brick-and-ivy clubhouses
scattered along Mount Auburn Street, the long and storied avenue
that runs through Harvard's campus.

These eight clubs dominate the college's social landscape. For
their male members, they provide meals, sprawling clubhouses, endless alumni connections, and rivers of alcohol. For the women who
flock to them late on weekend nights, after Cambridge's bars have

closed, they offer a clearinghouse of Harvard's most eligible and good-looking men, clustered in well-appointed, party-ready surroundings. Elitism is the order of the day: Male nonmembers who appear at final clubs are usually shunted into basement rooms, where they drink keg beer and compete for the affections of the party's less favored females. And when it comes to the grandest parties—fetes such as the Owl's Luau, the Spee's Pajama Party, the Fly's Calypso Party, the Fox's underwear-themed Boxer Rebellion—even the campus's most attractive women sometimes find themselves scrambling for invitations.

Harvard does have other social organizations. There are two underground fraternities—the university bans frats, officially—and several sororities; the Hasty Pudding Social Club, which dates to 1790 and admits only the best-connected Harvard freshmen; and three recently founded women's final clubs, the Bee, the Seneca, and Isis. There is also the Signet Society, the secretive literary club where the college's artistes congregate to dine with voguish poets. But none of these have the cachet and the connections that the final clubs provide—and none of them throw such great parties.

So membership in these clubs, which combine the elitism of an Eli secret society or Princeton eating club with the easy living of a state-school frat, is a much sought-after commodity. New members are selected every fall, usually from the sophomore class, through a lengthy process known as a "punch," which resembles an invitation-only fraternity rush, hazing included, except with ancient seals instead of Greek letters, and cocktail parties instead of beer-pong tournaments. "Punch" is a multipurpose word: People punch clubs, they are punched *by* them, and prospective members are referred to as punches.

The clubs are hated, of course. The administration, once hand-in-glove with the old boys' network, now regards them as an anachronism, an embarrassment, and a source of potential lawsuits. The campus's feminists and activist cliques regularly trot out the clubs as examples of how the patriarchy still suckles at Harvard's teat. And the mass of Harvard men, unpunched or unselected, linger outside the walls on weekend nights, listening to the music pulse, watching the girls flock to the doors, and storing up envy in their hearts.

And yet, and yet—they endure, they thrive, they prosper. Denounced as havens for sexual misbehavior, attacked as islands of unearned privilege, and warned against as breeding grounds for binge drinking, the clubs still soldier on, each year punching another generation of Harvard sophomores and ushering a chosen few into the ranks of the social elite. Because, after all, everyone wants in.

I know I did.

❖

My (entirely unexpected) punch invitations arrived in the fall of my sophomore year, through an unlikely source of social capital: the *Salient,* Harvard's always embattled conservative paper, where I became a deputy editor early that autumn. The editor in chief in those days was August Quintana V, a handsome Cuban-American whose grandparents fled Castro's Havana and settled, like so many penniless immigrants before them, on New York's Park Avenue. He was a member of the Spee, which was reputed to be one of the classier final clubs, free from drunken mud wrestling and constant satellite pornography, and closer to a real gentleman's society than a glorified frat. Or so said some people. Others said it was the Eurotrash club, filled with rich, Armani-wearing foreigners. (Apparently such club identities shifted constantly. By the time I graduated, the Spee was being referred to as the New York Jew hangout.) August, who had charm and good looks and wealth enough to overcome the social disadvantage of being a Republican, and who had chosen the Spee over two other clubs, told me that he loved it.

The Spee invitation was printed on cream-colored paper, with a dignified brown bear—the club's sigil—above the tastefully fonted lettering. But my other punch invitation was far more impressive. August was not the only clubman on the *Salient*, it turned out: There was also a former editor named Dunster, a sharp-faced junior whose full name, I later learned, was Wilfred Lowell Dunster Prendergast. (Harvard, it should be noted, boasts a Lowell House *and* a Dunster House among its residential colleges.) It was Dunster—trying to meet some club quota for punches, I assume, since I barely knew him—who was responsible for the hand-addressed envelope and the handwritten note, penned in flowing green calligraphy and sealed with a boar's-head stamp, that invited me to spend an evening with the "President and Members of the Porcellian Club."

The Porcellian is like the other final clubs, yet unlike them as well. It boasts a pedigree dating back to 1791, a roster of members rivaling Skull and Bones, and a clubhouse that may be vaster than any other final club's digs, encompassing all the upper floors of a long shop-filled building that runs along Massachusetts Avenue. The Porc, as it is sometimes called, has Harvard roots so deep that the Harvard Yard gate across from the clubhouse's inconspicuous door is carved with the same slavering boar's head that graced my invitation.

But no one has seen the inside of that clubhouse—not the gaggles of girls who flock to the Owl, Spee, Fox, and A.D. every weekend, not the wide-eyed, blazered punches, and not even the members' nearest and dearest. No male nonmembers can enter (although presumably there is a staff of servants), and the only women allowed in, the rumor goes, are members' wives, and then only on their wedding day and fiftieth anniversary. The Porcellian is also wealthier than the other clubs: It is supposedly the second-largest landowner in Harvard Square, surpassed only by the university itself, and every member, according to apocrypha, is guaranteed a cool million at the age of forty (or maybe thirty) if he has failed to attain millionaire status on his own.

I knew nothing of these rumors when the invitation appeared in my box. Indeed, I had only the vaguest conceptions of what punching a final club meant. But the card said "semi-formal attire," so I dressed neatly in a jacket and tie and tromped down Mount Auburn Street to the Harvard Skating Club, a mysterious place located well west of campus, in the shadow of Mount Auburn Cemetery.

A few blocks from my destination, I fell in with Forth and some of his Groton friends, headed in the same direction. They were all punching three or four clubs at least, I quickly realized, and the discussion revolved around which would be better to join—the Fly, with its nifty clubhouse? The Spee, with its swinging social life? The Porcellian, with its traditions?

"So what's actually going to *happen* tonight?" I was finally bold enough to ask Forth.

"I think," he said, "that it'll be like a cocktail party. All the members will be there, and all of us, and they'll talk to us and we'll talk to them, and later they'll get together and decide which ones they'll want to bring on for the next round. And then we'll get a call or another invitation if we've made the cut."

"Oh," I said. "Do you know a lot of people in the club?"

"No, no, not that many." Forth paused, as if doing calculus in his head. "Not that many at all."

And then we were there. There was a greeter at the door, a junior (and a Groton boy from the class ahead of Forth) named Jon Park, who was to sign us into a ponderous book—part of his duties, I later learned, as the club's punchmaster.

I passed a moment of intense social agony as he backslapped

with Forth and the other Grotonians, exchanging prep-school gossip. Then they passed in under low-hanging pine branches, and I stepped up to the book.

"Oh, Ross . . . you're on the *Salient* with August, right?" Jon said when I told him my name.

"You know August?" It was a thin straw, but I grabbed at it desperately.

"Know him? I'm in Eliot House with him. We were at Groton together," he added, scribbling my name and gesturing me in with the air of a father pushing his reluctant son into the deep end of the pool. "Go, get a drink. Have fun!"

It was anything but fun. I found a beer and accustomed myself to the crowds of tall, broad-shouldered young men, all dressed up and hobnobbing furiously in the shadowy lodge, under the antlered gaze of various trophies. Amid the well-stocked bar, the waiters carrying expensive hors d'oeuvres, and the sea of jackets and ties—all recently purchased, no doubt, at preppy boutique stores like J. Press or the Andover Shoppe—I felt adrift, like an interloper at a conference of business tycoons or political leaders, people accustomed to dividing up the world over cocktails.

Even worse, I knew almost no one there—Forth and his friends having vanished into the throng—and the people I did know, I hoped to avoid. They were acquaintances from the first month of freshman year, who had all moved up into more fashionable circles as Harvard's social hierarchy shook itself down: people like Henry Freck, a painfully pretentious German kid given to wearing Middlesex School scarves in all seasons; or Crawford Larch, a beefy rugby player from the first floor of Straus B with blistering, sunburned skin; or Lane Morgan Whittier, a blond Adonis, already the star pitcher for the Harvard baseball team.

There were far more punches than members, and even with every member—who sported identical ties, I realized, to distinguish them from us—claimed by four or five would-be Porc-men, numerous unattached punches circulated nervously through the room. To appear vaguely social, I latched on to one particularly pathetic specimen, an unshaved fiasco with curly, unkempt red hair, a Deadhead in a sea of bluebloods, and one of the few people in the room to whom I felt immediately superior.

We talked for a minute, exchanging the usual Harvard information—*So where are you from . . . What House are you in . . . What courses are you taking*—and then he brayed his first laugh, and said, "I don't know *anyone* here. I'm *so* weirded out."

"Yeah," I commiserated. "Neither do—"

"No, *no*," he cut in, "you *can't* be more freaked out than I am. I've *got* to get out of here."

"Well, there's free beer," I said, trying a smile.

"I don't drink," he said, and laughed again, exposing an unfortunate overbite. "I don't drink *anything*. I'm drinking *soda,* and I don't even like soda."

"Well—"

"Who punched you? I don't know *who* punched me. Maybe it was a mistake."

"I don't know—I think it was a guy I know from . . ." I trailed off, suddenly not wanting to admit to having any connections in the room. But my companion wasn't even listening.

"It *must* have been a mistake," he said, and his eyes lit up, as if the prospect cheered him considerably. "It must have."

"I'm sure you know somebody."

"Nope, nope, nope." He swept his gaze around the room, like a tuna in a school of sharks. "Nope, you're the first person I've talked to."

Beside us, a Porcellian man broke away from a knot of punches, and I turned, a little desperately, and stuck out my hand. "Ross," I managed. "I'm Ross."

He looked at me, looked at my hand—and then, mercifully, smiled. "Nice to meet you, Ross. I'm Clay."

Somehow it all became easier after that. In the space of an hour, I had met at least seven more members, told them my life story, jawed about Harvard, and even had them jaw enough about the Porcellian—*Much more respectful of women than the other clubs . . . More of a real "club" feel . . . I like having the private clubhouse . . . Less of a frat*—that it actually seemed like some of them wanted to impress me.

Perhaps not incidentally, I'd downed two more beers, both Harpoons, a microbrew peculiar to Boston, which someone told me was *founded by a couple of Porcellian guys, you know, about five years ago . . . that's why we always serve it at these things . . .*

The names and faces blurred into one another, Clay became Colin became Mike became Roger. Finally, late in the evening, I found myself talking to Oswald Sapperstein, an eccentric figure in that preppy room, tall, beak-nosed, and long-faced, with snazzy black glasses and curling red hair that exploded out in either direction from just above his temples. He wore a long green scarf with his suit, and was constantly smoking.

"So, what do you want to do with your life?" he demanded when I approached him gingerly and proffered my hand.

I admitted that I wanted to be a writer.

"That's fabulous! Fabulous! Great! What do you write? Do you write now?"

I said that yes, I wrote, and allowed that I did so for the *Salient*. This was an unfortunate thing to admit even in this setting—for I had learned quickly that even the old-money types were usually Democrats now.

"The *Salient*—yeah, yeah, uh-huh, Dunster used to be an editor there, didn't he?" He gestured toward the bar, where Wilfred Lowell Dunster Prendergast was taking a turn mixing drinks. "I never read it, honestly . . . I don't like politics much, and I wouldn't agree with anything you write, I'm sure. Probably, I mean. But is that what you want to do, be a journalist, be a conservative, be William F. Buckley?"

I told him about wanting to be a novelist, but how hard it was to write anything substantial during college.

"Sure, sure, I totally feel that. That's why I took time off. Took six months, traveled, you know the drill. It really helped my art."

What was his art, I asked politely.

"Oh, I'm a filmmaker. I make films—I'm in VES."

VES stood for Visual and Environmental Studies, the Harvard department that annually produces an array of agents of the avant-garde.

"Yeah, I'm actually working on my thesis now. I'm a second-semester senior, because of the time off I took. So I get to go through one last punch."

I asked him what his thesis was about.

"About? About? Well, it's about the experience of Asian-Americans on the Upper West Side of Manhattan. It's part documentary, part fiction."

"I see," I lied.

"It's my— My girlfriend is Asian-American. She's at Oxford now. But the film was inspired by her experience. Part of it is sort of a . . . sort of a . . . sort of a roman à clef, except it's not a *roman*, about us. About our lives."

"Your lives together?"

"About society, you know. And us—and Manhattan."

There didn't seem to be much more to say about that, so I asked him what he had done with his time off. Had he studied abroad?

"Studied? Christ, no. It was a semester *off,* totally and completely. I traveled, went to Spain, bummed around. Stayed in Lisbon for a while. I had the greatest love affair of my life there."

I nodded sagely, pretending that I knew exactly what such an affair was like.

"It was nice. And then I bummed around more, ended up on Malta."

"Malta?"

"Yeah, I hung out at the embassy, at the ambassador's house. It's a beautiful place, Malta. Just beautiful."

Finally—or suddenly, perhaps, with the alcohol working in my veins—the evening was winding to a close, and I was stumbling home through the lamplit streets, my tie loosened and my face flushed.

By the time I reached Quincy House, a pleasant haze had descended, and I was feeling very good about this whole Porcellian business. The club was pretentious and absurd, I decided somewhat tipsily, and the punch process was sickening—social climbing at its most naked. But I was glad to have seen it in action, glad to have had a brief window on that particular slice of Harvard. Now I knew what life at the very top was like, and I wanted no part of it.

Yet as I congratulated myself on being superior to all the over-dressed sophomores I had rubbed shoulders with that night, there was still something about the whole scene that attracted me. After all, wasn't this part of what had drawn me to Harvard—the pomp and splendor, the old traditions, the antlers on the wall and the high-branched family trees? I *was* a conservative, after all, and what was more conservative, more rooted in the past, than the final-club world?

❖

This was a grand illusion, although it took a while for me to figure it out. The final clubs are many things, but bastions of the ancien régime, of Harvard traditions dating back generations, they are not. Like the university itself, they are exquisitely adapted to the needs and realities of the twenty-first century, which embraces entitlement but not noblesse oblige, and champions class over, well, *class*. The clubs are Harvard in miniature, homes to the privileged among the privileged, the rulers of the ruling class.

Traces of the former world do remain. Within the Porcellian, there are plenty of old Harvard names to be found—Dunster and Lowell, for instance, and Roosevelt and Winthrop and Saltonstall. But even there, the real bluebloods are in the minority, crowded out by names that came late to America's upper crust. Some of these are the heirs of meritocracy's first wave, which flung a generation of bright young men into government service's elite realm—like Forth, for instance, whose grandfather served in Nixon's cabinet but whose family is only fifty years removed from anonymity—or Paul Nitze, the Porcellian's president during my punch year, and the grandson of the Paul Nitze who drafted cold-war blueprints for Harry Truman. Others are Upper West Side money, assimilated Jews and the gentile (and even, in a few cases, African-American) nouveau riche. Others still are internationals, part of Harvard's ever expanding global sweep: diplomats' children and the sons of Asian and European magnates, come to America as the sons of Mediterranean kinglets once went to Rome.

And the Porcellian, which stands almost alone in its continued defense of old Harvard's values—masculine solidarity and reverence for tradition—is almost alone in the number of hallowed Harvard names that grace its membership rolls. For the most part, the clubs are open to anyone with money and connections, be they Asian arrivistes, Manhattan-Hamptons royalty, or ordinary well-off suburbanites, doctors' and lawyers' children making the jump from haute bourgeoisie to just plain haute. The Delphic and A.D. and Owl are for kids who play the preppier sports, like lacrosse and rugby; the Phoenix is for the cool internationals, blacks and Asians especially;

and so on, down the list. A place for everyone, in other words, as long as you can pay.

Not that the clubs don't pretend (again, like Harvard) to have moved beyond class and filthy lucre in picking their members. There is financial aid, in almost every club, so anyone can join, final-club members always protest, when their institutions are accused of elitism. And anyone can—so long as you lived in the right suburb, vacationed in the right windswept part of Long Island or Maine or Nantucket or the Vineyard, and attended the right high school, with the right fellow students, who just happen to be the same people who decide, each year, who will become the next generation of Spee-men, Delphites, and Foxes.

There is diversity here, of a sort: The African ambassador's son, the Jewish lawyer's heir, the Indian doctor's pride and joy all have a place in these clubs, so long as their pre-Harvard lives have prepared the way. Indeed, the whole world is represented—the whole world that matters, that is.

❖

Three nights after that first Porcellian event, I attended the Spee punch's opening cocktail party. This was a grander affair. Instead of using the modest, piney confines of the Skating Club, they invited us to the Algonquin Club, one of the ancient, ossified upper-class establishments that line Boston's Commonwealth Avenue, replete with sweeping staircases, thick Persian carpets, and Brahmin portraits gazing from the walls. It was much more polyglot as well, with fewer long-chinned WASPs, fewer last-names-as-first-names, more Hong Kongers and Europeans, more brown skins and less blond hair.

And we were expected to bring dates.

That, ultimately, was what separated the Porcellian from the other clubs. It didn't just decline to admit women, it declined to pursue them, and to make their seduction (if getting women hammered and then having your way with them counts as seduction) one of its raisons d'être. The other clubs had no such scruples; there was a joke (or was it?) that made the rounds at the Algonquin that night, to the effect that punches were being judged on the beauty (well, "fuckability" was the word that people used) of their dates, which was, in theory, indicative of their ability to lure similarly lissome girls to future Spee festivities.

I went with Natasha, a sweet, slender Sri Lankan girl from my freshman entryway whom I asked at the last possible minute, after August told me that female escorts were expected. We did not precisely cut a swathe through the room. After five minutes in a sea of punches, Spee-men, and smoking, swan-necked women, I was floundering. For some reason, approaching members seemed twice as hard in mixed company as it had at the Skating Club—perhaps because there were too many introductions to be made, or perhaps because every Spee member seemed to have an intimidating, faux-blond girl attached to his arm. Natasha did her best, pulling me here and there and introducing us, but she was intimidated, too, I could tell, by the chilly first ladies of the club. Worse, the absurdity of the whole scene kept giving her the giggles.

So we stood together, Natasha and I, drinking and laughing at the splendor around us, and generally failing to make contact with any of the people I was supposedly trying to impress, or at the very least meet. August swept by a few times, resplendent in a bear-decorated tie, and did his best to drag me into the game, introducing me to his roommate and various other Spee-ers of note. But I was pathetic. There were too many people, too few members, and too great a disconnect, maybe, between the ancient, moneyed confines and the hip, brassy youth of the Harvard crowd.

Still, you can't say the Spee didn't put on a show. After the Algonquin, they hauled us all out for a night of barhopping—*IDs? We don't need no stinkin' IDs!*—that lasted well into the morning hours. Natasha and I ended up at Dad's Beantown Diner, a Boylston Street establishment that is not a diner at all. There we found ourselves (quite literally) dancing the night away, fortified by round after round of shots on the Spee, or at least on its free-spending members. I still had met only a few of these generous souls, but by the time "Dancing Queen" came on for the second time that night, I no longer cared.

By four we were back in Cambridge. Outside Quincy House, dressed up and dead drunk, Natasha and I stopped and looked at each other.

"You know," she said after a long pause, "I have class in four hours."

We both burst out laughing.

The following week, I missed the next Spee punch event in order to watch the Red Sox lose the fifth and deciding game of that year's League Championship Series to the Yankees. I was not, needless to say, tendered another invitation.

To my great surprise, my quest for the Porcellian had sturdier legs. A few days after the Skating Club cocktails, there was a phone call inviting me to the club for lunch—which really meant, I realized in disappointment, that three punches and three members would gather in the clubhouse foyer (the only part of the building that outsiders were allowed to see), have a drink or three, and then toddle out for a meal at a Harvard Square restaurant.

These lunches happened twice in the space of a week, and each time I was sure I had either made an ass of myself or absolutely no impression at all. The conversation at the first luncheon revolved around black holes, time warps, and various other quasi-scientific topics that the cold-eyed club president, Paul Nitze, raised in passing, only to have one of my fellow punches seize on them and worry away at the subject for nearly thirty minutes. The kid was still halfway through his explanation of how time drags out infinitely as you approach a black hole when the check finally came, and I had barely said a word.

My showing was only marginally better at the next lunch, which was held in the noisy, beery confines of John Harvard's Brew House, a hideous campus landmark where unimaginative students held birthday dinners. I was sandwiched between two other punches, a strapping rower who forgot to wear a tie and a fat-faced Norwegian with gel-plastered hair. We talked about crew, about which I knew nothing, and then about pursuing freshman girls, about which I pretended manfully to know quite a bit. I remember faking at least a dozen laughs.

"It didn't go well," I told my roommates after the first lunch, and again after the second. But somehow I kept getting invited back. Maybe it was my name that did it: Ross Gregory Douthat, seemingly ripe for a Roman numeral. Maybe I looked the part—tall and thin, and clearly WASPish even with my newly sprouted beard. Or maybe keeping a low but dignified profile, and hanging around with people who were obviously well connected in the club, like Forth, was the best way to avoid getting cut, at least in those early rounds.

Then the field trips began. *The President and Members of the Porcellian Club invite you to an outing*, the invitation insisted, so we dutifully piled into rented school buses on a drizzly Saturday morning, our ties freshly knotted and our cheeks glistening with aftershave. We drove for an hour, out through Boston's fading suburbs, which gave way to damp, puddled countryside, narrow lanes, and hanging tree branches that scraped at the buses—and finally the home of one Alistair Woolvington, Esq., a Porcellian man two generations removed, and a great, sagging wreck, with jowls and liver spots and burst blood vessels, and the strange, vulpine look that so many aging bluebloods seem to acquire.

Mr. Woolvington shook hands with each of us gravely, pausing only when a name stirred the waters of his well-connected memory. *Reardon Leary*, he said as he pumped hands with one of Forth's roommates. *Knew your grandfather, young man—he was in the club, too . . .*

There were Bloody Marys on the porch, and still more Harpoons, served up by a bartender. I was near the end of the line for drinks, and the members were largely claimed by the time I picked up a beer. So, as at the Skating Club, I fished around for lonely-looking punches.

"I'm Ross," I said to a blank-faced Asian kid, who was hovering near the silver-framed photographs of our host's grandkids. "What do you think of all this?"

"I don't know," he said. "But shouldn't we be talking to the members?" And then he was gone, leaving me marooned beside a shelf of black-and-white Woolvingtons.

It was good advice, and eventually I sidled up alongside Forth (something I became quite adept at during those weeks) and wormed my way into conversation with a tall, distinguished-looking senior named Todd Smythe, who was just back, I learned later, from two years on a Mormon mission.

They were talking about the Owl Club's event the previous night, which had ended in disaster when the cruise ship that the club had rented to sail its punches and their dates around Boston Harbor failed to show up.

"I was out with Jon Park," Todd was telling us, "and Jon got a call from a guy from the Owl. He was desperate, and he wanted to know what the heck there was to do that night."

"To do?" I asked.

"You know, like clubbing and stuff. What clubs were happening that night. Jon knows all about that. He goes out like three or four times a week, to Lansdowne Street or wherever."

"So did he help the guy?"

Todd shook his head. "There was nothing great that you could take a hundred people to. Some of them didn't even have fake IDs. So the Owl was pretty much screwed."

I, who didn't have an ID, sniffed at the thought of attending a punch event so horribly unprepared.

"Typical of the Owl," Todd added, and we all laughed knowingly.

A few minutes later, I found myself sitting down to lunch in between Forth's roommate Tyler Sheridan and a member named Geoff, a dark-haired junior who sang in the Krokodiloes, one of Harvard's countless tuxedo-clad a cappella groups.

Geoff and Tyler clearly knew each other from before, somewhere, so they talked past me for a long time while I racked my brain for something amusing to say. Finally there was a pause, and I reached for my Harpoon and said, "Did you guys hear about the Owl event last night?"

"I heard something," Tyler allowed. "Didn't their boat not—"

"It never showed up," I said hastily, cutting him off before he could steal my thunder. "And everyone was waiting on the pier, and they started calling people, trying to figure out where to go. Apparently they called up Jon—Jon Park, I mean—and asked him to tell them what to do. Because I guess he's really plugged in to the club scene."

"Really?" Geoff laughed. "Jon didn't tell me that. That's really funny."

"Isn't it?" I said, swigging beer and feeling terribly pleased with myself.

"Typical of the Owl," he said reflectively.

After lunch, cigars were passed around, and then we all went upstairs to change into rough-and-tumble clothes. We weren't told why, but rumor promised a touch-football game—which there was, on a marshy field below the Woolvington manse, near the pens where he kept his pigs and chickens. People dragged big plastic tubs filled with microbrews down to the field, and we drank and raced around in the mud for hours, playing ridiculously messy games of twenty-on-twenty, in which I never touched the ball, and then splitting everyone up into two games of ten-on-ten, each occupying one half of the field. I acquitted myself better in this second dispensation, despite playing on the "skins" team, which exposed my scrawny frame to the elements and left me looking askance at the muddy, Abercrombie-&-Fitch-worthy WASP beefcake of my teammates. I remember wondering, after I broke up a potential touchdown pass and nearly turned it into a brilliant interception, whether it was possible that the members were noticing my stellar play and thinking, *He'd be a damn good fellow to have around the next time we take on the Fly in a game of two-hand touch.*

Delusion is powerful.

"So what do you think of all this?" Forth asked me, after we had gone in and changed back into jackets and ties.

"It's fun," I said brightly. "What do you think?"

He grimaced. "I just like it so much better than the Spee. I don't want to offend August, but I'm really not that interested in joining his club."

"So you definitely want to be in the Porcellian?"

"Well, that or the Fly. I like the Fly, too. Have you seen their clubhouse? It's great. And they're the most like the Porcellian in terms of traditions and so on, except they do throw parties, which is nice."

"Yeah," I said, feeling a stab of envy at his apparent slew of options. "Parties are key."

"But you—the Porcellian is great for you," he said thoughtfully. "You fit in here, don't you think?"

"I guess," I agreed, feeling horribly flattered. "I mean, if I get in."

"Oh, you'll get in," he said. "Don't you think so?"

Outside in the rain, we thanked Mr. Woolvington, piling into the school buses again. And I suddenly thought that maybe I *would* get in after all. Forth thought I might—and he would know, wouldn't he?

❖

Other clubs' outings were far less restrained. My roommate Nick was punched for the Delphic, a rowdy, lacrosse-playing club, and he reported proudly that they played *tackle* football, and played it wildly, thanks to innumerable keg stands. The Porcellian's punch was absurdly luxe by any standard—the endless spreads of hors d'oeuvres, the catered dinners, the alcohol, the servants, the alcohol—but there were limits and decorum amid the excess. There was copious drinking, but no one got really drunk, and I never caught even a whiff of marijuana, let alone anything else, whereas other clubs passed around joints during the long bus rides. And the absence of women kept the sexual element entirely offstage (aside from homoerotic undercurrents, that is, and the whispered rumor that initiates would have to engage in sexual congress with a pig), so the events weren't marked by the drunken gropings and sloppy make-out sessions that dominated other clubs' punches.

Even outside the punch process, the other final clubs were famously dissolute. There were endless stories of debauchery: final-club boys helping strung-out prostitutes into the clubhouses late at night, people taking portraits of John F. Kennedy down from the wall and snorting coke off the presidential forehead, and on and on.

To take one example: Every year Harvard's Hasty Pudding Theatricals (not to be confused with the social club of the same name) puts on an all-male drag musical, written by students and intended to be a masterpiece of self-conscious camp. The Pudding show is world-famous: It runs for weeks at Harvard, then goes on tour in the Caribbean for part of the spring. But one night's show each year is reserved for members of the seven final clubs (the Porcellian has its own night) and their female guests. Perhaps "club night" began harmlessly enough, but by the time I came to Harvard, it had degenerated into a drunken nightmare in which plastered final-club boys threw things at the stage and heckled the performers with cries of "Faggot!," "Queer!," and uglier phrases. I remember a senior-year *Crimson* article in which the cast members told reporters that they lived in dread of that night, that it got worse each year, and that they were sure it would eventually turn violent.

"Why do they go through with it?" I asked a friend whose boyfriend managed the show.

She shrugged. "The clubs pay them a fortune."

And while it was easy to sneer at the campus feminists who annually filled the *Crimson*'s editorial pages with dire warnings about patriarchy and gender discrimination and the oppression of women, they did have a point—you could argue over definitions and degrees, but there was no doubt that sexual coercion of some sort took place inside the walls of those clubs.

In the basement women's room of Harvard's Science Center, one of the stalls had scratched in the door: "I was raped in the ____ Club," and with it a date. That message remained for months, and then another scrawl was added—a different club, a different date, but otherwise the same message. Eventually the administration had the door painted over.

It wasn't always thus. The clubs are relics of a time when Harvard College was entirely male, and they were founded to serve as junior versions of Boston's gentlemen's societies: places where members gathered to drink and smoke and dine, safe from the riffraff of the lower orders and the petticoats of the opposite sex. But the anti-establishment spirit of the 1960s, coming on the heels of the post–World War II wave of meritocratic admissions, was hard on this older understanding of club life. Membership dropped, dues fell off, smaller clubs (the Bat, the Iroquois) expired ignominiously, and even the more established clubs felt the pinch of the times. In 1969 a *Crimson* article noted that the Porcellian had attracted just four new members. "Either the steward is trying to cut down on the electricity bills or the A.D. boys play in the dark," the reporter went on, "because the A.D. looks totally deserted at night. . . . The Fox Club is dying from a lack of money and members . . . and the Phoenix is nearing financial doom."

It was women, ironically enough, who saved the clubs—specifically, an influx in the early 1970s of Radcliffe girls who were admitted to the clubhouses not as members but as guests and partygoers. Save for the Porcellian, which held to the older restrictions, the clubs happily traded in their old role as custodians of male fellowship for a new identity as campus party places where women in tight black pants are guaranteed a good time on Saturday nights. It was the entire drama of post-1960s Harvard played out in miniature: The clubs accepted the sexual part of the revolution and put the rest of it aside, and their membership rolls rebounded immediately.

Indeed, it's almost astonishing how easily the transition from Brahmin snobbery to meritocratic snobbery was accomplished, especially compared to Princeton and Yale, where elite clubs kept their elitism but at least made a nod to feminism by going co-ed. (By the early 1990s, even Skull and Bones's tomb was open to women.) There have been lawsuits and feminist protests, and Harvard officially severed its ties with the clubs in 1984, but the final clubs are still proudly all male and likely to continue so. And on weekend nights, when the dance music blares from the upper floors of the Spee and Phoenix, the women of Harvard are still lining up to get inside.

The only real challenge to this new regime comes from the alumni of earlier decades who sit on the club boards and manage the money, and who are distinctly uncomfortable with the turn that their institutions have taken. (Or perhaps, like Harvard's administrators, they are just uncomfortable with the possibility of alcohol- and sex-related lawsuits.) So there is a constant battle between the members and the graduate boards, with the latter threatening, regularly, to shut down the clubhouses if the current undergrads don't clean up their act. As I write these words, there has been another crackdown, and the clubs are supposedly sealing their parties, admitting only members and their guests (which still means that hundreds of people attend). It's a dance that has happened before: The clubs will put limits on partygoers for a while; the alumni will be mollified (and will probably feel pressure to attract new members); and gradually the debauchery will be cranked back up until it reaches a level that the graduate boards can no longer ignore. Then the whole pantomime begins anew.

It will go on indefinitely, if only because there are no other social outlets on Harvard's campus. There is no student center and there are no official fraternities; dorm parties must end promptly at one A.M.; and our country's already draconian alcohol laws are enforced with a ruthless zeal by administrators and cops alike. (My four years, which took place in the wake of a drinking death at an MIT frat, were particularly rigidly policed.) Harvard could hamstring the clubs at any time by investing in a co-ed social infrastructure, but the college doesn't seem to want alternatives to the final clubs; it wants them to disappear, with absolutely nothing springing up to take their place. Only then, secure in the knowledge that there is nowhere on campus to drink alcohol socially, and no way for underclassmen to obtain it, will Harvard's administrators sleep soundly at night. For now their rest remains uneasy—but at least they know that whatever goes on at the Fox and the Owl, the Spee and the Delphic, *they* aren't financially liable.

❖

The last Porcellian event that I attended was another outing, this one to the Percy Estate, a multiacred spread somewhere west of Lexington. Who exactly Mr. Percy was, I never learned, but we approached his estate after nightfall, under a full moon—two long school buses rolling down an empty, tree-lined lane while the October wind keened against the windows and dead leaves crackled beneath the tires. Then, suddenly, a mansion loomed between the trees, with a lamplit, graveled drive sweeping up to the doors. As we pulled in, I half expected to see the household servants lined up to greet us, a bowing butler at their head.

The reality wasn't so different. Within the manor, the punches—our numbers considerably thinned from the first night at the Skating Club—circulated through a downstairs filled with immaculate rooms, expensively furnished and devoid of personality. Servants wandered about, freshening drinks and serving appetizers, and so, too, did various Porcellian alumni, all looking dignified and splendidly well fed. The whole place had a curious unreality: It felt like a stage, its inhabitants picked out by a casting agency and its furnishings by a well-paid set crew. Nobody really lived here, it seemed, any more than they did in David O. Selznick's Tara or Robert Altman's Gosford Park.

There was a floating quality to the evening, a sense of being out-side my body and watching everything from a great distance, a buoy-ant feeling that only increased after I had downed several drinks. I walked on air through those elegant rooms, among those elegant people, like someone drifting through a dream, and my memories from the evening retain a fragmentary, dreamlike quality. . . .

. . . Two alumni, their voices quavering somewhere in the George Plimpton range, are holding court with a cluster of punches.

"Here's a story," one of them says, swirling his drink. "The two of us, we were coming to a Harvard reunion, and they assigned us guides, or something like that . . . can't remember exactly what. Anyway, they were current students, and when we got their names, we noticed that they were two young fellows named Walker and Pitcairn."

"Of course," the other one interrupts, "we both knew a Walker and a Pitcairn who had been at school with us—so we said, 'I wonder if these boys are their sons, or nephews, or something.'"

"And then we arrived and met them," the first alum finishes, "and they were black."

Cue general merriment . . .

There were glass double doors in one of the living rooms, and they opened out onto an Italianate sunken patio and a pond where lily pads jostled for space and goldfish swam in the depths. Beyond the pond, a flight of overgrown steps rose to a lawn and the full moon. Carrying my drink, I pushed through low-hanging tree limbs and trailing forsythia and found myself on a sweeping green that ran away from the lights of the mansion toward scattered willows and night-mantled hills, where the lights of distant homes climbed to-ward the pinprick stars.

. . . Two punches are talking near a curving stairwell. They are both wearing red ties, one striped and one dotted.

"No, I spent most of my time in Bridgehampton," one is saying.

"Well, Jesus," the other returns. "It was crazy. The ambassador was gone, of course, so the kid had the run of the place . . ."

"It's a nice place."

"Yeah, but eventually we all went out to bars, and came back, and somebody tried to steal some street signs or something crazy like that. I don't know who—I was pretty drunk at this point."

"Probably fucking Sebastian."

"Probably!" They both laugh. "But anyway, the cops were coming, so we all ran into the ambassador's place, and they couldn't do shit!"

"Because of . . ."

"Because of . . ."

"Diplomatic immunity!"

A gravel path led away from the house, across the lawn and toward the woods, and after dinner a whole crowd of punches and members carried their drinks out into the autumn night and went walking around the Percy Estate. The grass was dry, and mounds of leaves were piled in the shadows of the scattered copses, like strange animals set to guard an enchanted castle. The breeze burned cold on my cheeks, and I stared at the stars, feeling the conversation buzz around me. Connections were being forged, friendships cemented, memberships sealed—the vast and shining web was throwing out more strands, crisscrossing and tying them off, wrapping the world in silver filaments. And I was looking at the sky.

. . . I am inside, hovering on the fringes of a conversation. Colin Masterson, a member with frosted hair and a ruddy tan, is talking to a punch I have met once before, a stout, flushed creature named Roger Yarbrough. They are both on the Harvard sailing team, I realize.

"Do you know Rachel Polley?" I ask, naming the sailing girl I adored all through freshman year.

"Sure, yeah," Yarbrough says. He has close-cropped dark hair, a sharp nose, and a vanishing chin. "Yeah, she sails with Eric Allenby."

She dates Allenby, too, a fact that rankles me that fall. But I smile and nod and say that Rachel was in my entryway freshman year.

"Oh yeah?" Masterson says. There is a frozen pause, and it's clear that they will retreat back into their own conversation quickly.

"Yeah." I smile weakly, and then I think of something funny: "She always said that you guys joke that you're on a drinking team that likes to go out sailing."

Colin looks at Roger. Roger looks at Colin.

"No, I wouldn't say that," Roger says flatly. "Not at all."

At the woods, the Percy Estate gave way to wilderness, and the long post-dinner stroll came to an end. People began to turn back, climbing the lawn toward the lights of the mansion. I stood for a while there, on the fringes of the night, and eventually Forth passed by with Jon Park, the punchmaster, and several other people.

"What are you looking at?" Forth asked me.

"Have I told you about the croquet?" Wilfred Lowell Dunster Prendergast asks idly as we serve ourselves from the long, splendid dinner buffet.

"The croquet?" I say.

"Sure," he says. "It was a few years ago. Harvard doesn't have a croquet team, but a lot of other schools do, and there's a whole national college tournament or something. So a bunch of guys from the club decided to form a Harvard croquet team."

"You can do that?" I asked. "The athletic department would let them?"

"Sure," Dunster says, "why not? Maybe because they promised to pay for all their equipment, so it was just a question of Harvard recognizing them."

"No, no," Oswald Sapperstein interrupts, coming up to us with a wineglass in his hand. "They were just a club team, and this tournament was all clubs."

"Well, fine, whatever," Dunster says irritably. "The point is, they

went to this tournament, having never played another college in a match, ever. Some of them had barely played croquet before. And they all wore tuxedoes and stood around drinking and smoking in between turns. It drove the other colleges nuts—and then they ended up winning the whole thing! And Harvard hasn't fielded a team since."

I was looking over the trees toward a nearby hill, where a narrow stone tower with a peaked roof thrust upward into the sky. It was an incongruous sight, like something from a fairy tale dropped down in the middle of eastern Massachusetts.

"What is it?" Forth asked, staring at the tower. "Does somebody live there?"

"Something on the neighbors' land, maybe?" Park said. "I don't know anyone who's been in it. It's not part of this property."

"We should climb it," I said. "That would be fun . . ."

For a moment I had a vision of all of us climbing together, pushing open a creaking door and clambering up the stairs, passing between crumbling stone walls toward a tower room that no one had seen in hundreds of years—an ancient, secret place, more secret even than the hidden mysteries of the Porcellian.

"Too far away," Park told me. "Come on, let's go back. The buses will be leaving soon."

And so we went.

There were no more invitations. There were no more phone calls. There was only silence, and the days became a week, and more than a week, and I realized that my run at the Porcellian was over. Only then did I understand how much I had become invested in it— how much I desperately wanted to join, or rather to be *accepted,* and to enter the ancient rituals and hallowed halls of the society. It didn't matter, by the end, that I didn't truly like most of the members, that except for Dunster and maybe five others, I had difficulty remembering their names (well, that might have mattered, but in a different way), that I found their wealth and connections and casual privilege off-putting, that I had spent many of the punch events feeling tense and alienated and horribly excluded. No, nothing mattered except that they, the Porcellian boys, were part of a magical, pampered ruling class, and I wanted in.

And they had rejected me.

It left me feeling as if I had sold my soul to them and received exactly nothing in return. (Unless you count the free drinks.) I had felt contempt, initially, for the wealth and luxury that these *kids*, these teenagers and early twenty-somethings, seemed to take for granted. But by the end, my contempt had vanished, replaced by naked need. I wanted to wander the rolling lawns of the Percy Estate, to hobnob with Alistair Woolvington, to vacation in Barcelona and Malta, to crash croquet tournaments, and to party at an ambassador's house. I wanted to see the vast, semi-mythical recesses of the clubhouse, to be acquainted with the ancient rituals, to attend the secret retreats and tag along on the European tours.

These desires are latent in almost everyone, I imagine. But it was still something of a shock to feel my adolescent convictions about the unimportance of money, the tackiness of upper-class youth, and the shallowness of picking your friends for the sake of connections, all melt away under the heat from a final club's flame.

At least I wasn't alone. My roommate Nick—who read Howard Zinn and E. P. Thompson for fun—made it about as far along in the Delphic punch as I did in the Porcellian, and as the weeks rolled by and his chances of getting in seemed to increase, poor Nick tied himself in rhetorical knots trying to justify joining the Harvard elite. He would insist, outrageously, that the Delphic was the most "working class" of the final clubs, declaring that because the members were mainly lacrosse players and other jocks, the club was somehow less elitist than the Fly and the Porcellian. Or he would claim that joining

the Delphic would give him a chance to bring the whole rotten structure down from the inside, that he would use his membership in the
club to get other people in, his real friends, the people who deserved
to have a clubhouse of their own.

I don't think my roommate ever really believed these arguments.
But when he didn't make the final cut, Nick was heartbroken. He had
been certain that the Delphic boys really liked him and really wanted
him in their club. For the next three years, he always referred wistfully to the Delphic clubhouse, with its (unused) library and pool tables and posh, mahoganied rooms. It was worse for Nick, too,
because he wanted to work for an investment bank or a consulting
firm, so all through the senior year recruiting process he watched the
final-club guys sail upward, borne to impossible heights by their endless array of alumni connections.

I never had to compete with a Porcellian man for a job, or sit at
a recruiting session and feel the weight of my failure to make those
particular connections dragging me down. But I still had to pass
them on the streets and see them in dining halls, and at parties and
bars. No one ever said anything to me about it; when I ran into the
members, they were friendly enough, in a tense sort of way, but
there was no acknowledgment that they had deemed me unfit to join
their club, no word of explanation or apology. But then why should
there have been? There was no need to apologize, no need to feel
guilty. This was, after all, how the punch process worked. Some people got in, and everyone else got over it.

Only Dunster, months later, standing in the rain outside the
ghastly modern Science Center, made any mention of my failure. We
were talking about the Red Sox, I waiting for a *Salient* layout session
to begin, and he lit a cigarette and suddenly said, "I'm sorry about
the club, by the way. It wasn't anything you did—you just didn't
know enough of the members going in, probably."

"Don't worry about it," I told him. "I understand."

And I did. Forth was accepted, of course, and so were his room-mates, Tyler Sheridan and Reardon Leary. Who else? There was a Hornblower, a Scandinavian billionaire's heir, a Harvard dean's son, and several others of similar eminence. Compared to such people, why did I think I might merit consideration? I had not attended Gro-ton or Sidwell or Exeter or Milton, and even some who had attended those schools lacked the touch of class, the squash-racket swing, that made a Porcellian man.

Franklin Roosevelt didn't get into the Porcellian, in spite of his pedigree, and he would later say that it was the greatest disappoint-ment of his life. For my part, I decided later in my Harvard life that *not* getting into a club was a blessing in disguise: I doubt I would have liked the person I might have become as a member in good standing of the Porcellian Club. By the end of college, Nick and I could sit together in Charlie's Kitchen, Harvard Square's seediest pub, and talk about how lucky we were to have kept our good friends, our real friends, instead of trading them in for Delphic and Porcellian brothers. Harvard was privileged enough, we agreed, and sufficiently detached from the real world, without going a step fur-ther and entering the charmed circle of final-club brats.

But we would say that, wouldn't we?

The following fall, as we walked back from the Yard toward the river and the upperclass houses, Forth mentioned to me uneasily that the Porcellian's first punch event was coming up the following week. If I wanted him to, he would be happy to punch me again.

"But," he added quickly, "since you didn't get in last year, it probably means that someone in the club didn't like you—voted against you, I mean. And, well, I don't think anyone has ever gotten into the Porcellian after being voted down the year before. I really wish you were in the club—more than anyone else. But—"

"Yeah," I agreed, imagining the humiliation of returning to the Skating Club and Alistair Woolvington's home, of trying to ingratiate myself with people who had voted me down and people who had been voted up in my stead. "Yeah, it'd be weird. Don't worry about it."

He looked relieved, and no more was said.

CHAPTER THREE

The Strange Career of Suzanne Pomey

I HAVE ALREADY MENTIONED the Hasty Pudding Theatricals, the ancient Harvard acting troupe that puts on a bawdy, all-male musical every year. The Pudding is one of the college's most famous institutions, boasting a world tour and a stellar record of sold-out shows. So sacrosanct is the Pudding that its casting calls are the last place on campus where an official Harvard organization is allowed to discriminate, blatantly and cheerfully, against the fairer sex.

It's worth wondering why, exactly, the Pudding is so famous, since the shows—written, composed, and directed by students—are good-natured but tedious, filled with horrible double entendres and campy drag. (The titles tell it all: "Fangs for the Memories," "Jewel of Denial," "I Get No Kick from Campaign," and so forth.) Perhaps it's the costumes, a gaudy sea of splashy colors, elaborate wigs, and well-padded bustiers. Or perhaps it's the Pudding's practice of picking—at random, apparently—a celebrity Man and Woman of the Year (recent selections include Sarah Jessica Parker, Bruce Willis, and Anthony Hopkins) and inviting them to campus for a festive ceremony. The female celebs are given a parade through the streets of

Cambridge, and the Men and Women alike are favored with a good-naturedly vicious roast and the bestowal of the prized pudding pot. All in all, it makes for an irresistible media spectacle, mixing movie stars, the Ivy League confines, and garish cross-dressing, served up with a dash of sophomoric wit. The musicals themselves are almost incidental to the fun.

During my junior year, the producer of the Hasty Pudding Theatricals was a blond, well-dressed girl who would have been pretty had it not been for the ghostly, heavily made-up pallor of her skin and the coldness of her eyes. Her name was Suzanne Pomey, and she was a Harvard queen bee. During her sophomore year, Suzanne was president of Kappa Alpha Theta, considered the classier (or at least the prettier) of Harvard's two sororities, and later she co-founded Isis, a women's final club. She was a stalwart at Phillips Brooks House, the campus community service organization; she ran their well-staffed summer program and was famously popular with the underprivileged grade-schoolers she tutored. She loved the spotlight: In her most glorious campus moment, she invited Anthony Hopkins—then Pudding Man of the Year, fresh from playing Hannibal Lecter—to devour her, and he responded with a public grope and a greedy French kiss. A photograph snapped just after their embrace, in which a wolflike Hopkins nibbles at the fingers of a mock-horrified Suzanne, made the front page of the next day's *Crimson*.

So it was quite the sensation when, midway through our senior year, Suzanne, together with her close friend and fellow senior Randy Gomes, was arrested and charged with grand larceny. She and Randy had used her position as producer, it turned out, to embezzle nearly a hundred thousand dollars from the Hasty Pudding.

Everyone was initially shocked. But after a time, it became clear that no one who really knew Suzanne, or the nature of her social world, was terribly surprised.

❖

I came to know Suzanne through Sally Maddox, a brassy, red-haired Kentuckian who appeared in my room on the very first day of college in search of my Kentucky roommate, Davis Hendricks, with whom she had attended various smart-kid camps in their native state. At first I found Sally wildly eccentric—she was rich and bossy, pert and petulant, and she seemed to drag Davis around by the scruff of his protesting neck. I pitied him, imagining that he dreaded the rap on the door and the cheerful, Dixie-inflected cry of "Dayyy-vis!" (Other Harvard southerners dropped their accents quickly; Sally treated hers as a prize.) Later on, Davis became her boyfriend; later still, I became her great friend, realizing that while Sally might drag you from one end of campus to another for the most trivial of reasons, she was fun enough to make the trip worthwhile.

Sally was in Kappa Alpha Theta, along with a number of southern girls who, having left a culture where sorority-joining was de rigueur, were undeterred by Harvard's paucity of Greek societies. She had known Suzanne—likewise a Kentuckian—only casually, through the high-IQ network, but they became close friends during freshman year, then roommates the following fall. From the outside, it was a perfect match: Suzie and Sally, two southern sorority girls, both flirtatious and both (seemingly) with money to burn. When I became real friends with Sally—when, more aptly, she adopted me midway through my sophomore year—they seemed to be having the time of their lives together.

I was at a low point then, just rejected by the Porcellian and adrift in upperclass life, which seemed arid and bleak after the coziness of Straus B, where a good chat (or a long argument) was only a landing away. Quincy House was vast and ghastly and intimidating; many of my friends from freshman year were scattered in other houses, and I spent countless Saturday nights listening to the pulse of other people's parties, other people's fun.

So it was a bad time to meet Suzanne, who was a fabulous ignorer, blessed with a radar that unfailingly tuned out those who didn't merit her friendship and attention. She could sweep into a room where Sally and I were talking, have a ten-minute chat with her roommate, and sweep out again as if I didn't exist. In her clinical, social-climbing mind, I was barely worth a hello; at best, I earned a nod and a stare that seemed to slide off my skin, as if there were nothing there worthy of her gaze.

The stare is what I remember best about Suzanne from those early days. I remember the way she talked, too, although little of what she actually said; just the torrent of names and gossip and parties and hookups that rolled from her lips, filling the Winthrop room with the sense of sophistication, of connectedness, of *cool* that she always carried with her. I was never attracted to her, though she was attractive to many. She had sex appeal, but there was something off-putting in it, something that was wanton without being warm.

But most of all I remember the stare, if only because the rest of her features had an indistinct, vanishing quality. Perhaps it was the makeup she always wore, but the lines of her face seemed to fade into the pallor of her cheeks and forehead, leaving only a thin line of mouth, a hint of nostrils, and the holes of her eyes, small and dark. In black-and-white photographs, the effect is accentuated, so she seems to have no cheekbones at all, and no nose—just a pale blob of a face that fades into a head of paler hair.

She made me think, above all, of Hans Christian Andersen's Snow Queen, coldly sensuous and unapproachable. Her presence was intimidating, and after a time, whenever I visited Sally's room, I began to pray that Suzanne would be out, so I could avoid the feeling of utter insignificance that her glassy stare bestowed on me.

. . .

When she didn't dismiss you out of hand as beneath her notice, I am told, Suzanne was as solicitous as a friend could be, buying gifts, remembering birthdays, and sending perfectly timed e-mails containing perfectly worded messages (a joke here, a personal touch there). Yet many people later claimed that there was something a bit *too* perfect about her conduct, as if everything she ever did was calculated; as if friendship were a contract with specific duties on each side, specific transactions to be carried out, and specific rewards expected. She made enemies aplenty over the years, and even many of her supposed friends regarded her with a mixture of distrust and fear—or so they claimed after it all came crashing down.

But perhaps it is better to be feared than loved, and Suzanne seemed to do well enough for herself on that account. She was voted president of Theta, and most of her other leadership positions were elective as well; whatever people really thought of her, they voted for her again and again. She was a dogged worker, people said—in Theta and the Pudding, she took on the most thankless positions during her freshman year, so that people remembered her devotion when she ran for higher offices. And she was a capable politician, plucking out the important people in every organization and cultivating them until her ascent came to seem an inevitability.

It helped, in all this, that she spent money like water, lavishing presents on her friends, helping to sponsor events for her often cash-strapped sorority, and taking her community service program's "little sibs"—girls from the impoverished schools of Boston's poorer districts—on outrageous shopping trips to vast suburban malls. (No wonder, people said later, she was so popular in the after-school programs.) Pouring one's own money into the mix was a time-honored tactic among Harvard's would-be campus leaders: The *Salient* was floated for months on a loan from Dunster's ample pockets, and all through my junior year, the *Advocate*, Harvard's trendier-than-thou literary magazine, held rocking parties that were well beyond its budget, thanks to the Upper West Side lucre of its leadership.

One of Suzanne's financial splurges was sufficiently outrageous, even by the standards of high-class Harvard, to earn her a photo and a brief write-up in *Fifteen Minutes*, the *Crimson*'s weekly magazine. (Better known as *FM*, it is a delicious tabloid-style paper; its 1970s founders named it *What Is to Be Done?*, after a pre-revolution Lenin pamphlet, and the change to a Warhol-inspired title says everything about the difference between that generation and mine.) The occasion was her twenty-first-birthday party, for which she and her friend Randy rented out the local T.G.I. Friday's, transforming the chain restaurant into a teeming dance party complete with an open bar and a tab that ran to two thousand dollars.

The e-mail invitation to this party was penned—largely in verse form—by Randy, a handsome, well-liked kid, who was supposedly famous in Boston's gay club scene. On Saturday night, the invite announced, "Suzanne, Miss Pomey if you're nasty, will turn 21 / And since now she's in control we're going to do it her way / part sugar and spice and everything nice / part naughty vixen hell-bent on vice"—but mainly naughty vixen, given that the party's theme was "Skin—the 21-Inch Party," a reference to the (rough) amount of clothing each attendee was permitted. "Bare what you dare," Randy's e-mail suggested, and "cover what you must / The twenty-first century will be ruled by lust." Oh, and "don't worry 'bout the benjamins, this party is on us."

The *FM* photograph from the party—which appeared in an issue devoted to Harvard nightlife—shows Suzanne in the bathroom at T.G.I. Friday's, applying her makeup à la the famous snapshot of Marilyn Monroe. I was not invited that evening, alas—that pesky lack of social clout rearing its ugly head again. But by all accounts, Randy's e-mail promises were right on target, and Suzanne rang in her twenty-first year with a sweaty, sex-drenched, pell-mell dance party at which every drink and mozzarella stick was on her.

Six months later, she showed up in *FM* again, this time for an annual issue devoted to Harvard's "Fifteen Intriguing Seniors." The profile of the Theta prez and Anthony Hopkins canoodler began by noting that amid her myriad activities, "Suzanne Pomey did not make it to her own bed last night," having accidentally locked her keys in Phillips Brooks House. When you are "a leader of a multitude of Harvard community organizations and social clubs," *FM* fawned, "those little tribulations are bound to happen." The story concluded with a line from the rhyme that Suzanne wrote and read aloud when the chosen fifteen were summoned to a pricey French bistro and everyone was called upon to make a brief, self-referential performance. "Now Theta, now Isis, now the Pudding and more," Suzanne's poem ran. "I guess I became a kind of social club whore."

Or as *FM* put it, before setting out into the world, Suzanne "may as well take a breather and reflect on an illustrious career as Harvard's ultimate do-gooder wannabe socialite."

A month later, she was placed under arrest.

❖

Gradually, the truth came out. Suzanne was not rich, of course—indeed, by the standards of Harvard, she was almost poor. Thanks to the dogged post-arrest research of two *FM* reporters, Angie Marek and Amit Paley, the campus learned that she grew up in a one-story three-bedroom home in Vine Grove, Kentucky, a small town in the northern part of the state; her father was a retired army officer, and her mother, an immigrant from the former Yugoslavia, sold cars at the local Pontiac dealership. (The year before her daughter's arrest, she was the dealership's saleswoman of the year. "I don't have fear," she told a local paper. "I love a challenge, and I hate to fail.") Suzanne was an only child, and her parents seem to have been the doting, hyperinvolved sort typical among aspiring Harvard families. Michelle McCombs, one of Suzanne's friends from the time, told *FM* that Suzanne's father "would make up little math and history questions to answer when we came over, and of course Suzanne knew the answers because he taught her, but we didn't." McCombs added with a touch of pathos, "I think it was designed to make her look and feel better than us."

From such beginnings, Suzanne went on to become a high school achiever par excellence. She was president of the student council, co-president of the Kentucky United Nations Assembly, vice president of the National Honor Society, and vice president of Youth in Charge, an anti-drug and anti-alcohol group. Her list of extracurriculars also included Girls' State, the Governor's Program, the Academic Team, Students Against Drunk Driving, the Octagon Club, the Senior Advisory Board, the Spanish Club, and the Fellowship of Christian Athletes: all in all, a typically jam-packed Harvard résumé.

She also made her share of enemies, like the grade-school friend who refused to talk to *FM*, saying, "Suzanne has caused enough pain in my life. . . . I'm afraid of what she'll do if she sees my name in an article." Then there was the petition that Suzanne circulated after she failed to make valedictorian or salutatorian, demanding that the student body be allowed to vote on who was to give the graduation speech. (It failed.) Suzanne, one of her teachers said, was "a student who was always willing to find a shortcut."

Judging by a conversation she had with a high school friend just before leaving for Cambridge, Suzanne had a good idea of what awaited her at Harvard. "She always needed to be just a little different," the friend told *FM,* "and in high school being the best [academically] did make her different. . . . But she said at Harvard everyone was the best in their high school and so she needed to be different in another way."

❖

So how *does* one distinguish oneself amid a carefully culled, selecter-than-select population? How does one rise to the top at Harvard, where everyone is just as ambitious as you, if not more so?

All through college, my classmates and I were told, ad infinitum, that we were ever so lucky, because we were surrounded by an incredibly talented and interesting cross-section of classmates: hence the oft-repeated cliché about the best Harvard education taking place "outside the classroom." This promise was meritocracy's bright side. But there was a darker side as well. To reach the commanding heights of American education, we had to be, by nature, incredibly ambitious and incredibly driven. Harvard is a social Darwinist's delight, an ecosystem filled with creatures superbly adapted to vanquish every competitor.

Within this Harvardian hothouse, the advantage often goes—at least in the short term—to the manipulative and dishonest, those willing to backstab and lie and cheat their way upward. The internal politics of every large campus organization, from the would-be diplomats on the Model United Nations team to the ink-stained wretches of *The Harvard Crimson,* are permeated by this spirit of success at all costs. Everyone comes to college having padded their high school résumé, Suzanne-style, with an endless array of offices and honors, and so they naturally try to do the same in college, only to find the competition far stiffer. The result is a culture where mean-ingless club elections swirl with intrigue and rumors of unethical conduct—a place where everyone joins up and runs for office and then drops out if they can't run the show, because what would be the point? Only saps join activities for their own sake; you join them be-cause being student activities chair on the Undergraduate Council or associate publisher of *The Harvard Independent* makes for another line or six on the résumé that will eventually be sent to law schools or investment banks or prominent newspapers or whatever next rung you favor on the ladder of success.

At the Institute of Politics—the undergraduate arm of the Kennedy School of Government and a major feeder for summer in-ternships and post-grad jobs in Washington—things became so bad during my senior year (the politicking so intense, the scramble for in-ternships and recommendations so fierce) that the ex-politician in charge, David Pryor, dissolved the student committee that ran things, appointed his own slate of leaders, and announced sweeping changes in the way officers were chosen and internships divvied up. There was an immediate outcry—at least among the student bigwigs who had lost their clout—against Pryor's anti-democratic behavior, but his reforms were long overdue. The organization was well on its way to becoming Harvard's own Tammany Hall, where every junior in-ternship coordinator fancied himself a new Boss Tweed. Once I was taken aside by one of these student bosses after I penned an article that he didn't like and asked if I ever planned to apply for an IOP-subsidized internship. I was naive enough then to still imagine a po-litical career, so I allowed that I might.

"Let me be frank, Ross," he told me. "When I read something like that"—a gesture at the newspaper—"well, if I were in charge of deciding whether you get an internship, as I could well be, some-thing like that is likely to affect whether I'd recommend your application. If your name came across my desk"—a shrug—"I'm just saying that you should be careful what you write."

So there is a scramble for power, for petty perks and résumé-padding titles and the rush that comes with deciding your fellow students' fate. But when it comes to Harvard's cutthroat culture, this scramble is only half the story, since the boundless ambitions of the students are undergirded—especially during my four years, when the dot-coms hummed and the economy bubbled—by an astonishing foundation of wealth. It was astonishing to me, at least, and I came to Harvard from a suburban childhood spent at a private school where most people were comfortably moneyed. But I had never seen anything like the conspicuous consumption that fills Harvard to its Ivied brim.

Not everyone is well heeled: Need-blind financial aid sees to that. But poverty is rare at Harvard, as at every elite school, and financial aid is more likely to boost upper-middle-class students than it is to lift up the truly poor. Of the 47 percent of Harvard students who receive some financial assistance, only a fifth come from families making forty thousand a year or less, whereas fully a third belong to families with incomes in excess of a hundred thousand. Assuming that most people eligible for aid apply for it, these figures imply that roughly 70 percent of my classmates boasted parents earning over a hundred grand a year—and only 9 percent came from families making under forty thousand.

True, not everyone can match the free-spending ways of the super-rich, the final-club boys and their female counterparts. But the majority are well off enough, especially in a world where meals and lodging are taken care of, and where everyone, even the poorest student, can trade in some sense on the promise of future riches—and not riches accrued during a patient, painstaking twenty-year career in law or medicine. No, the magic of Harvard is that it promises to make you rich next year, when you graduate, or even *now,* if you and your roommates happened to come up with the Next Big Thing.

So it doesn't matter if you pile your room with expensive electronics, eat out frequently at Cambridge's overpriced restaurants and down expensive mixed drinks at the overpriced bars, and take the expected spring break trips to Barcelona, Paris, Cancún, and South Florida. Sure, you might have to absorb some college loans and maybe run up a Visa bill, making the most of the credit-card industry's eagerness to furnish elite collegians with extensive lines of credit. But soon you will be in New York pulling down seventy thousand a year for McKinsey or Goldman Sachs or J. P. Morgan . . . or perhaps, in those halcyon dot-com days, in Silicon Valley, enjoying a cosseted, lattéd life doing Web design for your roommate's start-up. After that there will be law school or business school, and then a still more lucrative job and onward, up a ladder that can be climbed as high as you want to climb, given world and time enough.

❖

This was the world that Suzanne entered—the world in which she thrived, at least for a time. She had the requisite ambition, and she was a talented enough operator to launch herself up the hierarchy of Phillips Brooks House, the Hasty Pudding, and Kappa Alpha Theta. She didn't have enough money to support her lifestyle, but neither did many people who moved in her circle, and if she had only toned things down a little—fewer femme fatale outfits, fewer presents for her community service kids, no "social event of the season" twenty-first-birthday parties—she could have skated through, then stepped out into her oft-stated dream of law school and a bright financial future.

Perhaps the wait of years felt too long. She wanted to be a socialite, so there were parties to be thrown, outfits to be purchased, trips to be taken, and all of it was happening now, today, at Harvard, where everyone was young and fabulous. She managed to create an image of wealth even before she started stealing, but fooling everyone wasn't sufficient for someone of her ambitions. She wanted the real thing.

So Suzanne set out to improve her finances by whatever means were at hand. She started on a small scale, poaching from Sally—which made perfect sense, I thought later, imagining how Suzanne must have reacted to sharing a room with a fellow Kentuckian, a fellow Theta, who was seemingly everything that she desired to be. Sally was an only child, the much-wished-for daughter of a self-made multimillionaire banker from Bowling Green. "A miracle," her parents called her, and they treated her accordingly, denying her almost nothing, from coats to cars to Cartier. Shopping with her, which I did sometimes—and Suzanne must have done quite a lot—was a surreal and sometimes shocking experience, as her charm and checkbook cut a swath through Boston's boutique stores, where half the salesclerks seemed to know her name.

Sally handled her wealth well, in a sense; she was unflaggingly generous to her poorer friends (which was almost all of us), using her own money to fill the gap between her lifestyle and ours. It was on Sally's dime that I saw my first Broadway show; it was Sally's Mercedes that drove me down to New Haven to see my sister perform in *The Nutcracker;* and I still wear the Burberry scarf that she bought for me one birthday, and the Burberry tie that followed at Christmas. So I was grateful to her, but there was always a flicker of resentment, buried deep, that Sally could do all this without breaking a sweat, and that there was no way to repay her.

I never envied her, though, because I never aspired to *be* her. But Suzanne probably did; her later career of lavish spending and generous gift giving suggests that she modeled her moneyed self, at least in part, on the standard set by Sally Maddox. And then there was her method of stealing from her rich roommate—which was, in its own way, equally telling.

I heard the story later, after the two girls had ceased to live together but before Suzanne's Hasty Pudding escapade came out. Throughout sophomore year, Sally told me, Suzanne liked to take her clothes, wear them without asking permission, and forget to return them. Taken on its own, this would have been a minor thing; Sally was nothing if not generous with her possessions. But Suzanne went further: She didn't just wear the shirts and skirts and pullovers, she went so far as to write her name on the collars, so that when her roommate demanded their return, she could point to the permanent marker and say, *No, Sally, these are mine. See?*

Sally didn't, but it was hard to argue with someone in such determined denial, and Sally was easygoing enough (and blessed with a large enough wardrobe) to forgive her friend's eccentricities.

But then her ATM card disappeared. The local Fleet branch told Sally, when she called to report it missing, that $150 had been withdrawn from her account in the last day. But not to worry, they said—all the withdrawals were made at an ATM with video surveillance, so whoever had taken the money had likely been caught on tape.

Sally went home and told this story to a seemingly concerned Suzanne, noting that she would probably be allowed to see the videotapes within a few days. Then she went to bed, only to have her roommate burst in, wild-eyed and sobbing, a few hours later.

Sally, Suzanne supposedly said, *I just looked in my wallet and found your card . . . and I'm probably the one on that tape.*

Was she confessing to the theft? Hardly. She admitted to withdrawing the money, sure, using what she "now knew" was Sally's card. But she insisted that she had done so thinking that it was *her* card—a mix-up made possible by the fact that, wonder of wonders, she and Sally turned out to share the same PIN. Sally's number was 1134, and 11/3 (well, fine, 3/11) was Suzanne's birthday, and four, you see, was one of her favorite numbers.

What must have happened, she told her roommate, *is that someone broke into our room, stole* both *our debit cards, and then came back and replaced yours in* my *wallet.*

Nothing Sally could say would induce her roommate to budge from this story. Suzanne sobbed, pleaded for their friendship, and made frequent references to Jesus, but refused to acknowledge her guilt. It was an effective tactic. Not only did Sally decide against reporting Suzanne's theft, but she remained friends with her light-fingered roommate. They were never as close as they had been, but in the social whirl to which they both belonged, a superficial, see-no-evil friendship resembled a real one.

Along with most of Sally's non-Suzanne-related friends, I was baffled that she hadn't turned in her thieving roommate, or at least cut Suzanne off entirely. I'm still not sure why she didn't. It had something to do with Sally's general generosity and something to do with the sorority life and friends they shared, and the difficulties of effecting such a breach without causing far-reaching ripples. But I always remember what Sally said later when we talked about Suzanne.

I'm afraid of her, Ross, she told me. *Everyone is, a little. You just don't know what she's capable of.*

Later, it came out that Suzanne had told a number of people that Sally had stolen an ATM card from *her.* This in response to those who wondered why the two didn't live together anymore.

But shirts and shoes and even ATM cards were too petty for Suzanne. Being a true Harvard socialite required big splashes—a two-thousand-dollar birthday party, for instance—and as she ascended through the ranks of the Pudding Theatricals, she must have realized that the cash she needed sat right in front of her. Money was not just something out there, in the world of banks and law firms and technology start-ups. During my college years, students regularly managed budgets in the hundreds of thousands or even millions of dollars, whether the money belonged to the *Crimson* or the Pudding or the Model UN's parent organization, the International Relations Council, which boasted its own substantial investment portfolio (and, in the booming 1990s, did quite well with it).

There were incidents, inevitably. In 1992 two seniors embezzled $127,000 from An Evening with Champions, a student-run ice-skating spectacle held in Harvard's hockey arena, with the proceeds going to the Jimmy Fund. (Both were convicted; one spent a year in jail.) Two years later, student leaders were charged with stealing thousands of dollars from Harvard Yearbook Publications, and a similar sum was pilfered that same year from the Harvard Krokodiloes. Two years after that, the treasurer of the Currier House Committee was indicted for embezzling $7,500 for her own personal use. These were only the stories that came to light; countless cases of financial mismanagement were swept under the rug, like the *Crimson*'s business manager who resigned the autumn after I graduated, over abuses of her office's sizable expense account.

Suzanne served as business manager for the Pudding show during my sophomore year, then became the show's producer the following fall. Her large-scale thieving began midway through this long period of influence, in March 2000, and continued for fifteen months. She shifted ever vaster amounts of money from the Pudding bank account—which was large enough to absorb such losses—into four separate accounts. The amounts ranged from $213 up to $9,870; the average was $1,500 a week. By June 2001, when the police were first alerted, the overall take was roughly $91,000.

Suzanne's accomplice in all this was her friend Randy Gomes, author of the birthday invitation, who joined the Pudding's business staff during Suzanne's sophomore year and occupied the minor office of assistant Man of the Year/Woman of the Year Manager the following fall. He was a tall, handsome student from Massachusetts; like Suzanne, he came from a middle-class background but managed to give the impression of significant wealth. (Many people thought that he was related to Peter Gomes, Harvard's chaplain, a mistake that Randy did little to dispel.) He had fewer friends than Suzanne, and fewer enemies; he was unhappy at Harvard, people said, and spent most of his social time in gay nightclubs across the river in Boston, where he became addicted to various drugs.

This habit, it was later claimed by Suzanne's attorney, was the real impetus for the theft. Randy was using the Pudding's money to fund his addiction, and Suzanne was along for the ride. But nobody who knew the two of them believed that line—it was Suzanne who had access to the Pudding's resources, and Suzanne who was calculating and controlling. Randy was viewed as being in thrall to his strong-willed friend. And the birthday party wasn't the only event that Suzanne paid for out of the Pudding's pocket. There was also a mixer between her sorority and the Delphic final club midway through our junior year, held at Locke-Ober, a posh Boston restaurant, for which Suzanne bankrolled an open bar that ran into the thousands of dollars. (Afterward, people said that the entire evening was planned in an effort to recapture the heart of a Delphic member with whom Suzanne had enjoyed a summer fling. The attempt failed, but like her shopping splurges with the community service kids, it suggested that Suzanne wanted to be loved for her money as much as she wanted to be famous for it.)

In general, she spent widely but not too extravagantly, making purchases that included a five-hundred-dollar color-screen cell phone

(Randy owned a matching one), a guitar for a boyfriend, and an autographed baseball for a boy on whom she had a crush. She spread around the rest of the money carefully: a spa trip here, a salon appointment there, and a constant zest for clothes from stores like Victoria's Secret (where she dropped eleven hundred dollars over the course of a year) and Express (another thousand dollars).

In the end, perhaps because of his drug addiction, Randy transferred considerably more money to his bank account than Suzanne did to hers, but that fact may be misleading, since the line between their purchases was never clear. They shopped together, and Randy funded events like Suzanne's T.G.I. Friday's party. ("When people realized how high the bar tab was closing out," someone told the *Crimson*, "they all said that he really must be her best friend.") In addition, the array of electronics confiscated from Randy's room was understood by their friends to be Suzanne's as well (their senior-year rooms were connected by a fire door). The equipment included a flat-screen TV, a DVD player, DJ equipment, and ninety-one DVDs. It's worth noting that save for the DJ equipment, this was hardly an outlandish setup for a Harvard dorm room.

Amid all the spending, people were curious. The Delphic-Theta mixer mystified many of Suzanne's sorority sisters. Some were told that her parents had donated the money for the party, and others heard about a dying aunt and a pre-inheritance gift. On the Pudding's 2001 trip to Bermuda, cast members remembered Suzanne taking money to reprint programs and then appearing poolside with enormous shopping bags from Saks. On the same trip, Randy showed up with a state-of-the-art portable DVD player and a satchel full of DVDs. (Randy's equivalent of Suzanne's spurious dying aunt was a fictive Boston sugar daddy who supposedly lavished cash on him.) Then there was Suzanne's habit of pilfering from the Pudding's petty-cash fund, noticed during her junior year by one Cecily Flemings, who was business manager while Suzanne was producer. According to the *Crimson,* after the arrests, Pudding members learned that "Suzanne literally physically threatened and intimidated [Flemings], so much that Cecily didn't even feel safe coming forward with the full story until the police questioned her this fall."

It sounds absurd, yet "I was afraid of her" was something that everyone seemed to say about Suzanne after her fall from grace.

In the summer of 2001, three months after Suzanne's term as producer ended, one of her successors realized that something was seriously amiss with the Theatricals' budget. The police were called in, and Suzanne's fate was sealed. She and Randy had left too large a paper trail to cover up, even had they tried. Nevertheless, the investigation took a considerable amount of time to complete, dragging on all through the fall of senior year. Suzanne and Randy knew about it; so did various Pudding higher-ups. But the rest of campus didn't, and there was nothing in Suzanne's conduct to suggest that anything was amiss. She maintained her usual schedule, and it was during these months that she helped to found Isis with a group of her wealthier friends—all of whom would later insist, quite loudly, that Suzanne had done nothing, *nothing,* to help finance the group. Her involvement in this rival girls' club was a slap in the face to Kappa Alpha Theta; the sisterhood, with dues far lower than Isis's, found out about its former president's decision to start fresh only when Isis was unveiled, with fanfare, late in November. There was much muttering about her perfidy. But by that point, it hardly mattered, since Suzanne's bridges were about to be burned for good.

The hammer fell publicly in January, during exams. True to its Darwinian nature, the Harvard community turned on Suzanne with a vengeance. The *Crimson*'s breathless front-page story, accompanied by a reprint of the famous Anthony Hopkins photo, devoted twenty-five lines to Suzanne's pre-indictment career as a campus celebrity, noting almost as an afterthought that "little information was available on Gomes last night." The paper's columnists vied with one another to denounce the larcenous pair—"No doubt they got off on their glittering social calendars and their circle of tender, affectionate friends," snarked one classmate of mine, who was not exactly a wallflower herself—while every campus publication and open e-mail list was filled with quotes from people testifying to her years of manipulations and cruelties. Then there was a searing exposé in *Fifteen Minutes*, which dredged up all of Suzanne's adolescent dirty laundry, quoting high school "friends" announcing their intention to come to Boston for the trial "to see if she gets what she deserves." Even *Harvard Magazine*, the staid voice of the alumni establishment, weighed in with a disapproving account of the thefts.

I was a columnist for the *Crimson* by that time, and it would be nice to say that I put aside my personal feelings for Suzanne and took the high road. But her arrest delighted me—it offered a delicious story, seemingly vindicating the moral order of the universe—and I decided to get personal. *Everyone*, I wrote in a column that appeared four days after the arrests, *has their own story about Suzanne Pomey '02, the well-known Winthrop senior accused of embezzling a hefty chunk of cash from the Hasty Pudding Theatricals. Mine concerns invisibility— specifically, my own. We had good friends in common, Suzanne and I, and so we saw each other at parties, in Winthrop suites, at bars, on the street. But we never spoke to one another, beyond the barest pleasantries. Or, more aptly,* she *never spoke to* me.

"Suzanne Pomey's Harvard," as I called my splenetic denunciation of Suzanne and the cutthroat culture that allowed her to flourish, was by far my most widely read column. It made me a campus celebrity in my own right, however briefly: *You're the one who wrote that column about Suzanne,* people would say upon meeting me. *I loved that column!* I braced myself for a backlash that never came: Out of roughly forty e-mails I received (most columns produced about three), not a single one came to Suzanne's defense.

But one of these messages made me think twice about my glee at Suzanne's fall. It was sent by someone who loved the column ("screw the people who say it was too harsh, etc. cause the bitch deserved all of it") but who wanted to clear up a minor misconception. For all her queen bee-ing around, my correspondent explained, Suzanne never quite ascended to what he called the "real" Harvard social scene. She worked for the Pudding theatrical troupe because she wasn't invited to join the elite Hasty Pudding Social Club, and pledged Theta because she couldn't get into the far-more-exclusive Bee. Worse, "she was never from old money New York," but from "some random place" in middle-of-nowhere Kentucky. "Talking today with a few friends of mine from the Fly and Bee who barely even know her or care to know her and think she is just plain stupid, made me realize this today. . . . Even having the money couldn't do it as she didn't have the pedigree . . . oh so sad."

For the first time, reading this message, I felt a shiver of sympathy for Suzanne, and a sense of —what? Kinship, perhaps? I had an image of her trying to get into the Bee—a women's club formed in conscious imitation of the final clubs, filled with girls from New Canaan and the Upper East Side—and facing the same kind of glacial scorn that she had bestowed on me. Perhaps Harvard had been, in a strange way, far more cruel to her than I had realized.

Yet it was hard to pity her. The trial was delayed until the summer, and Suzanne continued attending classes, living in her room in Winthrop, and maintaining the same breakneck social schedule as in the past. Some of her friends—a small group, but a significant one— rallied around her, out of loyalty or a desire for vicarious notoriety, and she would go out with them night after night, as senior spring and the whirl of pre-commencement events began.

Once the rigors of thesis writing are over, Harvard seniors live it up. There is a booze cruise, a casino cruise, a last-chance dance, a trip to Six Flags, and almost every night the class committee sponsors a senior bar at one of Cambridge's watering holes, where discounts and free appetizers abound. Suzanne never seemed to miss an event—she was always out, always drinking, always surrounded by her coterie of (largely male) loyalists. Often they encountered people from the Hasty Pudding, who sang "Smooth Criminal" whenever Suzanne came near them. Sometimes these scenes turned ugly, with insults hurled across the room and people coming as close to blows as careful, career-minded Harvardians ever did. In spite of these incidents, or perhaps because of them, Suzanne kept on partying. And she was conspicuous, too: She wore a red jacket, always, that set her apart amid the black peacoats that everyone else at Harvard favored—a bloom of sin in a Puritan sea.

But she and Randy didn't walk at graduation, since the college declined to award them diplomas, pending the outcome of their trial—which got under way late in the following fall. Both defendants pleaded guilty: Randy blamed his drug problems and a shrink testified to his addictions and his "deficit in self-esteem"; Suzanne blamed Randy. Although she "did acquiesce to Randy Gomes's scheme to use money from the HPT, she did not initiate the plan," her lawyer claimed. "She did, however, allow Randy Gomes to go forward with his plan . . . because she wanted to help Randy, then a friend, with his drug related problems." The lawyer added that Suzanne had "maintained an unblemished record while at Harvard," and in what was undoubtedly intended as a tearjerking performance, Suzanne's parents were asked to stand. "These are people who lived the dream of their child being admitted to Harvard," Suzanne's lawyer declared, as if this alone was reason enough for the court to show mercy.

The judge didn't swallow it whole. "The court does not find that the motive for the thefts was simply a combination of the defendant Gomes's drug problem and defendant Pomey's desire to assist a friend," he said at the sentencing. "The thefts involved in this case were substantial, repetitive, and not uncovered as a result of the initiative of either defendant." But in the end, neither Randy nor Suzanne received any jail time, even though their crime, "felony larceny over $250," carries a maximum penalty of five years in prison. The judge sentenced them to probation, remarking that despite the prosecution's request for brief jail terms, "no purpose would be served by a sentence of incarceration." He added that he had been touched by Suzanne's and Randy's "sincere expressions of remorse and regret."

No doubt they did regret it, in spite of the lightness of the sentence. After all, a Harvard diploma was denied to both of them, and just after they were sentenced, the Harvard Administrative Board recommended them for dismissal, a penalty that expels the offender from the college for five years and lets them back in only by a majority vote of the faculty. (In other words, next to never.) They had "lived the dream" of "being admitted to Harvard," in the words of Suzanne's lawyer, and that dream had been taken from them. They were expelled from the paradise of the American overclass. How could jail compare with such a cruel fate?

❖

The mythology of ancient Greece—the Greece of Hesiod and Mary Renault—is rife with stories of ritual violence in which a chosen scapegoat is torn to pieces by a hysterical mob. From the Dionysian myths of bacchic mayhem to the custom of annual king killing, religiously sanctioned murder is treated as a common and even salutary practice. As religious scholar Rene Girard writes, "Even if they are not accused of any crime, mythical victims are still supposed to die for a good cause," since in such acts of "mimetic violence," societal fissures are papered over and divisions are healed. Since "everyone believes in the guilt of the victim," Girard notes, "they all turn against him—and since that victim is now isolated and helpless, they can do so with no danger of retaliation. As a result, no enemy remains for anybody in the community. Scandals evaporate and peace returns—for a while."

This is an unfair metaphor for the fate of Suzanne Pomey, admittedly. She was hardly an innocent, and even now I cannot bring myself to pity her, unhappy or unbalanced though she may have been. I did not know Randy, so I can muster sympathy for him, but I can still feel the contemptuous chill of Suzanne's gaze, and I remember how her eyes danced when her appearance at some senior spring event sent a stir of whispers through the crowd. She was notorious, but she was never ashamed. I think she loved every minute of it.

Yet why did I, along with all my classmates, turn on her so happily and so savagely? What she did was wicked, but her crime was largely victimless, and America has always loved a glamorous thief. Her bold act of self-invention—the rural nobody goes east, cuts a few corners, and becomes a somebody—has a powerful resonance in our culture. Jay Gatsby was a bootlegger and a trader in stolen securities, but nobody roots for the feds to swoop down on East Egg and drag him away, in handcuffs, from the fireworks on his gleaming lawn. Where was Suzanne's Nick Carraway, to celebrate her dream of the orgiastic future, her green light at the end of the Pudding's dock?

You're worth the whole damn bunch put together, Nick shouts to Gatsby just before his death. Suzanne wasn't worth more than all her classmates, exactly, but she was one of us, in her grasping and dissembling. She was Harvard's raging id: She had the ambition, the obsession with fame, and the desire for riches that animated so many of us, and like us she stored them up behind the facade of a pure heart and good intentions, of community service and academic excellence.

We brought out the knives when she fell from grace, but we couldn't kill her—she was too much a part of ourselves. She may have been a sociopath, but every society gets the sociopath it deserves.

So it was appropriate, perhaps, that she didn't go into hiding like poor, drug-damaged Randy, that she lived it up along with the rest of us until the bells pealed over commencement and our four years were officially over. We denied her a diploma and the chance to march with us, but she was there nevertheless, a pale-faced shadow flitting among the parents and alums, the ghost of Harvard Present amid the waterlogged festivities.

She even came back the following fall, a month before the judge's verdict was handed down, when we recent graduates returned to campus for Harvard-Yale weekend—still in red, still aswirl with controversy, still defiantly guiltless. Perhaps time will exorcise her ghost, but I doubt it. I imagine that she'll be back again and again, for all the games and reunions to come, until we are old and gray and as wildly rich and famous as Harvard promised to make us. The capricious gods of meritocracy cast her out of paradise, but she's still hanging around the gates, hoping that the angel's flaming sword drops a little and that she can slip back inside.

Maybe she will—who can say? If she keeps coming back, what she did might finally be forgotten: at our fiftieth reunion, perhaps, when senility has begun its slow assault.

And when that day comes, I may even raise a glass to her—to Suzanne Pomey, a member in good standing, now and forever, of the Harvard Class of 2002.

CHAPTER FOUR

Approaches to Knowledge

A T THE BEGINNING OF every term, Harvard students enjoy a weeklong stretch known as "shopping period," in which they are free to sample as many courses as they like, and thus—or so the theory goes—concoct the most appropriate semester of classes. There is a rustling, boisterous quality to these two weeks, a sense of intellectual possibility, as people spend mornings and afternoons popping in and out of lecture halls, grabbing syllabi and listening to twenty minutes or so of boilerplate from the professor before darting away to sample other classes that meet at the same hour. Lectures are unusually well attended, and the more popular classes have shoppers crowding the doorways, leaning in for a peek at the legendary professor and—if enrollment is limited—jotting their names down on lottery forms, while trying, with typical Harvard competitiveness, to whip up the perfect case for why they should be allowed to take the course. This is the only time of year (exam weeks aside) when classes are the chief subject of dining hall and dorm room discussion, and when people seem actively excited by education, by the possibilities of a brand-new semester.

The enthusiasm evaporates quickly: The empty seats in the various halls and auditoriums gradually multiply as the semester rattles along, until rooms that were full for the opening lecture come to re-semble the stadium of a losing baseball team during a meaningless late-August game. There are pockets of diehards in the front rows, anxiously taking notes, and scattered observers elsewhere—students like me, perhaps, who have fought down the urge to hit the snooze button and hauled ourselves to the auditorium, only to realize that we've missed the last three lectures and fallen so far behind that tak-ing notes is a futile exercise. Better to doze off now and wait for se-mester's end, when we can do all the reading in a burst and then take frantic, exhaustive notes at the review sessions that are always help-fully provided, or simply go online to the course website and dis-cover that the professor has uploaded notes for every lecture, as if he understands all too well the character and study habits of his seldom-glimpsed students.

But during shopping period, late-semester torpor hasn't yet set in, the demands of extracurriculars aren't yet overwhelming, and the Harvard campus bubbles with academic energy. And so it was that Harvard Hall 101—a typical if smallish modern lecture hall, with perhaps a hundred seats arranged in a sloping semicircle around a blackboard and mini-podium—was packed with shoppers on the February day in 2001 when Harvey Mansfield gave the semester's first lecture on "Modern Political Philosophy: From Machiavelli to Nietzsche." Every chair was filled, and there were people in the aisles and on the windowsills, even spilling out the door and onto the linoleum of Harvard Hall's mezzanine.

It was a good day, in other words, for an act of political theater.

Mansfield cuts a distinctive figure on campus, both physically and intellectually. Short and trim, tanned and handsome, with an an-gular face, bright eyes, and a wide, sharklike grin, he is also unusually dapper in an age of professorial slovenliness, with his fedoras and pastel shirts and unusual ties—selected, he always insists, by his wife, Delba, who also assists on more intellectual Mansfield projects (their recently published translation of Tocqueville, for instance). He is famously conservative, a right-wing gadfly in the college's ointment, well known for his opposition to affirmative action and gay rights, and for his (sometimes cryptic) critiques of feminism and political correctness.

"Before I begin the lecture," he said that day, "I have a brief announcement concerning the class's grading policy. As many of you know, I have often been, ah, outspoken concerning the upward creep of Harvard grades over the last few decades. Some say that this climb—in which what were once C's have become B's, and those B's are now fast becoming A's—is a result of meritocracy, which has ensured that Harvard students today are, ah, *smarter* than their forebears. This may be true, but I must tell you that I see little evidence of it."

He paused, flashed his smile, and went on. "Nevertheless, I have recently decided that hewing to the older standard is fruitless, when no one else does, because all I succeed in doing is punishing students for taking classes with me. Therefore, I have decided that this semester I will issue two grades to each of you. The first will be the grade that you actually deserve—a C for mediocre work, a B for good work, and an A for excellence. This one will be issued to you alone, for every paper and exam that you complete. The second grade, computed only at semester's end, will be your, ah, ironic grade—'ironic,' in this case, being a word used to mean *lying*—and it will be computed on a scale that takes as its mean the average Harvard grade, the B-plus. This higher grade will be sent to the registrar's office and will appear on your transcript. It will be your public grade, you might say, and it will ensure, as I have said, that you will not be penalized for taking a class with me."

Another shark's grin. "And of course, only you will know whether you actually deserve it."

Mansfield had been fighting this particular battle for years, long enough to have earned the sobriquet "C-minus" from his suffering students in the government department, and long enough, too, that his frequent complaints about waning academic standards were routinely dismissed by Harvard's higher-ups as the out-of-touch crankiness of a conservative fogey. But the ironic-grade stunt changed all that. The next day, there was Mansfield on the front page of *The Boston Globe,* alongside a story on the decline of academic standards at Harvard and elite colleges in general. Suddenly what had been a minor, hushed-over embarrassment was big news, and Harvard was being mocked as the academic equivalent of Garrison Keillor's Lake Wobegon, where all the children are above average.

This was somewhat unfair, if only because Harvard was hardly alone. Grade inflation is rampant in elite universities, and in American higher education as a whole. Still, our numbers were particularly staggering. Over 90 percent of my classmates were on the dean's list, meaning that they had GPAs of B– or higher. Overall, half of all grades handed out in the year before Mansfield's ironic-grading policy were either A or A–, while just 6 percent were C– or below. By way of comparison, in 1940 more Harvard students had a C– average than any other GPA, and in 1955 just 15 percent of undergrads boasted a GPA of B+ or above.

No one disputed the numbers, or how drastically they had changed. But Mansfield's comments still sparked controversy, because everyone wanted to debate the *why* of grade inflation. This quickly became a debate about the legacy of the 1960s, for although grades had been going up for a long time, the biggest spike by far came in the latter half of that decade. In 1965, around 20 percent of students earned B+ or above averages; five years later, the number was 48 percent. For Mansfield, who had taught at Harvard during this era, the explanation was obvious. "Grade inflation got started," he wrote in the *Crimson,* "when professors raised the grades of students protesting the war in Vietnam. At that time, too, white professors, imbibing the spirit of the new policies of affirmative action, stopped giving low grades to black students, and to justify or conceal this, also stopped giving low grades to white students."

Needless to say, it was the race argument that earned the most attention. There was a flurry of angry e-mails and editorials, and the Black Students Association picketed Mansfield's class, passing out flyers and staging a silent protest at the start of one of his lectures. The administration was even moved to respond. Dean Harry Lewis penned an op-ed in the *Crimson* that divulged some "official" numbers, purporting to show that the most dramatic burst of inflated grades hit campus in the late 1960s, whereas blacks weren't present in significant numbers until 1970. (Whether he was right depends on your definition of "significant numbers," since there were a hundred blacks in the freshman class of 1968, up from fewer than two dozen in 1965.) In addition, Lewis wrote, the period from 1970 to 1985 — the first fifteen years of a strong black presence on campus — represented "the only fifteen-year period in the past eighty years in which there was no increase in grades at Harvard." (Again, maybe: Other numbers suggest that the upward climb of the 1960s flattened out only in the mid-1970s, not before.) Thus, he concluded, "the racial theory of grade inflation is so spectacularly wrong that it is hard to know how or why it got started."

I thought at the time that Lewis's op-ed was brilliant, less for its analysis than for how it neatly focused attention on the Vietnam era, while obscuring the far more interesting question — namely, what about the grade inflation of the present day? Grade inflation exploded in the 1960s and leveled off in the '70s and early '80s, but it began to grow again in the go-go '90s, after the counterculture's tide had receded, and achievement, personal responsibility, and general good form were once again the Ivy League's order of the day. Indeed, it was the 1990s, not the '60s, that saw the final triumph of the gentleman's B+. In 1985, 43 percent of Harvardians earned GPAs in that range, down almost a quarter since the permissive year of 1970; by 2000, midway through my college years, 68 percent of all Harvard students boasted an average of B+ or above.

Why such a startling spike, in a time of peace, prosperity, and (moderate) racial harmony? Mansfield's op-ed offered an answer, specifically "the prevalence in American education of the notion of self-esteem. According to that therapeutic notion, the purpose of education is to make students feel capable and 'empowered,' and professors should hesitate to pass judgment on what students have learned."

There is something to this, but I think that the roots of grade inflation—and, by extension, the overall ease and lack of seriousness in Harvard's undergraduate academic culture—run deeper than the cult of self-esteem. Understanding grade inflation requires an understanding of the nature of modern Harvard, and of elite education in general—and particularly the ambitions of its inhabitants, students and professors alike.

The ambitions of the undergraduates are those of a well-trained meritocratic elite, brought up to believe that their worth is contingent on the level of wealth and power and personal achievement they attain. The pursuit of these goals, in turn, depends on high grades in a way it did not for an earlier generation. In the semi-aristocracy that Harvard once was, the gentleman's C was accepted by students because they knew their prospects in life had more to do with their family fortunes and connections than with their GPAs. But in today's meritocracy, the family fortune must be reconstituted in every generation. Even if you could live off your parents' wealth, the ethos of the meritocracy holds that you shouldn't, because your worth as a person is determined not by clan or class but by what you do, and whether you succeed at it. What you do, in turn, hinges on what you put down on your résumé, and often on the GPA that adorns it.

Thus the professor is not just a disinterested pedagogue. As a dispenser of grades, he is a gatekeeper to worldly success. With the pressures of capitalism pushing in on academic life, it's easy to understand why professors would shrink from "punishing" their students, as Mansfield put it all too aptly, by handing out C's and D's. During the Vietnam War, when flunking out meant risking death in the Mekong's rice paddies, countless professors bumped up their students' grades. Thirty years later, the stakes are lower, but the pressures are still there: the upward pressure from students to have their grades raised (*Look, I can't afford a B in this class if I want to get into law school,* people say before marching off to beg a teaching fellow for a boost into the B+/A– range); the horizontal pressure from the rest of the professoriate, to which even Mansfield eventually gave way; the downward pressure from the college's powers-that-be (*If you want to fail someone, you have to be prepared for a very long, painful battle with the higher echelons of the administration,* one professor told the *Crimson* during the controversy); and perhaps the pressure from within, from the part of the professor that secretly sympathizes with his students' ambitious careerism.

Academics, after all, have ambitions of their own, and they are well aware of the vicissitudes of the marketplace, coping as they do with the publish-or-perish culture of the conference circuit and the tenure track. It's a culture that rarely rewards devotion to undergraduate education. During my four years at Harvard, the campus was littered with the corpses of student-favorite junior professors, from neocon political theorist Peter Berkowitz, who launched a fruitless lawsuit against Harvard, claiming that he had been denied tenure for political reasons; to linguistics professor Bert Vaux, whose class I wandered into to fulfill a requirement, and who—though he never made me love the subject matter—was an inspiringly diligent teacher, the only professor I ever knew who tried to learn every name in a lecture class of a hundred-odd students. (When tenure escaped him, Vaux took his case to the students, mustering a futile petition and a public outcry that fell on deaf ears. Three months after he left Harvard, the school added insult to injury, stealing superstar linguist Steven Pinker—whose books Vaux had used, to great effect, in his classes—from crosstown rival MIT.)

Another tenure-track casualty of my acquaintance was Louis Miller, a young professor of European intellectual history. He was an intense and handsome figure, with short black hair and a faintly ascetic air; a relapsed Catholic, he seemed almost priestly, despite his wife and child, but in a tough, masculine way that belonged to an earlier, more ascetic Church. I never took a class with him, but some of my friends did, and he began having lunch with us at the wide sunlit tables of Leverett House dining hall, where we would talk endlessly about politics and philosophy and religion and anything else that came up. All through my sophomore spring, we met and chatted and listened to him ramble, and I, whose knowledge of philosophy in those days began with Hobbes and ended with Locke, was inspired to spend the next two years burying myself in Plato and Cicero, Rousseau and Tocqueville.

But by then Miller was gone. He hadn't published much since finishing his Ph.D. dissertation on Nietzsche, and he was replaced by another youngish star—his intellectual mirror image, a whip-smart scholar of American pragmatism named James Kloppenberg, with whom I took a class but never shared a meal. Miller went south, to Saint John's in Annapolis, a Great Books school. *The students might not be as wonderful as you are,* he told us, *but the intellectual climate will be better.*

Many of my better teachers were those who understood from the beginning that they had no future at Harvard, that one either had to be a minority or a master of petty personal politics to climb the greased pole of tenure, and they therefore put it out of their minds. I had an advantage because my own major—or "concentration," as Harvard calls it—was History and Literature, which was not a department in its own right but a "committee on degrees," relying on professors from the English and History departments to teach its lectures, and administered for the most part by youngish tutors, recent post-docs who were killing time at Harvard before setting out to seek their fortunes elsewhere. My thesis adviser, a smart and solid student of imperial Britain named John Mackey, was one of these; he picked up his doctorate during my junior year and lingers at Harvard even now, less than anxious to start battling for employment with the thousands of jobless humanities Ph.D.'s.

"I don't want to leave New England," he told me recently, over lunch in Boston's North End. "My wife and I are happy here. But I should probably take the first job that'll hire me, even if it's at Western Oklahoma State or something, shouldn't I?"

"So will you?" I asked him.

He shrugged. "Maybe. Or maybe I'll go teach high school, or prep school, somewhere in Massachusetts. I'm just not sure academia is worth it, you know?"

The two women who ran my sophomore tutorial—one a History Ph.D., the other an English tutor, to fit History and Literature's interdisciplinary approach—were similarly jaded. Midway through the tutorial (a seven-person class, and probably the best-run, most rigorous course I took in college), someone asked them if they were planning to stay at Harvard. One of them laughed a little bitterly, and the other said no, they were just lucky to be here now.

"Harvard never promotes from within," she told us, "or almost never. Especially in the humanities, junior faculty never get tenure. They like to hire superstars. So if you want to be a Harvard professor, you go out and become a superstar somewhere else. *Then* they want you."

Both had disappeared before I hit junior year.

For those who stayed, who thrived or at least endured—well, who can blame them if, when it came time to grade their students,

they sometimes took the path of least resistance, the path of the gentleman's B+? That is, if they graded at all: Many didn't, particularly
those saddled with the large, impersonal lecture classes for which
major research universities are famous, with hundreds of clamoring,
grade-grubbing students and only a staff of graduate student assistants (or "teaching fellows," in Harvard's pretentious academese) to
help. Who can blame the professors, in such trying circumstances,
for passing the grading buck down to those younger, less burned-out
teaching fellows? And who can blame the TFs in turn—themselves
only a few years removed from undergrad anxieties, and coping with
their own set of academic pressures—if their grading standards were
sometimes a trifle, well, *lax?*

I give out mainly A's, one TF announced to my section early in the
first meeting of the year. *A few B's, maybe. But I don't like to, you know?*

❖

It didn't help that my classmates and I were creatively lazy, gifted at
working smarter rather than harder, and determined to cut every
possible academic corner. We were faced every fall and spring with a
bevy of daunting, pages-long syllabi that bristled with frequent five-
to-seven-page papers and lengthy readings (a typical two-day assignment might read: *Prologue, Ch.1, Ch. 3, pp. 73–76, 88–102, Ch. 5,
pp. 180–225, Ch. 9, pp. 250–57, Epilogue*), all culminating in a final
fifteen-to-twenty-page research paper and/or a three-hour exam. We
quickly realized that it was best not even to try covering all that
ground, especially when the hours wasted trying to read every word
of the first three-hundred-page book on the list could be put to far
better use glancing over the exam review sheet, picking out the

salient topics, then going back over the readings and skimming selectively, packing your brain with just enough information to bullshit your way through whichever of the three essay questions best coincided with the little reading that you happened to have done. . . .

Or you could use the time, as many industrious students did, to organize study groups in which twelve or so students divvied up twelve or so books, with each reading one and producing a meticulous outline of the material, which was then passed around via e-mail to all the members of the group—including, inevitably, the one free rider who was just too busy to finish his or her outline, but neglected to mention this fact until all the other outlines were safely e-mailed his or her way. . . .

Or you could spend your time at office hours with the hapless teaching fellow who taught your section, and who would be only too happy to give you that extension, and maybe change your grade on the last paper, and, if schmoozed properly, might even spill some "suggestions" about the areas of the syllabus covered on the midterm. . . .

Or if worst came to worst, and you had a paper due in thirty minutes, not a word written, and a hard-ass instructor who brooked no delays, you could spend your remaining time creating a document filled with wacky characters plucked from Microsoft Word's Wingdings font (interspersed, if you were really clever, with a few random paragraphs of intelligible prose), which would then be e-mailed to your teaching fellow, who wouldn't get around to opening it until the next day, at which point he would write to you and say that he was sorry, but the Word file was corrupted and he couldn't read your paper, and you would apologize profusely, mention all the virus problems your computer had been suffering, and send him a second, "virus-free" copy of the paper you had finished writing not ten minutes before. . . .

Or if worst came to *absolute* worst and your TF didn't accept papers via e-mail, you could follow in the footsteps of my friend Tom, a curly-haired Rhode Islander whose capacity for brilliant procrastination was unmatched (he wrote his eighty-page summa-minus thesis in just four days). Faced with a non-negotiable Thursday-afternoon due date for a history essay, Tom finished an introduction and a conclusion, used them to bracket seven blank pages, and dropped off the whole package in his TF's box, planning to write the rest that evening and then blame printer problems for the "missing" pages. On his way out of the TF's office, though, Tom noticed a maintenance door ajar, and over the course of that night, with Nick and me standing as lookouts, he repeatedly sneaked back into the supposedly locked building and gradually filled in the missing meat of the essay, producing no fewer than five successive drafts, each of which was dropped in the box and then replaced, hours later, by an upgraded version.

And so it was that on Friday morning, bright and early, the TF strolled into his office and found a brilliant Tom Doyle paper ensconced in his mailbox, first placed there at five the previous day, largely written between the hours of midnight and four A.M., and completed just thirty minutes before.

It goes without saying that Tom received an A.

This picture is unfair to those students who took academics very seriously indeed, who never missed a lecture or a section, who always did the reading and posted comments in the online discussion groups and began preparing for the exam several months in advance. Some of these workaholics were budding academics, genuinely thrilled to be puzzling over the Riemann hypothesis or analyzing the writings of the Cappadocian fathers. Others were future doctors: Being a pre-med at Harvard is serious business, at first because of the rigors of introductory courses like Chemistry 10—designed explicitly to weed out the weak and unprepared—and then because of all the laboratory requirements, which kept my pre-med friends buried in beakers and test tubes until all hours of the night. Still others were just habituated to a grinding work ethic, having spent their high school years diligently overachieving in every class and on every assignment, to the point where they could imagine school no other way.

But these stalwarts were a minority. The rest of us were studious primarily in our avoidance of academic work, and brilliant mostly in our maneuverings to achieve maximum GPA in return for minimal effort. I don't mean to suggest that we never worked or went to class. By the standard of America's beery institutions of higher learning, I have no doubt that Harvard is a bastion of academic rigor, weekly preparedness, and sky-high classroom attendance. But there were so many other things to be done—punch events and sit-ins, extracurriculars and summer job applications—and it was easy for my classmates and me to believe, consciously or unconsciously, that the classroom was just another résumé-padding opportunity, a place to collect the necessary GPA (and the necessary recommendations) to carry us to the next station in life. If that GPA could be achieved while reading one tenth of the books on the syllabus, then so much the better.

Sometimes you didn't even have to go that far. The final paper I wrote in college was assigned in "The American West, 1780–1930," by a history professor named Catherine Corman. She first passed out a pair of journal articles on the theory and practice of "material history"—essentially, historical research based on careful analysis of objects—and then dispatched us to the Peabody, Harvard's museum of Archaeology and Ecology, where she had set out three pairs of objects from the frontier era. An object in each pair was crafted by Indians, and one by Europeans; we were to pick a pair and write a ten-page paper that compared, contrasted, and explored the relationship between the two. There was a catch: Aside from the essays on material history, and a general text, *North American Indian Jewelry and Adornment*, we were to use no secondary sources.

Of the three choices, I can remember only the pair I picked: a feathered Sioux war club and an American revolver with its carrying case. As I stood in the museum, taking notes on the club's colored striping and the gun box's patriotic scrollwork, it seemed an impossible assignment. How was I ever going to eke out ten pages when I knew nothing about the provenance of the weapons or the significance of their decorations and markings?

Sitting at my desk two weeks later, I realized how wrong I had been. The paper was pathetically easy to write—not despite the dearth of information, but *because* of it. Knowing nothing meant I could write anything. I didn't need to do any reading, know any history, or learn anything at all. I just had to be smart.

Some excerpts offer the flavor of what I came up with. *Chief Running Antelope's war club is less a weapon than a talisman of supernatural power. . . . The club's red paint and eagle feather link the weapon and its holder to sacred, invisible worlds; the "H.A. Brigham" inscription reinforces the revolver's connection to a capitalist order in which weapons are mass-produced, rather than individually crafted. . . . The case is clearly an impractical method of carrying the gun . . . it is, rather, an eminently practical method of displaying it, with the paradoxical corollary that the gun is displayed by not being displayed. . . . The book-like case, with its gold leaf and intricate images, transforms the gun by containing its potential for violence. . . .*

The gun is displayed by not being displayed . . . By the time I finished, I almost believed it. My professor must have, too; the paper got an A.

Memories like this reassure me that in the grand scheme of academic decline, we corner-cutting undergrads didn't have that much to apologize for. We were typical students, that's all, and whatever nostalgists may believe, there was never a golden age when students did all their work and attended every lecture. When Aquinas held forth in Paris or Heidegger in Freiburg, the Tom Doyles of those ages were probably squirreled away in their dorms, frantically skimming other people's notes to prep for the final exam.

What made our age different was the moment that happened over and over again at Harvard, when you said, *This is going to be hard* and then suddenly realized, *No, this is easy*. Maybe it came when you boiled down a three-page syllabus to a hundred pages of essential exam-time reading, or when you saw that you could turn in that paper whenever and your frazzled TF wasn't going to dock you, or when you handed in C-grade work and were rewarded with a gleaming B+. But whenever it came, it taught us that it wasn't our sloth alone that made Harvard easy, or our hundred and one ways to avoid overwork, or our constant pushing for higher grades and fewer requirements and endless extensions on our assignments.

No, Harvard was easy because almost no one seemed to be pushing back.

❖

This wasn't true everywhere. Not every class was easy, not every professor passed out peculiarly content-free assignments, and not every department was debilitated by grade inflation. Those that were tended to be clustered in the humanities, in history and English, classics and the foreign languages, government and philosophy—in those departments, in other words, that provide what used to be considered the meat of a liberal arts education. It was humanities students who did the least work, who got the highest grades, who cruised academically while their science- and math-minded classmates had to struggle sometimes to reach that magical B+ plateau. It was humanities students, above all, who let their studies slide in favor of time-sucking extracurriculars—the *Crimson* and the *Advocate*, the *Lampoon* and the debate team, the Model United Nations and the Institute of Politics.

Humanities professors who bucked this trend were rare. It was my junior year before I really encountered one, when Sally Maddox talked me into taking a seminar on Gothic literature in the Victorian era. The class was excellent, as it turned out; it had a superb reading list, and it was taught by John Picker, a slender young professor who was suitably Gothic himself, as if he had sprung fully formed from a tale by Stoker or Poe. He had a narrow face, a high forehead, and a twisting, almost sinister smile, and his hair was jet black, with a supernatural streak of white down the middle. There was only one difficulty: Professor Picker had just arrived at Harvard and didn't quite understand the rules of the grade-inflation game.

I discovered this when I turned in my first paper, a second-rate effort dashed off in a couple of nights, for which I expected—based on two years of experience with Harvard English essays—to get an A–, or at least a B+. Instead, Picker gave it a B–, and threw in some pointed comments about how badly I had misinterpreted "The Fall of the House of Usher." Stung, I tripled my efforts on the final paper, producing a lengthy treatise on *Benito Cereno* that was, I thought modestly, some of my finest work—good for an A, surely, which would boost my overall grade up to the expected A– plateau. Sure enough, Picker liked it, too. But he gave it a B+.

I was far too proud to talk to him about my grade, so I did what I usually did when such things happened, which was to gripe for weeks on end, mainly to Sally (who had managed an A– in the class).

"You know," she said to me at lunch, after exams were over and I was beginning to put the unpleasant experience behind me, "I talked to Professor Picker about your grade the other day."

"You did *what*?"

"Sure," she said blithely, then explained, to my mounting horror, that she had been to Picker's office hours and my name had come up. Picker had mentioned how much he'd enjoyed having me in the class, and Sally had replied, *Well, Ross didn't think you gave him a very good grade.*

"Good God," I muttered, my head sinking into my hands.

"Anyway," she went on, "he said that he didn't know what I meant, that he *did* give you a good grade, and that was when I figured it out."

"Figured what out?"

"That he doesn't understand about our grades!"

Picker, she explained, had gone to the University of Virginia for graduate school, then taught there, and come to Harvard with high expectations for his new Ivy League students. More important, he had come knowing next to nothing about our high GPAs.

"He doesn't know anything about it!" Sally crowed. "He probably thinks that a B-plus is really good, and that he shouldn't give out very many A's at all! Aren't you glad I figured it out?"

"I can't believe you talked to him about my grades," I groaned.

"Well, fine, but don't you feel better?"

"Sure, I suppose so . . . but even so, *you* got an A-minus, Sally."

"Well, yes," she said primly, then grinned and clapped her hands. "Which means I'm really, *really* smart!"

The theory is often advanced that grade inflation is worse in the humanities because grading English essays and history papers is more subjective than marking problem sets and lab reports, and thus more vulnerable to student pressure and professorial weakness. There is a teaspoon of truth to that claim, I suppose, just as there is some small truth to the notion, beloved of right-wing critics of academe, that the humanities are a hotbed of lesbian Chicano poststructuralists who consider grades of any kind to be part of the vast patriarchal conspiracy. But as with grade inflation in general, the problem in the humanities runs deeper than subjective grading or fashionable socialism; it runs to the roots of elite America, to the grinding gears of the free market.

When asked about the left-wing biases of his Harvard colleagues, the libertarian philosopher Robert Nozick once hypothesized that most professors are socialists because they consider themselves far smarter than boobish businessmen, and therefore resent the economic system that rewards practical intelligence over their own (ostensibly superior) gifts. It's not a bad theory, but I'm inclined to think that such academic *ressentiment* coexists increasingly, at least in money-drunk America, with a deep inferiority complex regarding the modern capitalist project, and a need, however unconscious, to justify academic life in terms of the fantastic wealth creation that takes place just outside the ivory tower. (Not to mention within it, in the form of fund-raising and endowment-building. It's hard to be detached from grubby monetary concerns when your university is forking over $34 million apiece to its top portfolio managers, as Harvard did in 2003.)

During the 1990s, especially, when the old gods of Marx and Engels had failed, when globalization promised to unite capitalism and socialism in the eschaton of the Third Way, when recruiters from investment banks and consulting firms swarmed elite campuses preaching the gospel of Midas to the next ruling class, I think that confidence in the inherent value of a liberal arts education slipped to an all-time low. Many professors came to believe, however subconsciously, in the cultural voices that whispered to them that what goes on in the classroom is far less important than what happens later, out in the "real world."

If I am right—if the marketplace casts a lengthening shadow over academic life—then it should be clear that *some* areas of university life aren't going to lack confidence in the importance of their work. The sciences, for instance, rest secure in the knowledge that even if their students don't get rich, their labors will help shove along the whole modern project of wealth and health creation. Abstruse genomic work could one day yield in utero engineering; mucking around with chemicals could produce a cure for AIDS or the next Viagra; computer science promises, even now, to make every nerd a zillionaire.

Then there is economics, the new queen of the sciences: a discipline perfectly tailored for the modern-market-driven university, and not coincidentally the most popular concentration during my four years of college. It's no coincidence, too, that economics was the only department at Harvard where the faculty tilted rightward—on issues of regulation and taxation, at least. (Marty Feldstein, who taught Economics 10, Harvard's most popular class, was a former Reagan economic adviser.) To tilt right is, in some sense, to assert a belief in absolute truth, and the only absolute truth that the upper class accepts these days is the truth of the market.

In this sense, the antinomian left-wing professors who crowd the humanities are unwitting servants of the very market their socialist dogmas claim to disdain. Their decades-long wade in the marshes of postmodernist academic theory—where canons are scorned, books exist only as texts to be deconstructed by eager theorists, willfully obscurantist writing is championed over accessible prose, and every mention of "truth" is to be placed in sneering quotation marks— amounts to a tacit acceptance of capitalism's ruthless insistence that only science is important, only science really pursues truth, because only science has tangible, quantifiable, potentially profitable results.

The results of this retreat into irrelevance are visible all across the curriculum. Philosophy departments have labored to purge themselves of metaphysicians and moralists; history departments emphasize endless primary research and micro-history, seeking not to educate their students broadly in the human past but to train up another generation of dusty scholars of esoterica who will exchange papers on iron-ore production in ancient Ireland and feud viciously over the relative significance of various documents from fourteenth-century China. As for English, outside of a few eccentrics like Harold Bloom, there is little pretense that literature matters, that it is valuable in and of itself and should be part of every educated person's life, rather than serving as grist for endless academic debates that resemble nothing so much as the medieval scholasticism that today's philosophy departments officially disdain.

Writing in *The New York Review of Books* some years ago, Andrew Delbanco had this to say about the study of English in American higher education:

> *The field of English has become, to use a term given currency twenty-five years ago by the redoubtable Stanley Fish, a "self-consuming artifact." On the one hand, it has lost the capacity to put forward persuasive judgments; on the other hand, it is stuffed with dogma and dogmatists. It has paid overdue attention to minority writers, but . . . it (along with the humanities in general) has failed to attract many minority students. It regards the idea of progress as a pernicious myth, but never have there been so many critics so sure that they represent so much progress over their predecessors. It distrusts science, but it yearns to be scientific—as attested by the notorious recent "Sokal hoax," in which a physicist submitted a deliberately fraudulent article full of pseudoscientific gibberish to a leading cultural-studies journal, which promptly published it. It denounces the mass media for pandering to the public with pitches and slogans, but it cannot get enough of mass culture. The louder it cries about the high political stakes in its own squabbles, the less connection it maintains to anything resembling real politics. . . .*

A self-consuming artifact. It's a perfect phrase, and one that could apply neatly to all of the humanities, which are increasingly engaged only with themselves, and believe only in the propagation of their own disciplines—in the production of more academics, not the education of the student body in general. Or as Delbanco says of English, the humanities exhibit "the contradictory attributes of a religion in its late phase—a certain desperation to attract converts, combined with an evident lack of convinced belief in its own scriptures and traditions."

Sure, historians believe in their periods and primary sources, English scholars in their textual debates, philosophers in their logic games. But many of them don't seem to believe that they have something to offer students who don't plan to be historians or literary theorists, or philosophers. They don't make the effort to translate their particular work—which may be excellent—to the most pressing task of undergraduate education, which is to provide a *general* education, a liberal arts education, to future doctors and bankers and lawyers and diplomats.

Or as one History and Literature tutor said, early in my freshman year, when I asked him to describe the concentration to me— *Well, you know, if you want to be a consultant or an investment banker, a degree in History and Literature won't stand in your way.*

❖

If an antidote to this stultifying status quo exists, one might hope to find it in Harvard's Core Curriculum, the large swath of requirements that awaits every undergraduate. If the humanities suffer from a crisis of confidence, if they cannot offer any vision of what an academic generalist might study, then one would expect the Core to step into the breach, offering a unified approach to a liberal arts education, a compelling account of the intellectual joys that every Harvard student should experience before he or she enters the wider world.

If only it were so! The Core Curriculum, the current centerpiece of undergraduate education at Harvard—though its days may be numbered, thankfully—is the 1970s answer to a traditional liberal arts curriculum, and it manages to be even worse than that description makes it sound. At its inception, in the not so halcyon year of 1978, it was hailed as a brilliant innovation, a more democratic answer to the Great Books programs that colleges like Columbia still maintain. To that end, it has no universal requirements, no prescribed texts or classes or reading lists. Instead, it insists that students take, before graduation, at least one class in nine of eleven subject areas—areas whose titles and subject matter *sound* suitably comprehensive. There is Literature and Arts A through C: A is given over to classes on literature, B to music and the visual arts, and C to the artistic achievements of specific cultures—ancient Greece or Augustan Rome, for instance. To these are added Historical Studies A and B; Sciences A (physical science) and B (life science); Foreign Cultures (classes on non-Western societies); Quantitative Reasoning (a recent addition, perhaps prompted by math department protests); Moral Reasoning (courses on ethics, religion, and philosophy); and Social Analysis, whose classes deal with the social sciences and include that ever popular standby, Marty Feldstein's Economics 10.

All in all, a sojourn in the Core would seem to provide a well-rounded (if perhaps slightly unimaginative) survey of human learning, neatly broken down by disciplines. But while the Core disciplines are theoretically general, their class offerings tend to be maddeningly specific and often defiantly obscure. The Core forces you to take a course on a foreign culture, for instance, but it doesn't make any attempt to distinguish between the importance of, say, "Understanding Islam" and "The German Colonial Imagination"; either one will satisfy the requirement. A student satisfying Science B might take

"Human Evolution," but he might also select "The Biology of Trees and Forests," or perhaps "Dinosaurs and Their Relatives." For his Social Analysis requirement, he might decide to study basic economic principles in Ec 10, or he might take "Food and Culture" or "Psychological Trauma" or "Urban Revolutions: Archaeology and the Investigation of Early States." And in Literature and Arts A, his one literature requirement, our hypothetical Harvardian might decide to take one of Marjorie Garber's two exhaustive Shakespeare courses—but then again, he might be drawn to "Women Writers in Imperial China: How to Escape from the Feminine" or maybe to "Theories of Authorship: Russian Case Studies" or even to "Lives Ruined by Literature: The Theme of Reading in the Novel."

This is not to denigrate the more whimsical and esoteric choices that fill a college's course catalog. A computer science major, his head spinning with endless lines of code, might be well served to take a break by dousing his head in "The Two Koreas" or "The Cuban Revolution: 1956–71." But under the current Harvard system, those could easily be the only two history classes he ever takes, and it seems at best deeply disingenuous to suggest that the study of Castro or Kim's regime should bear the same weight as, say, knowledge of the two world wars, or the French Revolution, or the American founding, in the development of a "broadly educated" student body. (It's worth noting that the history department didn't offer a single class on the American Revolution during my four years at Harvard.)

To this complaint, the authors of the Core's mission statement reply, with a touch of smugness, that "the Core differs from other programs of general education . . . it does not define intellectual breadth as the mastery of a set of Great Books, or the digestion of a specific quantum of information . . . rather, the Core seeks to introduce students to the major approaches to knowledge in areas indispensable to undergraduate education."

These words, which appear in the course catalog each year, are the closest that Harvard comes to articulating an undergraduate educational philosophy. They suggest, rather baldly, that the difference in historical importance between, say, "Chinese Emigration in Modern Times" and "The Development of the Modern State" (both offerings in Historical Studies A) does not matter, because both courses offer a "historical" approach to knowledge that is presumably more valuable than mere "facts" about the past. Comprehending "history as a form of inquiry and understanding," as the Core handbook puts it, trumps learning about actual events. There is a similarly pat introduction to each of the other disciplines—"Literature and Arts" classes "foster a critical understanding of artistic expression"; the Sciences "convey a general understanding of science as a way of looking at ourselves and our world"; "Foreign Cultures" aims to "expand the student's understanding of the importance of cultural factors in shaping people's lives, and to provide fresh perspectives on the student's own cultural assumptions and traditions." In each case, the emphasis is squarely on methodology, rather than material.

If the intellectual poverty of this system isn't apparent in theory, it certainly is in practice. The dream of the Core's founders, apparently, was for Harvard-educated scientists to know *how* Harvard-educated historians think, and vice versa—without knowing, necessarily, what those historians might be thinking *about*. The reality is that Harvard-educated scientists learn very little about the mind-set of the historian, while likewise failing to learn the basic facts of world, or Western, or even American history. And they do so in classes that manage to combine all the faults of undergraduate education at elite universities: The enrollments are huge, the lectures are poorly attended, the professors and TFs are harried, and the grades, inevitably, are stratospheric.

My own experience of the Core was typical, I imagine. I set out with the honorable intention of picking a roster of classes that would be somehow comprehensive, and that would lead me in directions at once interesting and essential, providing perspectives that were un-available in my coursework in History and Literature (which focused on modern Britain and America). I was looking, I now understand, for classes like the first Core course that I wandered into: namely, the "Concept of the Hero in Greek Civilization," which, in spite of its nickname ("Heroes for Zeroes"), proved to be a spectacularly fasci-nating romp through ancient Greece, with assists from such contem-porary films as *Blade Runner* and *When We Were Kings*. It was a survey course with a twist, with an enthusiastic professor—the wild-haired, turbulent scholar Gregory Nagy—pulling a reluctant crowd of students through what used to be called the classics.

For the next three years, I tried to recapture what Nagy offered in his whirlwind tour of Homer and Herodotus, Sophocles and Aeschylus: the perfect combination of Great Books and great teach-ing. What I found instead were disengaged professors and overbur-dened TFs, who—like their bored, oft-absent students—seemed to be marking time, waiting for the moment when they could return to the parochial safety of their departmental classes. Indeed, parochial-ism often overtook the Core classes themselves. A course on "under-standing Islam," for instance, involved only cursory analysis of the Koran, the history of Islamic civilization, and the rise of radical Is-lam; but it devoted weeks to readings on Muslim diaspora communi-ties in London and Muslim-animistic syncretism in Africa. I chose another class, "The Portrait," because it seemed to offer something approaching a crash course in art history. (The Core offers no tradi-tional art history class; instead, students choose from a collection of courses like "Art in the Wake of the Mongol Conquests" and "Chi-nese Imaginary Space.") For the first two weeks, "The Portrait" loped through E. H. Gombrich's comprehensive *The Story of Art*, and then the rest of the course was devoted to police photography in nineteenth-century France, to sexual fetishism in Victorian daguerreo-types, to aboriginal headshrinking . . . the list goes on and on, but I didn't. I had stopped going to the lectures by the midpoint of the course.

"The Portrait" deserves further attention, though, for managing to combine all the faults of Harvard's Core in one tidy semester-long package. The subject matter was largely abstruse and esoteric; the professor, a scraggly-haired Frenchman named Henri Zerner, was perpetually disorganized ("Theees eees eeentolerable!" he would cry whenever his slide projector jammed, as frantic TFs scurried to do his bidding). The assignments were pitched suitably low, and the grades skewed lower still—a necessity, perhaps, since almost no one was willing to wade through the impenetrable, jargon-heavy reading. The class was easy enough, but never fun, because even if you skipped the lectures, there were still the agonizing section meetings, in which long and awkward silences were spent leafing through un-read assignments, all the while avoiding eye contact with the well-meaning but ineffectual TFs.

Small wonder that the few Core classes that are actually well taught are swamped each year by hundreds of eager undergraduates, no matter how obscure their subject matter. The closest thing to a Harvard education—that is, an intellectual corpus that most Harvard graduates can claim to have in common—is probably obtained in such oversubscribed courses as "The Warren Court and the Pursuit of Justice" or "First Nights: Five Performance Premieres" or the ever popular "Fairy Tales, Children's Literature, and the Construction of Childhood."

Yes, an ex-Harvardian may not have read Shakespeare or Proust; he may not be able to distinguish Justinian the Great from Julian the Apostate, or tell you the first ten elements in the periodic table (God knows I can't). But one need only mention "Mass Culture in Nazi Germany" or "Constructing the Samurai," and his eyes will light up with fond school-day memories.

❖

Among such popular Core classes, perhaps the most beloved of all is "The Images of Alexander the Great," which boasted an enrollment of more than five hundred when it was offered in the fall semester of my junior year. On the morning of the Alexander final exam, half of these—two hundred and fifty of my classmates, with last names from A to G—were scattered across the auditorium known as Science Center B when an agitated young man carrying a satchel marched to the front of the room, hurled a brick at the blackboard, and announced that he was carrying a bomb.

At first this barely registered on the assembled exam takers, who were busy identifying slides of Alexandrine coins. Then the professor, a Hellenic historian named David Mitten, asked the man who he was, and didn't he know there was an exam going on here?

"I am Romanticist," the brick thrower declaimed loudly, and added that he was declaring war on the United States of America.

By now everyone was paying attention. The young man slung his satchel off his shoulder. "If anyone tries to leave," he shouted, "I'll set off my bomb! So put your heads down on your desks!"

It would be nice to say, at this point in the story, that a heroic Harvard student leaped up, wrestled young Romanticist to the ground, and perhaps defused his bomb. Instead, there was a hasty and ignominious stampede for the exits, as more than two hundred of America's finest college students clambered desperately over their seats and bolted from Science Center B, leaving their professor, a lone TF, and exactly one classmate behind to cope with the madman—who, for his part, began wandering the lecture hall, slurping from abandoned soda cans and water bottles.

There was never any bomb, and the story ended happily enough. The cops arrived, young Romanticist was carted off for a psychiatric evaluation, and Professor Mitten rescheduled the exam and complained loudly of the "insult to Alexander." But looking back on my Harvard education, I often think of that morning's chaos—the shouting lunatic, the flying brick, and above all, the pell-mell flight from the auditorium.

The disorder that grips Harvard's curriculum has a similar feel of windswept abandonment, of a lecture hall filled with scattered papers, pens, and bookbags, where the professor is powerless and every student is scrambling for the door. Like a great library ravaged by a hurricane, in academic Harvard the accumulated wisdom of mankind and the essential elements of a liberal arts education lie scattered everywhere, waiting to be picked up. But to separate the trivial from the significant, the wheat from the chaff, is a task for which little guidance is offered. If we look up for answers, there are always faces watching over us—the coins of Alexander projected over Professor Mitten's exam; the busts and stained-glass windows lining the freshman dining halls; the oil portraits on office and classroom walls; the statues dotting the campus and city. But they are stone and glass and canvas, and they are silent.

It's not that you can't get a marvelous education during your four years. With its wealth of resources, of brilliant professors and endless research opportunities, Harvard remains one of the best places on earth to educate oneself. But in that last phrase lies an unspoken truth—namely, that Harvard will not actively educate you, will not guide or shape or even push back in any significant way against entropy and laziness and careerism. Education, at the Latin root that few Harvardians study, derives from *educere*, "to lead out." But this is a function that America's elite universities have increasingly abandoned, becoming less schools than factories, you might say, assemby-lining the future bankers, lawyers, politicians, and doctors out into the wider world, while hoping to draw enough undergrads into academia to keep their disciplines afloat.

This is the paradox of the modern university: Out of drift and disorder emerges a herd mentality. *Every man for himself*, the students fleeing Science Center B must have thought that January morning, even as they all dashed toward the same waiting doors. *Every student for himself*, Harvard tells its undergrads, leaving them to their own devices; and they, too, all race in the same direction, into the same oversubscribed courses, the same practical-minded concentrations, and eventually the same careers.

Alan Bloom, writing a decade before I began my undergraduate years, offered this observation about university life:

> *Thus, when a student arrives at the university, he finds a bewildering variety of departments and a bewildering variety of courses. And there is no official guidance, no university-wide agreement, about what he should study. It is easiest simply to make a career choice and go about getting prepared for that career. . . . The real problem is those students who come hoping to find out what career they want to have, or are simply looking for an adventure with themselves. . . . This undecided student is an embarrassment to most universities, because he seems to be saying, "I am a whole human being. Help me form myself in my wholeness and let me develop my real potential," and he is the one to whom they have nothing to say.*

These words make me remember, vividly, the moment when Harvard's course catalog arrived in my family's mailbox, late in my high school's senior year. It was a doorstop of a book, a thick paperback filled with hundreds, maybe thousands, of classes. I pored over it avidly, unable to imagine how I could possibly choose among them all, how I could pluck out just thirty-two classes, four years' worth, from what seemed then to be a sea of fascinating choices.

To that question, perhaps the most important question facing any college freshman, Harvard never even attempted an answer. I chose my thirty-two classes as much by accident as by design, and there were spurts of time when some of them mattered to me, and even moments when I was intoxicated, when I felt that I was exploring new territory, and gaining what Bloom calls "a taste for intellectual pleasures." But achieving those moments required pulling myself away from Harvard's other demands—social, extracurricular, pre-professional—and shutting my ears to their siren song, which in turn took far more discipline than I was usually able to exert over my restless, ambitious soul.

Mostly I logged the necessary hours in the library and the exam room, earned my diploma and my solid (if faintly inflated) GPA, and used the rest of the time to keep up with my classmates in our ongoing race to the top of America and the top of the world. It was only afterward, when the perpetual motion of undergrad life was well behind me, that I looked back and felt cheated.

It was only afterward, too, that I began chuckling inwardly when some older person, upon discovering that I went to *Harvard,* would furrow his brow, nod gravely, and inform me that he was very impressed, but wasn't it *such hard work?*

And it was—but not in the way that most people mean. It was hard work to get into Harvard, and then it was hard work competing for offices and honors with thousands of brilliant and driven young people, hard work keeping your head in the competitive world of extracurriculars, hard work keeping your soul in the swirling social world, hard work fighting for law-school slots and I-banking jobs as college wound to a close . . . yes, it was heavy sledding all around.

But the academics—no, the academics were the easy part.

CHAPTER FIVE

Love Stories

I N JANUARY 1857 a Harvard underclassman named Francis Ellingwood Abbot met a Concord girl named Katherine Fearing Loring. "Was introduced to Miss Kate Loring, a charming and lovely girl," Frank wrote in his diary, which later found its way into the Harvard libraries, where an archivist named Brian Sullivan discovered it early in my senior year and eventually published it as *If Ever Two Were One: A Private Diary of Love Eternal*. "I danced with her twice or three times," the entry went on, "and found her very pleasant and well-informed, and very lady-like. I thought of her all night—instead of going to sleep. If there ever was a fool, his name was Frank Abbot."

Nine days after the dance, Frank's diary recorded that "Kate is apparently seventeen or eighteen, small and slightly made, and to me very beautiful; rather pale, with hazel eyes and that peculiar kind of light hair, that you do not know whether to call it light or dark." He went on, "She is certainly a sweet and lovely girl, but I am not in love with her yet." And yet—"Kate, Kate, Kate! My silly head will let nothing else in. Dear Kate . . . I would I might forget you, or else win your love. How happy that would make me! Oh what a fool, what a fool, what a fool!"

Just three weeks later, Frank kissed her for the first time, then dropped his head to her lap and burst out ecstatically, "O God! I thank thee! O God, I thank thee!" That same day he asked Kate's father for her hand in marriage and was rebuffed. "This is rather sudden, Mr. Abbot," he was told, but the two were allowed to continue courting, which led the young Harvard man to pass his beloved a note saying, "We can hope"—a note she kept for her entire life, and which he eventually pasted into his diary alongside a lock of her hair.

Two and a half years and countless ardent love letters later, they were married, and remained so through six children and all the fluctuations of Frank's career as a Unitarian minister. Kate died in 1893, and Frank wrote then that "my love [for her] is just as impetuous, as overpowering, as passionate—all the more because now its nature is grief."

As the tenth anniversary of Kate's death loomed, Frank felt that God had finally released him. He wrote a last entry in his diary, which concluded: "I thank the Master of Life that at last He calls me home to my wife." Then he took the train from Boston to Beverly, where Kate lay buried, went to her grave, drank poison, and died.

"They found Doctor Abbot cold in death," the *Beverly Evening Times* wrote, "stretched out, face downward on the grave of his wife. His hat, a derby, was pulled down hard over his face, and a handkerchief grasped in his fingers. Just in front of the marble headstone dedicated to the memory of Mrs. Abbot and inscribed: *She made home happy and was the world to her own,* was a bunch of pink and white carnations, tied with a bit of white twine and which were placed as a tender offering to one he loved so well."

❖

A century later, during the first week of school, every Harvard freshman attends a screening of *Love Story*, held in one of the dingy, scooping Science Center auditoriums and organized by the pretty and gung-ho members of the Crimson Key Society, which is the closest thing Harvard has to a school spirit club. *Love Story*, as any survivor of the 1970s knows, is the tale of Oliver Barrett IV and Jennifer Cavalleri's doomed Harvard romance—he the blueblood hockey star, she the Italian-American English major from the wrong side of the tracks. The film feels dated and dopey now, but it's possible to glimpse the themes that made it such a cultural phenomenon back in 1970: It rode the crest of the sexual revolution and the shift to meritocracy, and its great conceit is that the self-destructive, tough-talking preppy, once tamed by working-class love, settles down, studies hard, and graduates at the top of his class from Harvard Law School. She dies of cancer; he gets the memories and a really good job. It's probably no coincidence that *Love Story* was the last movie that the administration permitted to be filmed on Harvard's hallowed grounds.

To watch the film today, in an auditorium of Harvard freshmen, is a cultural phenomenon of its own. The screenings are the Crimson Keyers' moment of glory: The club's members, male and female and mostly drunk, fill the theater's back rows, and from the film's flickering credits, they yell and heckle the handsome protagonists. The movie is bad, but the heckling is always worse, tinged with a viciousness that seems disproportionate to *Love Story*'s artistic sins. To a shot of Memorial Church, or any similar building, the cry goes up: *Phallic sym-bol!* To just about every shot of Ryan O'Neal: *Where's his other hand?* To Ali MacGraw's every line of dialogue: *Shut up, bitch!*

Countless Harvard freshmen, I suspect, arrive at school with dewy-eyed images of a campus thick with potential soul mates: comely intellectuals sipping coffee and forging profound bonds, all set to a Nora Ephron script and a Sarah McLachlan sound track. For these idealists, the *Love Story* screening is an unpleasant two hours, the closest that Harvard comes to large-scale hazing. And for those—and there are many—who come to college with only slightly more sexual experience than, say, the young Frank Abbot, the night is particularly agonizing, since every sexual reference and lewd double entendre serves as a reminder of their own hapless innocence.

I was one of these squirmers, having arrived at college a virgin and more. I had never so much as kissed a girl, beyond a few chaste spin-the-bottle pecks, and an unfortunate stage smooch with an older girl during a junior-year production of *You Can't Take It with You*. It's true that my scarlet "V" was made more bearable by my on-again, off-again aspiration to the premarital chastity that my Catholicism demanded—but only slightly, since I was always aware that my virtue was largely fraudulent, having never been put to any serious test. As my roommate Julian liked to say, I was a virgin by choice: the choice of the women of America.

As it turned out, my anxiety over this embarrassing fact peaked during the *Love Story* hazing and declined thereafter, as I gradually realized that my relative innocence was typical among the high-achieving set. In high school, sexual precocity and academic achievement rarely go hand in hand: For some it's a matter of priorities; for others, like me, it's a matter of being fumbling, girl-shy dorks. Either way, by the jaded standards of American adolescence, incoming first-years at elite schools tend toward the virginal and the romantically naive. (It's one of the few qualities that we share, I imagine, with the Bob Jones University freshman class.)

To my great relief, my closest comrades, the freshman males on the third floor of Straus B, were typical innocents of meritocracy. Six of us were virgins, and at least half shared my monastic high school history—no girlfriends, little kissing, and much hopeless pining. So for a happy few months, the sexual playing field seemed to have been neatly leveled, and I went cheerfully from parties to classrooms, confident that lurking around the next corner was my one-and-only, the girlfriend/soul mate who had been denied me thus far. There were eight hundred young women in the class of 2002, after all. I was only asking for one.

What I yearned for in those early days was a safe and even boring college relationship: one forged not at a dance or dinner party but in the friendly confines of the dormitory, where the sexes are only doorways apart and regularly run into each other in states of undress that doubtless would have provoked innumerable *I thank thees*, or perhaps a heart attack, in young Frank Abbot. The typical freshman romantic pairing at Harvard begins with such fraught entryway encounters, proceeds through a few false starts and drunken conversations, and culminates when the amorous pair—let's call them Dick and Jane—admit to their friends, and to each other, that they are an official couple.

Often it's only at this point that love enters the equation, perhaps with Jane making the "L" word a condition of their transition from oral sex to the genuine article. It's a transition hampered at first by the close quarters and shared bedrooms of freshman dorms, but in sophomore year, Dick gets his own bedroom, and from then on they sleep together almost every night. Their lives thus intertwined, they fall into various routines: They eat breakfast together most mornings; they go out to dinner a few times a week (Dick pays, unless Jane is having a particularly feminist moment); they cross the river to Boston together occasionally; and each fall and spring they rent a car and drive to a bed-and-breakfast in Lenox or Great Barrington or Stockbridge, where the stodgy proprietors pretend to believe they are a married couple.

To many of their friends, they might as well be. Coming into the bathroom one night in sophomore year, Dick's roommate catches them in their pajamas, applying toothpaste to each other's brushes. *You're so married,* he bellows, and they grin and troop off to bed.

Their first breakup comes early in senior year, and Dick probably precipitates it, out of some nebulous feeling that the wild days of college are passing him by, and there will be plenty of time for monogamy later. By senior spring, though, they are back together, after both parties have taken unhappy forays into the wider dating scene. *I knew it wouldn't last,* everyone says.

But things are different as senior year draws to an end—less settled and less marital, or perhaps *more* marital, but in an uneasy, pre-divorce sort of way. They fight frequently, and worry constantly, over what to do after graduation, when Dick is planning to take a job in New York and Jane isn't sure what she is going to do, and the fights grow sharper as April becomes May, and June approaches. At the senior soiree, held every year in a tent near the buildings of what was once Radcliffe, Jane breaks down in tears, and at the last-chance dance a month later, they have a screaming fight—over some other girl Dick has been talking to—in the center of the dance floor at one of seven interchangeable Boston clubs. Their friends grow weary of it all: *Not this shit again,* people mutter amid the tears and slamming doors.

At graduation, though, they are all smiles, dining with each other's parents—who know each other well by now—and pretending, for a day or a week, that everything will work out. Then they go their separate ways, putting their careers first as both sets of parents had advised, and the relationship comes to a close—but amicably, very amicably, so amicably that many people predict they will get back together eventually, if neither meets someone else, and if they end up in the same city again: that six years later, we'll see them together on *The New York Times* wedding pages, smiling and happy and boasting advanced degrees, Dick from Wharton and Jane from Berkeley, and he will have taken a job at Morgan Stanley and she'll have founded a project devoted to tutoring underprivileged kids in the Bronx, and everyone will be pleased and will say to one another, as if someone somewhere had ever doubted it, *I told you so.*

Such is the college marriage, often ignored in the prurient accounts of casual blow jobs favored by the college scene's adult anthropologists, but a critical part of the undergraduate dating world nonetheless. Indeed, such starter marriages practically *are* the college dating scene, since random, drunken hookups hardly count as dates, and only established couples go out to romantic dinners anyway. Many such relationships won't have Dick and Jane's happy ending, expiring under the weight of a senior-year breakup or a post-college split, and a lucky minority will transition smoothly from the college marriage to the grad school engagement to the actual wedding. But as a representative tale of modern courtship, the story of Dick and Jane serves well enough.

But is it a courtship, in any sense of the word? When two people are living together, sleeping together, planning vacations and meals and classes together, can they really be said to be courting? Courtship implies that no commitment has yet been made, and you can't have a courtship, really, in a sexually active dating culture, because a woman with multiple suitors or a boy with multiple flames will soon enough have multiple sexual partners, which is not necessarily frowned upon but sharply limits the likelihood that any of those partners will stick around for the long haul. (For women, particularly, the term "slut" has not yet lost its sting.)

The ubiquity of sexual activity, then, has the paradoxical effect of limiting romantic options. Either you immediately cement your-selves with toothpaste, or you risk knowing that your beloved is spending Saturday night going down on someone else.

So nobody courts, or has love affairs, or goes a-wooing; instead, a successful college couple forms "relationships," a word that neatly captures both the sturdiness and the distinct lack of passion. There are many good things, from a purely utilitarian perspective, to be said about such relationships—they provide stability and a sort of low-key happiness to many people; they offer a monogamous sexual outlet that dampens the flames of eros and lets people focus on work; they reduce the risk of STDs; and perhaps their resemblance to actual marriage even provides a kind of practice that reduces the divorce rate among elite couples.

And of course, very few of today's Harvard grads end up drink-ing poison over the graves of their college loves.

But it's hard to escape the sense that we have lost, or put away, something that Francis Ellingwood Abbot and Katherine Fearing Loring once possessed, something that could make Frank break into prayerful paroxysms after a mere kiss. We are so practical now, so pragmatic—or better, you might say, we are *pragmantic,* since it's not that we lack for romantic ideals; not in a culture where finding "the one" is a secular religion, fed by romantic comedies and WB dramas pitched to soulful teens with overripe vocabularies; not in a culture in which the human hunger for transcendence often seems to look to others for the perfection that people used to seek in God. Yes, there are dreams of romance yet—but the college marriage of-fers to such seekers at best a shallow transcendence, a romantic path on which ardor is quickly satisfied, and thereby quickly cooled, quickly routinized, quickly assimilated into the larger pursuit of ca-reer and success.

Even so, I wonder now if there was anyone in my class—the

most promiscuous final-club jock, the leftiest, most transgressive bi-sexual art grrl—who didn't sometimes imagine him- or herself some-day safely, reassuringly, within this pragmantic model. Certainly I did, in the first weeks and months of Harvard. And as that fall rolled on, I was increasingly certain that I knew which girl I wanted there with me.

Her name was Rachel Polley, and she was from Brunswick, Maine, a small college town that hugs the coastline halfway between Portland and Mount Desert Island. Her father was a college profes-sor, a Slavic specialist who had returned from Yugoslavia with a Ser-bian bride and raised his daughter in the salt air of the Maine coast. Rachel grew up tanned and muscular, with dark curls and exotic fea-tures. Sally Maddox called her Seal, and the nickname was probably appropriate, because of both the strange glossiness of her skin and her affinity for the sea. She joined the sailing team and spent count-less college weekends whipping back and forth along the Charles, or defending Harvard's honor in more exotic waters.

Rachel was part of Straus B: She lived upstairs, and I met her on the second day of freshman year, when we gathered in our proctor's suite to make introductions and learn about condoms (good) and al-cohol (bad). At first I thought she was peculiar and even irritating, especially when her Internet connection didn't work and she came downstairs and planted herself in my apparently inviting chair and began using my computer to go online. My roommates made fun of her, but she made fun of them right back, good-naturedly—she was always laughing, in those first weeks, with none of the guarded self-consciousness that most of us had carried with us into college—and after a while they accepted her, and she became a fixture, watching television, reading on our green futon late into the night, and talking endlessly. Talking to me, mostly—she had singled me out, I think, as someone important, someone worth her time, and eventually I singled her out as well, as the person best suited for the distinct honor of becoming my first-ever girlfriend.

This was a recipe for folly, since Rachel (alas!) had brought a boyfriend with her, a fellow graduate of Brunswick High who had been salutatorian to her valedictorian, and who was now comfortably ensconced down the river at Boston University. His name was Adam, and he was a shambling doofus, or so everyone in Straus B agreed—he had a shaggy beard and an ingratiating slump, and he might have been a shining light in coastal Maine, but he should have been no match for my charm, my good looks, my raw Harvardian sex appeal. Yet Adam endured, visiting frequently, showing up in tuxedos for formals, or rain-drenched and bearing flowers at romantic intervals. So even though Rachel lingered in my room till all hours, and sometimes fell asleep on our futon—even though everyone else in the entryway assumed that "something" was going to happen between us; even though my roommates all assured me, soberly, that I was *on deck*—still, she and I limped into Christmas without any acknowledgment that anything beyond friendship existed, or might exist, between us.

On the day we left for holiday break, with the entryway half empty and her suitcases scattered across her cramped common-room floor, my shyness gave way. I asked her, with desperate nervousness, if she thought she might break up with Adam, and then, when she made some carefully noncommittal reply, I flatfootedly professed my devotion. This didn't produce the desired effect (a kiss, perhaps, or a swoon, or a swooning kiss), but the more she murmured nervously, the more I spoke passionately; the more she withdrew, the more I pressed onward. I liked her—no, I thought she was beautiful and wonderful—why not say it? I loved her. I *loved* her. We should be together. She should break up with Adam and go out with me. Didn't she think so? Couldn't she see it?

"Ross," she told me, "I like you very much, you know that . . . but I don't see how it can work out. Not now, at least."

So I became angry. *Not now,* she said. What was *that* supposed to mean? What about all the time we spent together? What about her falling asleep on my futon, what about her letting me give her back massages, what about us talking until five A.M. about nearly everything? What would her precious Adam think about that? Did she think he would approve?

"Look," she said with horrible calm. "This sounds weird to say, but . . . I like you. I really do. I could—I could almost—this sounds so weird, I'm sorry—I could see myself marrying you. I could. But I don't know if I could see us dating right now. Does that make any sense?"

It didn't.

"Merry Christmas, Rachel," I told her in what I thought was my most savage voice, and went quickly downstairs to bed, and tears.

So it was over, I told myself that night, and on the train to New Haven, and all through the misery of a Rachel-less Christmas break. I had failed utterly, as I always had in high school, and all that was left to do, if I was to salvage my dignity, was to give her the cold shoulder from now on. No more late nights on the futon, no more sexually charged massages, no more of her e-mails and music on my computer, no more of her at my desk, or in my room, or anywhere near me, if I could help it. I would be happily Rachel-free for the rest of the year.

Back at Harvard, my resolve lasted all of three days, and then she was back, curled up and pajamaed on a corner of the futon, or balanced on the arm of my desk chair, downloading another batch of chick-music MP3s.

"I thought you were going to get rid of her," Davis said to me late one January night, after Rachel had wandered sleepily upstairs to bed, leaving me moping at my desk, listening to the songs she had recently added to my collection.

"I thought I was, too," I admitted, removing my headphones, which were filled with the closing bars of "Leaving on a Jet Plane."

"You know what you should do?" Nate interjected, strolling shirtless to the bathroom. "You should forget about her *now*. This is college, for God's sake, and you've wasted, what, an eighth of it chasing Rachel? You need to get out there—get in the game!"

Nate's girlfriend had visited that weekend, flying in from the University of Chicago; they had gone to high school together and were currently attempting a long-distance relationship. For the two of them, it involved huge cell-phone bills and expensive airline tickets; for me, it involved being banished to the futon whenever she came to visit.

"Nate's right," Davis told me in his usual laconic drawl. He was instant-messaging with his own girlfriend, still in high school back in Kentucky.

"Look, it's easy for you guys to say," I protested. "You've both had girlfriends—you both have them! I haven't. I need to know what it's like. And I'm in love with her, guys. I don't *want* any other women. I only want her."

From the shower came Nate's voice: "Um, is that the Indigo Girls I heard coming from your headphones, Ross?"

"Whipped," Davis smirked, back to his computer screen.

Rachel decided to break up with Adam early in January, got back together with him two weeks later (*Maybe you aren't on deck after all, boss,* Julian said sadly), and then they broke up again early the following month. Through it all, Adam kept showing up at Straus, and they would hold long, impassioned late-night conversations while I paced around a darkened campus or fumed in my bedroom, snarling and barking at my weary roommates, or taking melodramatic draughts of whatever third-rate vodka I had squirreled away at the bottom of my dresser.

Adam even went with her to the freshman formal, held late in February. I had the flu that week, but—*just to show Rachel what I was made of!*—I dragged myself to the dance, where I spent the whole evening alternately staring daggers at Adam and regaling my luckless date with tales of the lovely, perfect, unattainable girl whose company I clearly preferred to hers.

"Don't you think that maybe you should, um, give it up?" Nate asked me a few days later, after his friend Nora—my date to the formal, at his urging—informed him that no, she had *not* had a good time, thanks very much.

"Give it up?" I said blankly. What was he talking about? Didn't he see how much progress was being made? Sure, it wasn't exactly a traditional romantic progression: We weren't leapfrogging from French kissing to heavy petting and beyond. But things were happening, I was sure of it. For instance: Instead of falling sleeping on our futon, she had begun taking early-evening naps in my bed. And it seemed, to my admittedly untrained eye, that she was wearing less and less clothing for our late-night deep talks on my futon, and that the backrubs I gave her were becoming increasingly erotic.

Besides, there were all sorts of signs that we were meant to be together. I was a Catholic convert—and so was her favorite high school teacher! I loved fantasy novels—and so did she! My mother's family was from Maine—and so was she! Most important, she really did *like* me—at least enough to sleep in my bed, and to let me give her late-night backrubs! Didn't Nate understand how imperishably rare these qualities were?

"Why don't you get her drunk?" he said, sighing. "If she got drunk and you actually hooked up, then maybe you'd stop bitching about her."

But that was another thing that I adored about Rachel. In a world of cheap beer and sweaty college parties, she didn't drink, had never been drunk, didn't touch the stuff. I found this charming, sweet, innocent, beautiful, and the last thing I wanted to do was kiss her for the first time in a drunken stupor.

No, our love had to pure, untainted, perfect. And it would be. I just had to be patient.

So I waited, and winter became spring, and her late-night pajamas became tank tops, and suddenly I found myself kissing her bare shoulders—I, who had never kissed a girl. Admittedly, she turned away when I tried to kiss her lips, but I could kiss her neck—and then, as April waned, her cheeks and eyes. She began to kiss me back, at odd times and in odd ways: She would come up behind me while I was working at my computer and nibble discreetly at my ears, or brush her lips and tongue across my fingers when I least expected it.

You give me butterflies, she said one night, *and nobody's done that for a long time.* Another evening, she asked if I thought we might be, *you know, soul mates?*

Don't get too attached, she said still another night.

❖

When Frank Abbot was wooing his Kate, he told her a story about a young man who loved flowers but was disappointed because they always died. Seeing his distress, the young man's guardian angel sent him out in search of the "living flower," and he wandered until he found three lovely flowers growing together, and knew that the middle blossom was the flower that he sought. "And he longed to pluck it, and place it at his breast, and cherish it dearer than all beside," Frank told Kate. "And now the young man wants to know if it will do any good to ask the gardener—can he have the flower?"

The story finished, the young suitor buried his head in his hands and "waited for an answer in the most agonizing suspense. . . . At last she said, very softly, and very sweetly—'I HOPE SO.'"

There was no gardener in our world, no father whose permission I needed, but it was a moment like this that I pined for with Rachel, a moment when I found the perfect words to melt all her misgivings. Maybe I didn't even need words, and the right confluence of events—like her noticing me with another girl, or seeing me make an impossible Frisbee catch, and so on down an increasingly delusional list—would do the trick. Or maybe there was something I could *do*, a gesture of some kind, a great romantic act that would accomplish everything in one fell swoop.

But no—romantic gestures were too difficult, too fraught with peril. There was always a chance that they would backfire, that I would end up like my friend Siddarth and his lost freshman love Vanessa.

They had met, Siddarth and Vanessa, during the pre-frosh weekend that Harvard holds every April for incoming students. She was the daughter of a prominent Boston family, with a town house on Beacon Hill and a place on Nantucket, in the miniature village of Siasconset, where the cottages were small and the speed limits oppressive (TWENTY IS PLENTY IN SIASCONSET, ran a popular local bumper sticker). Vanessa was willowy and gravely beautiful, with an interest in ancient Greek and modern poetry. When my friend first saw her, she was talking passionately about Virgil's Aeneid, and Siddarth—who had been president of his midwestern high school's Latin Club, and who knew Virgil as well as he knew anything—was smitten within minutes.

He flew home to Ohio clutching Vanessa's e-mail address, a promise in ballpoint ink that she and everything she embodied—class, beauty, brains, and grace—awaited him in his looming freshman year. But that was five months away. A stretch of high school remained, and particularly the senior prom, for which Siddarth still lacked a date. Contemplating the girls he knew, he found that he could think only of Vanessa, ensconced in her distant New England boarding school, like a preppy Rapunzel . . . and he began to carve out a fantasy in which he asked *her* to the prom, instead of some dull Columbus girl, and she flew in for the weekend, trailing glamour in her wake.

So Siddarth wrote to her, but the e-mail bounced back to him, and so did several variations. He probably should have let the dream die then, but he instead decided to make one last attempt. He picked up the phone and called the Freshman Dean's office.

"I'm sorry," he was told, "but this office does not give out students' numbers or e-mail addresses."

"Yes, but I'm a student, too," he insisted. "My name's Siddarth Kapoor. I'm class of 2002, same as her. You can look it up."

"I'm sorry, sir, but the information you've requested is confidential."

So all he could do was wait, telling himself that their pre-frosh meeting was probably mostly in his head, and that it was a big class and a big campus, and he wouldn't run into her again. But when he arrived at Straus in September, there she was, Vanessa Schuyler in Straus E, no less, a mere thirty yards and six vertical walls away. It was a touch worthy of Virgil, that out of all the dorms in Harvard Yard, the Dean's Office had placed her so close to him.

There was a party in Straus E that first week, and Siddarth and Vanessa ran into each other unexpectedly there. Or at least it was unexpected for her; he had planned for it carefully, down to the shirt he was wearing and the casual attitude he affected as they stood chatting over plastic tumblers of vodka and OJ.

"So," he said after a few minutes of small talk, "do you want to have lunch sometime?"

There was a long pause.

"You know," she said, staring hard at her screwdriver, "maybe we should get to know each other a little better first?"

It was all downhill after that. He was mortified, she was chilly, and he beat a hasty retreat to his room, where he suffered for days. "All I did was ask her out to lunch!" he stormed. *"Get to know each other better . . .* that's the whole *point* of going to lunch!"

His mood did not improve when we learned that Vanessa was going out with another boy from Straus E, a lacrosse player named Brian Messersmith. "Didn't take her long to *get to know* him, I guess," he muttered, and proceeded to mope all fall and winter, dating other girls halfheartedly and pining for Vanessa, who went everywhere with Brian and averted her eyes when they passed Siddarth on the stone walkways outside Straus.

Much later, we learned what had happened. Or rather, I learned it, from Vanessa's mother no less, at a graduation party four years after Siddarth's freshman heartbreak. I had been drinking a bit, and I fell into a conversation with Mrs. Schuyler about the boys Vanessa had dated in college, and before I could stop myself, I was saying that *of course, the guy who loved her first and best was probably my roommate Siddarth.*

Siddarth? Mrs. Schuyler said. *Oh, I remember him!*

It all came tumbling out then—how Vanessa had mentioned him when she came home from pre-frosh weekend, and she had said he was very nice; but then that summer, the Freshman Dean's Office called and said that they were concerned Siddarth might be stalking her, *and then, of course, he was placed in the dorm next to hers. So we were all a little concerned, as you can imagine.*

Sure, I told her, trying to be agreeable. *It all makes sense now.*

And so it did. Everyone's behavior made sense: The university was worried about the safety of its students and probably its own legal liability; Vanessa simply picked up on Harvard's fears, the attitude that such flagrantly romantic behavior wasn't quite normal, that this Siddarth character bore watching, and made those fears her own. It was all perfectly rational, perfectly pragmatic . . . and at the same time perfectly mad.

I guess he was just a little too aggressive, Sally Maddox said later, when I told her the story.

❖

"I've never met anyone as aggressive as you," Rachel Polley said to me one night, late in our freshman April, as I pressed my lips against the nape of her neck.

I laughed aloud. "You think I'm *aggressive*?" (I was at this point still not allowed to kiss her on the lips.)

She shrugged. "Never mind."

Eventually we did kiss on the lips—fleetingly, as if she wanted to hold back, to keep it from me as long as possible. We began to talk endlessly about the future, about whether I would visit her in the summer, about books that I would recommend to her, about visiting Europe together. We talked about being married, though not, it occurred to me later, about being girlfriend and boyfriend. At the time, though, I felt I could see our whole joint life spilling out in front of us, as consummation came and then gave way to great sex and a deep and complete emotional understanding, then on to our three upperclass years together, our off-campus apartment senior year, our overlapping but noncompetitive courses of study, our twin professional tracks, our first apartment, our second (larger) apartment, our splendid wedding, and then children, houses, suburbs, schools, prizes, lifetime achievement awards . . .

"Maybe you should be a lawyer," she said one night. "Or at least go to law school, you know? So that we would have a way to make money, just in case."

For eighteen years, I had watched the law wear my father down, the paperwork and the long hours, the moral compromises, the strain when cases went to trial and the boredom when they didn't. I had never wanted to be a lawyer.

"You know, maybe I should," I said.

Rachel looked at me strangely, then suddenly she bent and began sucking—slowly, languorously—on my fingers.

"This is completely surreal," I told her after a moment.

She released my hand and smiled—dazzlingly, I thought, in the dusty, after-midnight darkness of Straus, where an antique poster of John F. Kennedy, pilfered by Davis from the Institute of Politics, watched us with grinning, presidential eyes.

"I know," she said. "I don't know what I'm doing." Then she went back to work on my fingers.

Thinking it over the next day, I decided to take her remark about my aggressiveness as a compliment, a sign that I was doing well, that I was finally behaving like a real man instead of a fumbling adolescent. I was winning her, conquering her, even, and there was charm and modesty in her holding back, or so it seemed to me. This waiting was a test, that was all. I had always done well on tests.

What I lacked, unfortunately, was a real grasp of the essence of the pragmantic couple, which is that it requires unity of interest, unity of choice, far more than ardor and conquest and the other stuff of romantic fantasy. I had made *my* choice—for me, Rachel had no rival. But she hadn't made hers, and her withholding of affection wasn't a matter of modesty or coyness but of more practical concerns.

A successful college marriage, I realized later, isn't just a matter of finding the right person to suit your needs. For the relationship to work, for it to succeed—the language of capitalism is all too appropriate here—it's a matter of finding the right *kind* of person as well. There are exceptions to this principle, occasional examples where opposites attract, mesh, and mate for keeps. But generally it's only a matter of time before an odd couple stops being a couple at all.

The best illustration of this among my social circle came in senior year, when Nate—having long since shed his high school flame—began to date a polished Manhattan girl named Gail Simmons. It started as a senior fling, but Nate was quickly besotted, in spite of the unlikeliness of the pairing: he the brash Kansan, she the trust-fund girl from Central Park West. *Gail and I*, he told us all proudly, *are in deep love.*

Problems multiplied soon enough. Her existing friends—a collection of handsome, faintly effete upper-crusters, with an air of dissipation about them—disdained him; she didn't want him to meet her parents; she was uncomfortable being out in public with him. Nate was uncomfortable, too, with the parties where her friends did lines of coke in the bathroom, or with the nights when she was out with them and didn't return his calls. But he was in love, so he made excuses for her.

He made excuses in May when she held a graduation party and didn't invite him, claiming it was just her old friends when it was really everyone she knew. He made excuses in June when he visited her in Newburyport for a weekend and her parents introduced him, cuttingly, as Gail's "friend." And he made excuses in July when he went home to Kansas City and called her every day and planned trips up to see her, which she repeatedly vetoed, first because her mother wouldn't approve and then for other, more nebulous reasons.

Then August came, and she broke up with him, and the excuses were finally over.

For Rachel and me, the end arrived more suddenly. That freshman spring, as exams approached, there was a rash of sailing-team parties, and at these, for the first time, Rachel began to drink. The world of the sailing team had always been largely hidden from me, but all at once it was thrown into relief—the preppy names, the pub crawls, the windblown afternoons, the lengthy excursions to warmer climes. Rachel was going on one such trip after exams: to the Florida Keys, to sail against a bevy of southern schools. I had never worried about her at the parties or on the trips, never worried about sailing-team rivals, never imagined what might happen on a pleasant tropic evening after a long day on the water. I had focused, foolishly, on the hapless, fast-fading Adam.

The best sailor at Harvard that year was a blond California junior named Eric Swaggart Allenby. Rachel crewed his boat during my freshman spring, and she would talk about him on occasion—the girls he liked, the absurdity of his middle name, and other trivialities. I barely listened; I had other things on my mind. But after a sailing party in early May, Eric Swaggart Allenby walked Rachel home to Straus and kissed her on the first landing. I was on the second at the time, coincidentally, crossing to another room, and I looked down and saw the dip of his head, the rise of hers, the ruin of my hopes.

I didn't tell her what I'd seen, but she told me the next day what she'd done, that it didn't mean anything, and that she didn't want to have a relationship with him. That evening on the futon, she kissed me without any reservations at all, and my previous night's devastation gave way to sweeping, gorgeous triumph.

I remember striding across campus the following morning in brilliant New England spring weather, thinking that if I ever had a son—no, let me be honest, if *Rachel and I* ever had a son—and he wanted advice on women, I would tell him that the ticket was persistence and plenty of it. Sure, this whole business had taken me a good eight months of effort, but never mind that. I had emerged victorious, hadn't I?

That night, for the first time in what seemed months, Rachel didn't come downstairs to my room. She didn't appear the next night, nor the night after. I asked her roommates, oh so casually, if they had seen her. They had, but only briefly, sweeping through in the early evening to gather books and clothes and sailing stuff. Then Savina, who lived upstairs and dated my roommate Julian, said that she had passed Rachel in the Yard, walking with Eric Allenby and a whole gang of sailors on their way down to the river.

So I did what any technologically savvy, slightly mad college student would do: I fingered Rachel.

"Fingering" was a suggestively named quirk of our e-mail system, a frequently used stalking technique that allowed any user who knew Rachel's e-mail address to discover, by typing "finger rpolley @fas.harvard.edu" into the command prompt, where she had last checked her e-mail. By early morning, my computer screen looked something like this:

```
fas%:\ finger rpolley@fas.harvard.edu
:\ rpolley (Rachel Jasmine Polley) last known login at
10:47:13 from allenby.harvard.edu


fas%:\ finger rpolley
:\ rpolley (Rachel Jasmine Polley) last known login at
11:32:17 from allenby.harvard.edu
```

```
fas%:\ finger rpolley
:\ rpolley (Rachel Jasmine Polley) last known login at
12:13:55 from allenby.harvard.edu
```

As my fingerings became more frequent, more compulsive . . .

```
fas%:\ finger rpolley
:\ rpolley (Rachel Jasmine Polley) last known login at
12:13:55 from allenby.harvard.edu
```

```
fas%:\ finger rpolley
:\ rpolley (Rachel Jasmine Polley) last known login at
12:13:55 from allenby.harvard.edu
```

```
fas%:\ finger rpolley
:\ rpolley (Rachel Jasmine Polley) last known login at
12:13:55 from allenby.harvard.edu
```

```
fas%:\ finger rpolley
:\ rpolley (Rachel Jasmine Polley) last known login at
12:13:55 from allenby.harvard.edu
```

Somehow I held out hope that this wasn't what it seemed, that there was another, less heartbreaking explanation. But after a few days, I was at the end of my rope. I hadn't slept and couldn't eat; I began taking long midnight walks across campus. Sometimes I hung around outside Mather House, Allenby's dorm, a pale-faced specter in my windbreaker, trying to guess which window was his. Sometimes I stood, shivering, under the sprinklers that came on just before dawn, letting the freezing water burn my skin. I played Dire Straits' "Romeo and Juliet" obsessively; it was the last song she had downloaded to my computer.

On the fifth night after our final tryst, Rachel came to see me. We were alone, and she sprawled on the futon, as she had so many times, and told me that Allenby had asked her out on a date for the following Monday, and that she was going to go out with him. Just to see what it was like.

A date? I wanted to blurt out. *You've spent every night in his room, haven't you?*

"So . . . what does this mean for us?" I asked instead.

"For us?" she said blankly. "Well—I don't know. You know, it's funny. I actually told Eric about you, I told him all of it, everything that's happened, how much we have in common."

"You did?"

"Uh-huh. And he said it sounded like maybe I should be going out with you."

I laughed a little wildly. "He said that, did he? And what did you say?"

"Well I guess I didn't say anything. I mean, I've thought the same thing, all the time, for the last few months. I keep asking myself, *Why aren't you just going out with Ross,* you know?"

"So why aren't you?"

She sighed and looked away, out the window, into the late-spring light. "This is a really difficult time for me, you know. Adam's coming to visit tomorrow, and a bunch of our friends from high school, and I'm going to have to tell him that we aren't getting back together this summer. I don't know how he's going to take it."

It took me a moment to follow this. "You mean he thinks you're getting back together? This summer? Why does he think that?"

"Well, you know, that was our *plan,* I guess. That we'd break up for a while now, then get back together in June, when—if—when we both went back to Brunswick. So he thinks that's what we're doing."

"And when were you planning to tell me this? What happened to *us*—to me coming to visit you? Like we talked about?"

"You mean you won't come visit me if we aren't dating?" Her tone was petulant, mock-spoiled, a voice that I had always found terribly attractive.

"Well, *are* you going to be dating someone else? Like Eric Swaggart Allenby?"

"You know his middle name?" she said, drawing back a little. "That's kind of creepy."

Of course I know his middle name! I wanted to spit. *It's Swaggart, for God's sake!*

"Anyway," she went on, "I just want to try this, you know? To see where it goes. I mean, maybe I don't want to date anyone for a while. You're so intense, so certain about being in love . . . maybe that's why things haven't happened with us, why I couldn't decide if I wanted to date you."

"What does that mean? You don't want to date someone but you're going out on a date with another guy?"

"I did warn you not to get too attached, didn't I? Besides, Ross, when you think about it, would it really have worked out? I mean, be honest for a minute, and imagine the two of us being together—I'd be off sailing all the time, you know. You wouldn't really be happy, would you, dating me and always having to say, *Oh, she's off sailing*? Would you?"

"Why wouldn't I? What possible difference would that make?"

"No," she went on, seeming not to hear, "if I date anyone seriously, it should probably be someone on the sailing team."

By now a painful obstruction was swelling in my throat. "But what about everything we talked about? What about— You said I gave you butterflies, Rachel! What about that?"

"You know," she said, musing aloud, "maybe you should have gotten me drunk earlier, like back before spring break? Maybe things would have been different."

"Don't tell me that! Oh my God . . ."

"Well, maybe it's true."

"Are you going to have sex with him?"

"With Eric?"

"On the trip to Florida?"

"Ross, I really don't want to talk about this."

So it went, on and on, and I became ever more maudlin, more tearful, more pathetic. I wanted to be curt, chilly, above the fray; instead, I wept. I remember clutching her and saying something about not wanting to lose her, and her agreeing, but she seemed to be already sailing past me, past this scene, past freshman year and my seedy futon, into a brighter, less scruffy future.

"I keep thinking," I said at the end, "that if I just come up with the right thing to say, you'll be convinced. That you'll see how good we could be together."

"It doesn't work that way, Ross," she told me. "It just doesn't."

It ended there, except for my getting drunk on a bottle of cheap wine that night and hurling things around our common room, much to my roommates' dismay; and except for my moping and drinking my way through the rest of the school year while Rachel embarked on her new life with Swaggart, which eventually became a stable college marriage, and may even turn into a real marriage soon, for all I know—and except for the last day of school, when I rode the T to South Station and, crossing the Charles, looked out and saw the river speckled with gleaming, white-sailed boats, and the lump rose in my throat again and I cried, for the last time.

Yes, it ended there. I don't think I ever had a real conversation with Rachel Polley after that long and tear-stained night. There were e-mails, of course, some drunken, some pathetic, some approximating the dignity that I had so badly failed to preserve. But our friendship, such as it was, ended that spring, and then time and Harvardian bustle went to work, healing the wound and slowly transforming my memory of *l'affaire* Rachel into what it really was, a freshman farce, not a Greek tragedy.

I don't know what you saw in her, my long-suffering friends said that summer, obviously relieved that there would be no ear-nibbling, finger-sucking Rachel Polley cluttering up our room the following year.

After a long time had passed, I didn't know either.

CHAPTER SIX

Safe Sex

M Y FRIEND MARGARET WENT to Smith and hated it. Throughout freshman year, she begged me to visit her. *Bring other boys with you,* she always added. *I miss boys so much. Everyone here is either a lesbian or pretending to be one.*

Late in my sophomore spring, I obliged. My friend Tom volunteered to accompany me—but only after I assured him that yes, Margaret was reasonably good-looking, and yes, she had promised that we would find, amid a sea of man-hungry Smithies, someone to hook up with.

Tom and I left early on a Saturday, borrowing a friend's car, and reached Smith in the mid-afternoon of a melting New England spring day. The budding, bursting landscape exuded sex; the women of Smith did not. Margaret was in her sweatpants, unshowered and hungover, and so were her friends. We sprawled in her bedroom, watching Spanish soap operas and feeling tense, while the girls whispered to one another and shot glances our way. Tom kept trying to strike up a conversation, and when his efforts fell flat, he began talking to me in French, crafting choice insults—*Elle est vraiment une vache, n'est-ce pas?*—in what he seemed to think was our joint secret language.

After a few minutes of this, the girls rose and swept out en masse, issuing frosty see you laters like a flock of haughty swans. We were left alone with Margaret.

"What's their deal?" Tom demanded. "Do they not like us or something? What did we do?"

"You know," Margaret said dryly, "two of them major in French."

Later on, she took us to dinner in a half-empty Smith cafeteria. We were the only men in the room, and around us were scattered the lonely, supposedly desperate women that we had come here to ravish, or at least make out with. They seemed to have no trouble ignoring us.

"So," Tom said near the end of the meal, "when do we go out and stuff? What's happening later? Wild parties, right? Crazy lesbian orgies?"

"Well," Margaret said slowly, "you know, we had a big dance last night, an all-campus thing, and I'm kinda hungover. I think a lot of people are, and I'm not sure about any parties, unless you want to go all the way over to a frat party at UMass. We could do that . . . I think it's rush week. Does that sound fun?"

"UMass?" I burst out. "But we've traveled a hundred miles to get away from co-ed parties—to get away from other guys! That's the whole point! Why would we go to a UMass frat?"

"Sorry, sorry," Margaret said quickly. "I mean, I'm sure there's a party here, I'm sure there're a lot of parties. I just don't know exactly where they are. But later we can go out looking for them."

But later she was sleepy, so Tom and I went out alone and wandered the campus for an hour, chasing lights and noise through shadowed arches and empty courtyards, and down lamplit lawns where sprinklers hissed. We found no parties and few people—only scattered girls who avoided eye contact with us and darted tense glances at the emergency phones. It was like being in a foreign country, roving the streets of some European capital where everyone immediately marked you as an American and no one would admit to speaking English, let alone give you directions to the nearest hostel.

This, we agreed, sprawled in defeat beneath the statue of some founding bluestocking, was the absolute rock bottom.

"I mean, should it really be this hard?" Tom asked me plaintively. "We're at an all-girls' school. . . . Where are the ladies, Ross? Where are they?"

A Smithie happened to be passing at that moment, and Tom's plaintive *cri de coeur* turned her brisk walk into a trot, or even a lope, toward the safety of the nearest building.

"Yeah, you heard me!" he shouted after her. "Where are the *ladies*?"

"Nicely done," I said.

"Oh, right, because otherwise she was going to invite us back to her place and maybe introduce us to a few of her friends." He sighed. "No . . . we might as well have stayed at Harvard. Look at us, we basically *are* at Harvard—it's cold out, the campus is empty, and we're sexually frustrated, looking for the parties that aren't there, looking for good-looking women who don't exist. The night's a waste, the whole trip's a waste . . ."

"There's always Margaret," I offered.

He laughed. "That's nice of you, but she's really not my type."

Back in the room, Margaret was writing e-mails, having exchanged her sweatpants for pajamas. "Let's have White Russians," she said encouragingly when we flopped, downcast, on her rug. But there was no Kahlúa, so we drank screwdrivers, and when the orange juice ran out, we made gin and tonics, except that there was no tonic, so they were gin and Sprites instead. Then we decided to watch a movie, but all Margaret had was *Shakespeare in Love*, so we watched late-night TV, and then a slew of dating shows, and then the infomercials came on, and we knew it was time for bed.

"Are you guys having fun?" Margaret asked me when Tom had vanished into the bathroom.

"Does it look like we're having fun?"

"I'm sorry," she said. "My friends drove over to Mount Holyoke, I think. And probably everyone else went to Amherst, like I said they would. If you'd come last night . . ."

"If you'd *told* us to come last night . . ."

"Anyway," she flounced, "it's not like you fulfilled your end of the bargain! I was promised nice boys to hook up with, Ross."

"I brought you Tom, didn't I?"

She sighed. "Dear heart, Tom's not my type at all."

When he came back, we had a nightcap and then lay talking in the dark—Margaret in her bed, Tom and I on the floor alongside. Well past midnight, I turned away and announced that I was going to sleep, but they went on whispering for a long time while I tried and failed to drift off. At last there was silence in the room, and I thought, *Finally*, and rolled over just in time to see Tom sliding into Margaret's bed, his shadow gathered up in her quilted darkness, and then their noises began and I realized that no, *this* was rock bottom.

I crawled with my sleeping bag to a far corner of the room, which meant that I was five feet away, not two, from Margaret's overburdened twin bed. I huddled there while the minutes passed with agonized slowness, while the murmurs and sighs and damp kissy squelches merged with the squeal of the bedsprings, and when I thought they had to be nearly done, there was a strange *thwack*, and then another and still a third, like the sound of a high five or a slapped face . . . or maybe, I thought with mounting horror, a *spanking*.

I fled then, abandoning my sleeping bag and stumbling out into the hallway, where I blinked in the sudden blaze of fluorescence. I wasn't sure what to do next: The corridor was a row of locked bedrooms, and an all-female college's common room was probably a lousy place for a man in his underwear to hide out. But just standing in the hall seemed worst of all, so I made for the bathroom, where I stood for a long time staring in the mirror, trying to recognize myself in the wild-eyed insomniac glaring back at me, and trying to decide how angry I could be at Tom come morning.

Not very angry at all, came the unwelcome answer. After all, wasn't this why we were at Smith, why we had traveled all this way— to get drunk and crawl into bed with girls we didn't know? I had even said he could hook up with her not three hours before, however much I regretted it now. And wouldn't I have done the same thing? Or if not, wasn't it only because I was too self-conscious, too inhibited and nervous around women, not because I could claim any special virtue?

Still, I reassured myself, if I wanted to be angry about something, there was always the ass slapping. Surely *that* was beyond the pale!

There was a padding of slippers in the hallway then, and girlish voices. I froze for a moment, then dove for the nearest stall, where I crouched on the toilet seat and listened to the noise of running water, the *scritch-scratch* of toothbrushes, the soft sounds of gossip.

"You know, I thought there was someone in here earlier," one of them said while the other spit and gargled.

I carefully lifted my feet above the stall door, out of sight.

"I think it was a *boy,*" came the conspiratorial reply.

"A boy? I wonder where he went."

It was more than I could bear. "I'm still here!" I bellowed from the stall, and they squealed and fled.

When I was sure they weren't coming back, I ventured out and stood in front of the mirror again, then paced in the hall, and finally decided to brave Margaret's room. There was no noise, no movement from the humped shadows on her bed, and I crawled back into my sleeping bag and lay there for a while, attuned to every squeak and sigh, ready at any moment to hear the slap of flesh on flesh, to have the agony begin anew.

Mercifully, I slipped into a dreamless asleep just as dawn began to break over Smith.

"Are you going to tell everyone about this?" Tom asked me on the next day's drive home, after a breakfast at which he and Margaret resolutely refused to look at each other, while I made cracks about how happy I was for them, how I thought they had a bright future together, how I really wanted them to fight for this relationship . . .

"Oh, I don't know," I lied. "Can I ask you a question about last night before I decide?"

"No, Ross, we didn't have sex, if that's what you mean . . ."

"Nope," I returned blithely, "that wasn't it. I wanted to know about *this*." And here I began slapping at my left hand with my right, as if swiping away a troublesome fly. *Thwack, thwack* . . .

"What are you . . ."

"From last night, Tom—remember? And what I want to know is, were you slapping her ass?"

"Was I *what*?"

"You know, it's a pretty simple question," I said, secure in my own righteousness. "Were you slapping"—*thwack*—"my friend Margaret's"—*thwack*—"ass, Tom, while I was lying five feet away, trying to sleep?"

He stared ahead at the road, his knuckles white on the steering wheel. "Well, it wasn't exactly . . . I didn't . . . it was an accident."

"An *accident*?"

"Well, yeah, at first. But then, you know, it seemed like she liked it, so I thought, *Why not keep going?*"

"So what you're telling me," I said, my voice rising, a prosecutor building to his triumphant summation, "is that we drove a hundred miles to an all-girls' school just so I could spend the night hiding in the bathroom so as not to have to hear one of my friends slapping the other friend's *ass*?"

"I guess—" he started, and then cut off suddenly. "You went and hid in the bathroom? Really? Why?"

I stumbled, caught off guard. "Well, I had to . . . I mean, I . . ."

"What, were you just standing in there? Or were you sitting on the toilet? Did you actually *use* the bathroom?"

"I guess . . . I don't know . . ."

"Did anyone come in? Did girls come in? They did, didn't they! What did you do, Ross? What did you say? And my God—what were you *wearing*?"

His laughter drowned my helpless shriek.

❖

There is precious little sex at Harvard, if you believe what you hear, at least for those who aren't ensconced in the comforts of a college marriage. The absence of sex is a running joke and an ongoing gripe. Students complain about the unattractiveness of their classmates; proctors pass out condoms with a condescending air, as if expecting them to languish for years at the bottom of a sock drawer; and everyone agrees that Harvardians are too busy, too driven, and probably too uptight to spare the time and energy for casual sex. Alumnus Conan O'Brien began a recent Class Day speech by saying, "Fifteen years ago I sat where you sit now, and I thought exactly what you are now thinking: *What's going to happen to me? Will I find my place in the world? Am I really graduating a virgin? I still have twenty-four hours, and my roommate's mom is hot. I swear she was checking me out.*"

This is somewhat unfair. According to one annual survey, only 30 percent of my classmates reached senior year still clutching their virginity, and I am willing to bet that a large percentage of these holdouts disposed of theirs somewhere during the frantic, drunken run-up to commencement. But Conan's one-liner captures, almost perfectly, the smog of sexual frustration hanging over Harvard's campus, where almost everyone seems to feel they are being cheated—by themselves, by the opposite sex, by the administration or the campus culture—out of a four-year spree of sexual adventures that would make Wilt Chamberlain blush.

It isn't supposed to be this way. After all, my generation is easily the most sexually liberated in Harvard's history, more so even than our make-love-not-war predecessors, who still had to contend with puritanical administrators, disapproving parents, and a stifled, I-like-Ike cultural framework. Today's administrators are still worried about sex, but only in a self-interested *Let's keep rape and STDs to a minimum* way; parental disapproval is a fast-fading phenomenon; and as for the culture as a whole . . .

So with everyone from condom-distributing deans to Christina Aguilera urging us to fornicate away, it's odd that there was so little sexual activity warming Cambridge's wintry nights. Maybe it was the workload, or the pressures of careerism and competition, which left little time for the pursuit of sex. Or perhaps it was the fact that much of Harvard's student body wasn't terribly far removed from their high school careers as dorks, grinds, and nerds, and an adolescent legacy of social awkwardness and sexual frustration wasn't easily shaken. Or maybe, as many people claimed, it was the fault of the administration, whose puritanical alcohol policy kept my uptight classmates from body-shotting their way to sexual fulfillment.

But maybe the whole problem was a matter of expectations. From the first stirrings of puberty, we had been spoon-fed a sexual catechism as rigorous and wide-ranging as anything dreamed up in the most scholastic alcoves of the Vatican. Our high school sex-ed classes assured us that intercourse could be at once safe, hygienic, and fun; our television shows promised us an adult world where every-one toppled thoughtlessly into bed with everyone else; our popular musicians urged us to take off all our clothes and rub them the right way. The pages of glossy magazines gave us guidelines for Mind-Blowing Sex, and Eight Ways to a Better Orgasm, and How to Make Her Scream All Night, and all the other *Maxim-Cosmo* refrains. All the while, the more sensitive among us were promised that none of this casual sex would stand in the way of our desire for deeper at-tachments, for soul mates, for true love.

If the cult of sexual satisfaction is the opiate of the American adolescent, then college is the eschaton, the promised land where every dream will be realized, every desire catered to, and all the fum-blings and false starts and parental interference of high school will be left far behind. Incoming freshmen are assured, by a wide variety of commentators, that old-fashioned dating is dead—students today don't date, supposedly, but roam instead in co-ed packs and pair off, casually and often drunkenly, for the hookup, that nebulously de-fined romantic encounter that runs the gamut from chaste necking to what a simpler time called "going all the way." Then there are the movies, from the brilliant *Animal House* down to its unfortunate latter-day spawn, in which the four years of higher education are de-picted as a gleeful, good-natured bacchanal.

When my classmates and I came to college, there was plenty of sex to go around—but it never quite lived up to its advance billing. We were promised a utopia, a landscape of erotic plenty, a place where, as in Huxley's *Brave New World*, everyone belongs to everyone else. Instead, we had to deal with confused relationships, mixed sig-nals, hang-ups and violence and jealousy and misery—with all the un-pleasant stuff of human desire, which sexual rebels long traced to the pernicious effects of repression and patriarchy and old-time religion, but which had endured despite the slow demise of these bogeymen.

We had to deal with the danger of sex, in other words, and our overachieving souls were ill equipped for it. Danger didn't help you get good grades, or run the *Crimson* or the Undergraduate Council; it didn't add any lines to the résumé, or give you a leg up in recruiting or medical school applications; it didn't help you push on into the bright and successful tomorrow that we were so often promised. All danger did was add a layer of complication, of emotional tumult, of uncertainty and potential misery to our competitive, planned-out lives—and we didn't have time for any of that.

So the pattern was set. People arrived at Harvard expecting sexual fulfillment, found the going rougher than expected, and retreated quickly into books and extracurriculars and the familiar paths that had dominated their high school lives. True, a lucky minority forged joined-at-the-hip relationships, whose stability provided a safe sexual outlet and interfered not at all with careful career-mindedness. But the rest of us, the lovelorn majority, were left to float alone through the strange, strained sexual culture that holds sway among the young American elite, in college and beyond, through the long adolescence of our twenties.

This culture pretends to be libertine and licentious, but it's neither. Real eros and real passion are kept at bay, a strange combination of the crude and the clinical holds sway—and at Harvard in particular, a thick and corrosive helping of irony is stirred into the mix. My classmates and I fancied ourselves intellectuals, after all, and there is nothing intellectual about the way sex is pitched and preached and sold in America. We were too smart for such lowbrow fare, yet we wanted it anyway, wanted the leering magazines and the panting songs and even the idiotic porn. So we sought refuge in a calculated self-consciousness that made it socially acceptable to subscribe to *FHM* or *Stuff,* or organize a "pimps and hos" party, or belt out 2 Live Crew amid Model UN festivities. Once a year, at Winthrop House's Debauchery dance, you could even strip down and exchange sexual favors for Mardi Gras beads. But you always had to make it clear that you were self-aware, that you were slightly above it all, that you were doing it, sure, but you were doing it *ironically*.

In such a culture, the sexual intercourse that does take place tends to have a transactional rather than a transcendent quality, and it's far more likely to produce retrospective embarrassment than any sense of liberation or fulfillment. Indeed, there isn't much left to be liberated *from* in a sexual culture like ours. The old restrictions have fallen away, creating a landscape shorn of every taboo—against sex before marriage, against oral sex, against cohabitation, against pornography watching and masturbation and homosexuality and bi-sexuality and cross-dressing, with everything allowed so long as no one cries rape. But such a landscape often feels shorn, as well, of sexual idealism, of romance and passion and the excitement of love that earlier, more repressed generations seemed to have in abundance.

Thou shalt not disrupt thy career is the only commandment left, but it feels as restrictive as a thousand biblical prohibitions.

What remains is farce: the comedy of the random hookup. "Hooking up" is a tired term by now; it was tired even during my college years. It had already been discovered by social critics like David Brooks, who depicted jaded undergrads discussing meaning-less sexual encounters in "the tone one might use to describe commut-ing routes"—or Tom Wolfe, whose essay on the subject announced that "in the year 2000, in the era of hooking up, 'first base' meant deep kissing, groping and fondling; 'second base' meant oral sex; 'third base' meant going all the way; and 'home plate' meant learning each other's name."

There is some truth to these alarmist reports, but among elite students, at least, it's easy to overestimate the frequency of the casual hookup, which serves as a not so Platonic ideal for single men, some-thing that they know is real and have even tasted from time to time, but for the most part remains tantalizingly out of reach. The hookup is usually the goal of a single guy's Friday or Saturday night, but despite decades of bold talk about the unleashing of the female libido, the pool of women willing to go along with a sweaty, consequences-free grope session remains far smaller than the pool of interested men. Worse, at Harvard, at least 70 percent of that already meager pool of women will end up beating down the doors of final clubs by two A.M. on a weekend eve, in search of the touch of class and the free alcohol that the final-club boys are only too happy to provide. This leaves, for the hordes of lusty males who set out, coiffed and cologned, to bars and parties in the hopes of picking someone up, an available female population of the drunk and desperate, the weird and reckless. Even then most men go home empty-handed, since there aren't enough such women to go around.

The random hookups that do occur are much treasured phenomena for the male undergrad, but they often involve women he considers (rightly or wrongly) well beneath him. This tendency creates an odd mix of self-congratulation and shame. "I got that piece of ass I was looking for," Tom was fond of saying after a night of pseudo-passion—yet for years afterward, we could get his goat merely by dropping the names of the various gorgons he'd invited into his bedroom. "Yvonne!" we'd cry as he cringed. "Marisa!" (An audible moan.) "Alison!" (An agonized yelp.) And as he sank below the table in shame, *"Veronica!"*

One can only imagine what poor Veronica thought of Tom. Nothing good, I imagine. The comedy of the hookup isn't quite so funny for women, for all that the sexual revolution has supposedly released them to behave as caddishly as any man. In part, it's that women still tend to expect something more from a hookup than fleeting release. They are more likely than men to imagine a relationship blooming from a one-night stand, and more apt to be disappointed when it doesn't. But there are pitfalls even for women who lack such illusions, since a version of the old double standard endures, weakened dramatically but still potent enough to keep them walking an uneasy tightrope between frowned-upon prudery and frowned-upon promiscuity. The latter still exacts a steep social price. "Final-club slut," with its tidy intersection of class resentment and misogyny, was usually the epithet of choice at Harvard, and there was no real male equivalent. Calling a guy sleazy or sketchy didn't have the same ring, the same venom, as calling a girl a whore.

In the age of hooking up, even using a word like "sketchy" pejoratively is rather silly. Whether you're making a late-night booty call to an old flame, necking drunkenly with a stranger at a Boston club, or heading west to Smith in search of women more desperate than the typical Harvard girl, hooking up is always a deeply sketchy business. Alcohol is inevitably involved, strange and sloppy behavior is expected, flight at the break of dawn is practically required. Pride and shame swirl in near-equal measure: You may leave your room on Saturday morning pledged to hook up at any cost, but if your quest is successful, the Sunday-morning stroll home is still known as the "walk of shame." And over everything hangs the specter of rape and sexual assault, defined in Massachussetts law and university policy as any form of sexual contact in which the woman is legally intoxicated—a classification that could apply to scores of Harvard encounters every Saturday night.

Naturally, amid all this sketchiness, truly bizarre happenings abound: the drunken girl whose bowels voided just as she and her swain were getting down to business; the girl who insisted that her would-be paramours perform a set of naked jumping jacks; the girl who swept into my roommate Nick's room late one night, announced "I always wanted to do this," made out with him for thirty minutes, and never spoke to him again. The abortive encounters were often stranger still, like the night when a girl of my acquaintance managed to be taken home, drunk out of her mind, by the man of her dreams. While he went into the bathroom, she undressed and arranged herself provocatively on his bed. Coming into the bedroom, he looked her over and grinned.

"So, do you want me to FUCK YOU?" he demanded.

"Yes, oh God, please . . ." she panted.

"Do you want me to FUCK YOU . . . in the ASS?"

"Oh, yes, *yes*!"

"Well then," he said cheerfully, "have a nice night." He turned on his heel and departed, leaving her to scramble home as best she could.

My favorite strange story took place on a humid spring evening when Nick, out walking in Harvard Square, ran into an acquaintance from a New York internship who was now a student at MIT. She seemed unusually glad to see him, and soon they were having dessert together, and she was confessing that she'd thought he was really cute and nice when they had met before, and he was happily confessing that he felt the same way, and then they were taking a nice romantic stroll along the Charles River at dusk, and kissing in the shadow of Weeks Bridge, and she was whispering that it would be so fun if they could . . .

". . . go for a swim together!"

Beside them, the Charles lapped, peaceful and polluted, sweeping syringes and broken glass against its banks. Boston traffic roared on either side, and on the nearby footpath a jogger darted past, and a cyclist. Then, before Nick knew it, his companion had doffed her shirt, dropped her pants, and begun breaststroking her way out into the twilit water.

"What did you do next?" we asked him, breathless.

"What could I do?" he said. "I stripped and swam out after her. And then we made out."

"In the river?"

A slightly dazed grin. "In the river."

That Charles River swim, we all agreed, never could have happened if the girl in question hadn't gone to a different school. Hooking up with people from outside the Harvard bubble was *always* easier, or so everyone knew ("dropping the H-bomb" is the campus term for luring a girl to bed by casually telling her where you go to school). Or at least it was easier for men. A double standard lingers here as well: The same qualities that supposedly make Harvard men irresistible, our brilliance and ambitions and bright prospects, tend to stereotype Harvard girls as intellectually intimidating, unappealing, and unfeminine. We males may be scorned as cocky and snobbish, but that's far better than being dismissed as frigid, freakishly smart ballbusters—which explains why girls are more likely to hide their Harvard affiliation than to flaunt it. (Even within the college there was an unspoken bias among certain parts of the male population against getting together with someone from Harvard, a discomfort with the idea of a girl who was as high-achieving and personally ambitious as we knew ourselves to be.)

Not that the H-bomb was foolproof even for us men. Outside girls never seemed as awed as campus legend would have you believe. Still, a number of people I knew cut a Casanovan swath through the population of Wellesley, the girls-only school that was once Radcliffe's rival (*Wellesley to bed, Radcliffe to wed,* runs an archaic saying) and has lately imbibed the same ethos of lesbian chic that my friend Margaret so hated at Smith. The lesbianism only added to the allure, and many of my more desperate male classmates happily piled on board the so-called Fuck Truck, a shuttle running from Harvard Yard to Wellesley's campus in suburban Boston. Or they donned drag to attend the annual Dyke Ball, where they watched young women grind and strip and French-kiss each other, and hoped against hope to meet a girl like Teresia, the Wellesleyite who hooked up with my roommate Siddarth one weekend and then called him the next to invite him to her campus for what she promised would be a full-scale, scheduled orgy.

"I don't know, guys," Siddarth mused to us that night. "I'm almost tempted. But I'd have to leave soon, if I'm going at all—so should I?"

I gave him the Catholic answer, which was a regretful no. Everyone else gave him the *Maxim* answer, which was *Hell yes, brother*. But then doubts began to creep in.

"You know, if it's a *scheduled* orgy . . ."

". . . the sort of people who'd show up . . ."

". . . would be weird . . ."

". . . and ugly . . ."

". . . and they'd probably all be . . ."

A chorus—*"Men!"*

Siddarth stayed home that night.

My own attempts to drop the H-bomb peaked the summer after my grand freshman failure. I wasted fruitless hours at UConn frats and seedy basement parties, making desperate conversation with various young women—"Beer Slut," my friends called one; "Stumpy," they nicknamed another—in the hopes of burying Rachel Polley's memory with a string of conquests.

One successful foray ended on the guest bed of a high school friend's parents, with a girl who resembled a chunkier Reese Witherspoon drunkenly masticating my neck and cheeks. It had taken some time to reach this point—*Do most Harvard guys take so long to get what they want?* she had asked, pushing her tongue into my mouth. I wasn't sure what to say, but then I wasn't sure that this *was* what I wanted. My throat was dry from too much vodka, and her breasts, spilling out of pink pajamas, threatened my ability to breathe. I was supposed to be excited, but I was bored and somewhat disgusted with myself, with her, with the whole business . . . and then whatever residual enthusiasm I felt for the venture dissipated, with shocking speed, as she nibbled at my ear and whispered—

"You know, I'm on the pill . . ."

❖

I'm on the pill. . . . She wasn't from Harvard, but on that night, in that dank basement bedroom, she spoke for all of us, the whole young American elite. Not *I love you,* not *This is incredible,* not *Let's go all the way,* but *I'm on the pill.* Because that, after all, was the critical information.

Formal sexual education is thick with charts and diagrams, statistics and gruesomely cautionary photos. *This is what chlamydia looks like,* my high school biology teacher would tell us, shoving a picture of a chancrous penis in our face. *These are the odds of getting pregnant if you don't use birth control—this is how you put a condom on a banana— this is the vas deferens, this is the urethra, this is the fallopian tube, and this is the clitoris.* Little of this information sticks. Nobody remembers the exact risk of pregnancy, or the timing of the menstrual cycle, when they're fumbling in the dark with a naked woman, and nobody thinks back to that Trojan-and-banana demonstration when it comes time to put on the condom. Sex ed works, if it works at all, because of the underlying message of those classes, which has less to do with clinical details than with economic and social imperatives. Remember what matters, the young elites are told, first by high school teachers and then by college administrators, parents, and even peers: Remember your career, your parents' hopes, your grad school applications, your earning potential as a single Ivy grad in your early-to-mid-twenties, remember all this, and be careful whom you screw and how.

This culture of safety begins with birth control, the Harvard administration's main contribution to keeping students out of harm's way: condoms in every residential bathroom, birth-control pills from University Health Services, the morning-after pill if things go slightly awry, abortions in Boston if all else fails. *Do whatever you want, but remember your rubbers* is the message that our once religious school hands down, and the message is dutifully echoed, in more graphic language, by the socially conscious student groups that cater to their classmates' appetites and anxieties. "Peer Contraceptive Counselors" was my personal favorite: They had workshops and counseling and a hotline for emergencies, and they advertised it all with cheerfully colored posters promising to teach you how to put on a condom, how to use a dental dam, and other necessary skills. "You can do anything after you've learned to handle Woody the Wooden Penis," their website promised.

But being safe goes far beyond the prophylactic. After all, we were in college—people got drunk and forgot their pills, their condoms, their very senses. Hence the rise to prominence, if you will, of mutual masturbation and its close cousin, oral sex. Such techniques are the stock-in-trade of the young and privileged. They reduce the risk of STDs considerably, the risk of pregnancy entirely, and neatly satisfy the orgasm imperative. If you get bored with lips and tongues, there are always other twists: breast sex for the bosomy, for instance, or old-fashioned hand jobs for the truly boring.

Everybody wins: You can have oral sex with a stranger without worrying about morning-after pills; you can have it with an acquaintance or friend and tell yourself that it didn't mean much beyond the gratifying of a brief spasm of desire; and you can have it indefinitely, as a number of couples I knew did, either to preserve something for the wedding night, to satisfy vague religious fears, or simply to avoid the cumbersome necessity of a nightly condom or daily birth-control dose. You can lead the liberated, orgasmic life that young, upwardly mobile Americans believe themselves entitled to, and you can do so without ever putting that upward mobility at risk.

Safer even than oral sex, though, are sex toys, once the tools of courtesans and lonely housewives, now safely mainstreamed and available to everyone who wants sex without any real mess. What pornography is to young men, sex toys are to young women: stimulation without risk, titillation without danger, orgasm without the stickiness of a partner.

"Well, you may have heard the rumors," began an e-mail to the membership of the Radcliffe Union of Students, a feminist-minded undergrad group, during my junior year, "and, yes, RUS will be having a sex toy party in the coming weeks." Sadly, the writer assured RUSers that "everyone will remain fully clothed" during the festivities. "This is essentially a Tupperware party with sex toys," she promised them, or even a "product demonstration," in which "someone from outside, who does this for a living"—at a local "women-owned" sex shop called Grand Opening, to be exact—displays and demonstrates "a range of sex toys," in the hopes that "women who may not be comfortable going into the mainstream sex shop [will] see what options are out there for broadening their range of sexual experience." After all, the e-mail explained, "female masturbation and the reality of female sexual desire is really an affront to and a challenge to the patriarchy," since "women who can get themselves off don't need men to fulfill themselves sexually . . . which removes female sexuality from the idea that it only exists for the purpose of reproduction and male satisfaction."

The e-mail's self-conscious feminist spin was two decades late. Women masturbating might have affronted the patriarchy once upon a time, but most of the men I knew were happily on board with "the reality of female sexual desire." The notion of having "a good relationship with a sex toy," though, was admirably of the moment—a moment when a vibrator is a typical twenty-first-birthday present among roommates; a moment when it's perfectly respectable for college marrieds to bring sex toys into their beds; a moment when there often seems to be a kind of quid pro quo being hashed out, in which women expect men to allow contraptions between the sheets, or at least to be accepting of their private use of dildos and other, less threatening devices. The goal of sex, after all, is the orgasm, not any antique ideal about "one flesh" or "mystical union," so whatever helps the two parties proceed to the peak of physical pleasure should be welcomed. Especially since the future ruling class has so little time to spare for sex.

We usually use a vibrator when we're in a hurry, a friend informed me once. *You know, when we have to be somewhere or something.*

In return, men expect women to be okay with pornography, which is, after all, the safest sex there is. Thanks to the VCR, cable TV, and now the DVD, pornography has taken American life in general by storm, but smut is a particularly pervasive presence on college campuses, where the current crop of students has grown up with the Internet, and with the attendant knowledge that instant erotic gratification is only a mouse click or two away. Today's Harvard man is as likely to know the oeuvre of an adult-film star like Jenna Jameson as, say, the novels of Ernest Hemingway or the chronology of the Civil War—while down I-95, at decadent Yale, a group of students formed an adult-video-watching organization called Porn and Chicken, then tried to film an adult movie themselves (working title: "The Staxxxx") using undergrad actors. Casting problems put an end to the venture, but the banner of Ivy League porn has recently been picked up at Harvard, where a student-run sex magazine has begun publication. The title, naturally, is *H-Bomb.*

Pornography has long been among us, with young men as its target audience, but you had to at least leave home for the smut of the recent past, which was confined by the disapproval of law and custom to a demimonde of strip clubs, adult theaters, and bookshops. Even the material that was widely available, like pinup girls and *Playboys,* had a kind of coyness about it, or an aesthetic innocence.

None of that endures. What exists in its place is prostitution in all but name, an endless stream of copulation and cum shots, with vacant-eyed men and siliconed women servicing their partners—and us—through the magic of the high-speed Internet. For my generation, such hard-core porn is the real sex education, a squalid curriculum in which every desire can be realized, every sordid itch scratched. Even pedophilia, the last taboo, shows signs of weakening. It's chafed at in the ubiquitous banner ads and pop-ups promising "teen sluts" and "barely legal" girls, and it's easily circumvented by the determined and web-savvy. Just ask Antonio Lasaga, the former master of Yale's Saybrook College, or Ronald Thiemann, the former dean of Harvard's Divinity School, both of whom had extensive child-porn stockpiles exposed during my years at Harvard.

The dark diversity of Internet porn offers, ultimately, a kind of sexual leveling, asserting boldly that every desire is worthy of cultivation, and that every man (and every woman, too, it's increasingly insisted) deserves to dally, via DVD, mpeg, and streaming video, with the quivering, moaning object of their fantasies. Porn strokes, quite literally, the very Harvardian (and very American) sense of entitlement, telling us what we have always known: that we should be able to have whatever we want, whenever we want it, and without any risk at all.

❖

What's remarkable about the whole system is how well it works, at least among the youthful overclass—how easily the regimen of diaphragms and dental dams, masturbation and oral sex and porn, has replaced the older forces of family, religion, and shame that policed the sexual landscape for generations. Instead of telling young people to save sex for marriage, the new sexual orthodoxy tells us to have as much as we want, but to do it carefully, lest our bright and happy futures be set back by disease and unwanted children. It's a cost-benefit equation, in the end, and my classmates and I understood it perfectly and followed the code nearly to the letter. Why not, when the benefits are immense, and the costs—a blow job instead of the missionary position, a vibrator instead of a penis—are relatively small.

This equation doesn't work so well for everyone. If you don't have the prospect of a six-figure salary awaiting you after college, if you don't have the grades or board scores to rise high in the ranks of the meritocracy, if your horizons are limited by your neighborhood, your dysfunctional family, your poverty, then being told to curb your natural appetites for the sake of your future may seem absurd, unreal, or even insulting. It's easy to remember to use a condom when your post-college address will be in lower Manhattan or Beacon Hill or Santa Monica. But it's hard to remember—and hard to see the point—when the world you know, and the future you can expect, lies far beneath the floating cosmopolis of the overclass.

So there *is* a price to be paid for belonging to Harvard's most sexually liberated generation. But it isn't paid by us. Nearly one in three children in the United States is born out of wedlock, and a third of those are born to women twenty-two and younger; in the black community, the illegitimacy rate is close to 70 percent. But there are almost no babies born, illegitimate or not, to Harvard students (the university system is famously hostile to them). We are far too careful for that.

There are 1.2 million abortions every year in the United States, and half of all Americans will contract an STD before they turn twenty-five. But again, Harvard students are careful: None of my friends had abortions—unless you count the morning-after pill—and few of them contracted STDs, save perhaps for the ubiquitous human papilloma virus (*which is totally harmless,* we lied to one another). Even the family structures of Harvard students seem remarkably stable, for a broken-home-ridden country in which half of all marriages end in court. An informal tally of twenty of my college friends finds that exactly two have divorced parents.

But why *should* we have to pay a price for our freedom? We practice safe sex, after all, an ethos perfectly tailored for the privileged student, because keeping sex safe requires only motivation, self-control, and a healthy self-regard, which we have in abundance. These motivations don't exist everywhere, but it's not our fault if other people don't have our bright futures to remind them to pull that condom tight and take the morning-after pill. We live in a meritocracy, don't we? We deserve to be where we are, don't we? And aren't a few illegitimate children, born to other, poorer people, ultimately less important than our sexual liberty, our inalienable right to do whatever, and whomever, we want? Especially since we're generous enough to tutor some of these same kids in Harvard's admirable after-school programs.

Few of my classmates think this way, at least consciously. But our sex lives are sufficiently insulated, sufficiently "safe," to make it naive to imagine, as conservatives often do, that the excesses of the sexual revolution may yet produce a reaction among the young elite, a revival of courtship and chivalry and chastity, a return to modesty. There are excesses, yes—excesses that tend to fall disproportionately on women, who are stuck having the abortions, bearing the fatherless children, and enduring the sterility and cancers that bloom from chlamydia, from human papilloma virus, from pelvic inflammatory disease. But these excesses rarely touch elite women, or elites in general; *we* don't get pregnant young or married too early, *we* don't get STDs, *we* don't have abortions—though we find it comforting to know that we always could, if it came to that.

All that we suffer, in the end, is the dissatisfaction I have already mentioned, the sense that something is missing, that the culture's promises haven't quite been fulfilled. But such tepid frustration is hardly the stuff of which social change is made. We are now a generation away from the sexual nirvana that our parents' generation hoped to usher in, and leafing through the pages of Alex Comfort's *The Joy of Sex* and other ur-texts of the 1970s is like reading dispatches from a foreign country, a place where sexual activity was supposed to be transcendent, religious, or at least memorable. But nobody's even thinking about turning back now.

The year after I graduated, a couple of twenty-something sex columnists turned out a hip new sex manual pitched to the younger generation. Entitled *The Big Bang* and billed as "the definitive guide to the new sexual universe," it aimed to be artsy, edgy, funny, and totally different from the manuals of an earlier era.

"Those books aren't particularly out of date information-wise," one of the authors told *The Boston Globe*, when asked about Comfort's famous volume, "but they are far too earnest for us. The prevailing assumption is that 'lovemaking' should last for hours and always be a beautiful interpersonal experience.

"That's not the sex we and our friends are having!"

CHAPTER SEVEN

The Liberal Civil War

O
N A SPRING AFTERNOON late in my junior year, a band of students emerged from the basement of a freshman dormitory and raced into the office of Harvard's president, which occupies the first floor of the venerable brick building known as Massachusetts Hall, near the entrance to Harvard Yard. Carrying sleeping bags and laptops and a week's worth of granola, they dashed past bemused campus policemen, past the secretary's desk, and planted themselves in the president's office, whose occupant, Neil Rudenstine, was mercifully absent. There they took out their cell phones, hooked up their laptops, and prepared to wage a twenty-first-century sit-in.

Their demand went out the same day: *All Harvard workers, whether directly employed or hired through outside firms, must be paid a living wage of at least $10.25 per hour, adjusted annually to inflation, and with basic health benefits.*

On campus, everyone already knew what they wanted. The students were members of the Living Wage Campaign, an arm of the Progressive Student Labor Movement (PSLM), and they had spent the last three years participating in a steadily escalating stream of protests, op-ed writing, teach-ins, rallies, more op-ed writing, sleep-ins, more rallies, more op-ed writing—all of it aimed at convincing the administration to agree to a living wage. First it was ten bucks an hour; later, thanks to inflation, a less slogan-ready $10.25. Through it all, the powers-that-be had barely budged, and their fellow class-mates had watched the antics with either apathy or irritation—so it was hard to argue, in a sense, with the official reasons for sitting in. *We are sitting in because we have exhausted every avenue of dialogue with the administration that could lead to a living wage*, they announced, and it was essentially true. *We are sitting in because we have exhausted every other strategy when dialogue with the administration has failed,* they announced, and this was also true.

We're sitting in because it makes us feel cool and important, they didn't say, but many suspected that this, too, was part of the truth.

The campus yawned and disapproved. The *Crimson* editorial-ized against them and ran a hotly contested poll showing that two-thirds of students opposed the sit-in. The president and deans refused to negotiate. The cops stood outside and bantered with the protestors, showing no signs of reaching for their nightsticks. With no showers, Mass Hall began to stink.

But the students had their laptops, they had their cell phones, and they had plenty of sympathizers—other PSLMers, and some of the local union leaders, and also a usual-suspects collection of Cam-bridge residents, the sort of shaggy-haired people for whom the rev-olution had been postponed but not necessarily canceled. A variety of fellow travelers converged on Harvard Yard, and soon there was a daily protest, thick with drums and placards and chants of "Hey hey ho ho, poverty wages have got to go" outside Massachusetts Hall. Then a tent city sprouted on the venerable lawns in front of John Harvard's statue, and the endless line of Japanese tourists who shuf-fle through the Yard each spring day had a new photo opportunity.

Hard on the circus's heels came the media. Which had presumably been the plan all along.

❖

Campus protest at Harvard has a distinguished pedigree. Student rebellions were commonplace in the early nineteenth century, when rowdy undergraduates were wont to smash windows and furniture, light bonfires, and set off explosions in Harvard Yard, often in protest of some onerous academic requirement, or a flagrant injustice committed against a student. In 1823 over half the senior class swore to leave college until a dismissed classmate was reinstated; in response, the faculty expelled forty-three students (out of a senior class of seventy), including the son of John Quincy Adams. In 1834 the freshman and sophomore classes went on strike, apparently to protest a Latin professor's demand that they memorize something called *Zumpft's Latin Grammar*. Harvard's president that year was Josiah Quincy, for whom my house was named, and he tried to crush the revolt by suspending every sophomore for a year, while promising to haul those responsible for an outbreak of vandalism before a grand jury. This tactic backfired, and more protests ensued. The junior class donned black armbands and hanged Quincy in effigy, an explosion was set off in chapel, and a group of seniors wrote a bill of grievances so convincing that the Harvard Overseers, after stripping the bill's authors of their degrees, felt compelled to issue a forty-seven-page rebuttal. The grand jury produced few indictments and declined to punish the offenders; Quincy's popularity was shattered; and Harvard's enrollment dropped off sharply. (The Class of 1836 was the smallest since 1809.)

By the twentieth century, Harvard was more orderly, and protests diminished during the sobering years of depression and world war. Beginning in the 1950s, though, the old habits reasserted themselves: Students overturned streetcars and clashed with police when Pogo cartoonist Walter Kelly was late coming to campus for a speech; and they turned the campus upside down for two nights to protest a decision to begin printing diplomas in English rather than Latin. Such uprisings were wild, but they were also innocent and a little silly. They would seem even more innocent in the wake of the following decade's disasters.

The president of Harvard throughout the 1950s and '60s was Nathan Pusey, an Establishment figure (albeit a midwesterner, not a Boston Brahmin) who neatly embodied the genteel liberal ideals of his generation. He had opposed Joe McCarthy in the early fifties, presided over the expansion of meritocracy at every level of Harvard, welcomed Jews and Catholics into the university, increased ties to Radcliffe and paved the way for the eventual merger, and basked, however briefly, in the glow of Camelot, when a Harvard man was in the Oval Office and all was right with the world. Pusey was handsome, too, in a strangely ageless way; his face was unlined well into his sixties, and it looked, Roger Rosenblatt wrote in his memoir of the era, *Coming Apart*, "like a police artist's sketch of a good-looking man." He was a tremendous fund-raiser—the alumni adored him—and Harvard grew rich and confident during his tenure.

By the late 1960s, though, Pusey's brand of liberalism looked stodgy to many faculty and students. The former thought him pompous and unintellectual, the latter out of touch and puritanical, particularly on matters sexual, where Harvard's rules governing female guests in undergrad rooms were increasingly attacked as out of date. The pill had appeared, so had Timothy Leary, the cheerful consensus of the previous decade was on its way out—and that was even before it became clear just how bad Vietnam would turn.

Still, as the crisis decade wound on, and things turned sour and violent on college campuses across the nation, Harvard prided itself on being immune to the chaos. There were incidents, of course. In November 1966, Robert McNamara came to debate the war, and protestors from Students for a Democratic Society (SDS) disrupted the speech and hounded him so that he was forced to escape through the college's network of steam tunnels. But McNamara himself downplayed the matter, and twenty-six hundred students signed a letter apologizing for the conduct of their classmates. As late as 1968, Pusey and his peers could brush aside the massive protests surging over Columbia and Berkeley as merely localized problems. At Berkeley, Pusey insisted, the spark was "uneasiness about the quality of undergraduate education," while a commission chaired by Harvard Law professor Archibald Cox smugly concluded that Columbia was "deficient in the cement that binds an institution into a cohesive unit." While everyone agreed, in principle, that Harvard should be prepared for the worst, nobody seemed to believe it would ever come to that.

Meanwhile, student radicals were making plans of their own. There were attacks on the Harvard curriculum (a group that included *Crimson* president James Fallows planned a student-taught counter-curriculum called "The Conspiracy Against Harvard Education"); protests against recruiters from tainted corporations (a luckless shill for Dow Chemical was trapped for several hours in Harvard's Mallinckrodt Laboratory, where he had been conducting interviews); and petitions against the presence of ROTC on campus. On this last issue, the faculty seemed prepared to give ground. In February 1969 they voted to withhold college credit for ROTC courses, which would have transformed it into an extracurricular activity. Later that same month, another committee recommended ending all ROTC programs within two years.

This wasn't fast enough to suit Harvard's chapter of SDS. On

April 9, around midday, a group of roughly three hundred students, tutors, and various outsiders seethed into University Hall, the nerve center of Harvard's administration. They evicted the deans who occupied the building, pushing and dragging them outside if they resisted and meting out particularly violent treatment to the lone black administrator, Archie Epps, an Assistant Dean of Freshmen. (Epps outlasted them; he rose to be Dean of Students and was still serving at Harvard when I arrived on campus.) Some of the occupiers rifled through Harvard's files, eventually publishing the juicy bits in the SDS paper, the *Old Mole*; others defaced the walls of the offices and posh Faculty Room, though this activity was kept to a minimum; still others gave impromptu speeches from the steps and windows of the building. They issued demands, too—the immediate purge of ROTC from Harvard's campus, and the rolling back of rent on university-owned property in Cambridge's poorer neighborhoods (a bid for working-class solidarity that offered a foretaste of my generation's obsessions). But the real focus, as everyone knew, was the Vietnam War. As SDS put it, "we consider the ROTC as a life-and-death issue for the people of the world whose lands are occupied by U.S. troops, whose social revolutions are fought viciously by the U.S. military."

Campus sentiment was generally against the occupation, and the protest might have fizzled out if the administration had let it run its course. (John Kenneth Galbraith said later that "twelve hours of patience" would have ended the matter, and James Q. Wilson concurred.) But like Josiah Quincy before him, Pusey was a man of authority, not compromise, and his instinct—buttressed by what were then seen as the lessons of Berkeley and Columbia—was to come down hard on the radicals, and come down fast.

So it was that at five A.M. on April 11, about four hundred local and state policemen stormed University Hall and evicted the occupiers. The police, working-class Bostonians with little patience for cosseted Ivy League peaceniks (*Fascist pigs,* the students screamed; *Long-haired commies,* the cops shouted back), were less than gentle. They wielded a battering ram on the doors, tear gas on the students assembled outside, and Mace and nightsticks inside University Hall. More than fifty students were clubbed before the building was cleared, and dozens staggered out with bloodied heads and faces. The defining image of Harvard in the 1960s was set that morning: shaggy-haired, bleeding students going down under the coshes of helmeted staties.

The media lapped it up; the faculty—though divided over the sit-in—was largely horrified; and the student body, previously cool to the protests, turned out by the thousands to protest Pusey's violent solution. For the first time, revolution seemed to be in the Harvard air, and most people expected a new, more violent wave of protest to follow, either that spring or the following fall, and that a radicalized student body would be the rule for many years to come. The bloody morning in the Yard was a watershed moment, or so everyone agreed, and nothing would ever be the same again.

Nothing was, but the revolution itself never materialized. There were more protests, including a fracas over the establishment of African-American studies, in which one black student wielded a butcher knife outside the faculty meeting that voted on the new discipline (it was approved); and later a variety of strikes and vigils and protests as American involvement in Vietnam wound to its miserable close. But nothing ever approached the drama and violence of the University Hall takeover, and what many had imagined to be just the beginning of a revolutionary wave turned out to be its crest.

It quickly became clear that the April violence's long-term importance would be as a political Rorschach test, one that neatly defined the cleavage in late-1960s American liberalism. Was the takeover a dark day, a lesson in the perils of puerile far-left radicalism? Or were the protestors to be lionized as martyrs, offering a heroic response to the evils of America in general and Harvard in particular? The argument began almost as soon as the last screaming SDSer was hauled from the hallowed confines of University Hall; it has not been settled yet.

Pusey, having lost the confidence of faculty and students alike, slipped sadly into retirement in 1971, two years after the decision that defined his twenty years in office. ROTC vanished from Harvard, the Vietnam War came to an end, peace broke out on college campuses. But the chasm that the 1960s opened is still there, dividing not left from right (conservatives on elite campuses boast the approximate clout of Methodists in Mecca) but left from far left, Democrats from Socialists, *The New Republic* from *The Nation*—and, most fatefully, Al Gore from Ralph Nader.

Call them parlor liberals and street liberals, if you will; on college campuses, they are still at war, still fighting the battles that SDS began and Nathan Pusey failed to finish.

There has been movement, since the spring of 1969. The old generation of parlor liberals retired or died off (or got with it, posthaste), and with them vanished certain ideas that were once liberal but were quickly recognized, in the bright dawn of the Age of Aquarius, as essentially reactionary—ideas about sex, for the most part, which on college campuses meant ideas about visiting hours and single-sex schools, which became single-sex dorms, which became single-sex floors, which became single-sex rooms, and even that idea was regarded, by the late 1990s, as essentially antiquated and ridiculous. Then there was abortion and *Roe* v. *Wade*, and everyone understood what they were supposed to think of that; and then the issue was homosexuality, and colleges became the first "safe space" in a country that was at first rigidly homophobic and then somewhat less so, and then suddenly was watching *Will & Grace* and *Queer Eye for the Straight Guy* by the millions.

So the street liberals won some victories in the bedroom—but they lost everywhere else, as the 1960s generation grew up and went to work and began to make money, which led them to consider that maybe the whole business of capitalism wasn't so bad after all. This realization didn't set in for a while, because there were the 1980s, and Reagan was president, and greed might have been good, but right-thinking Harvard grads from the generation of 1969 could still look down their noses at moneymaking, still associate it with those terrible, tax-slashing, bomb-building Republicans. But then came Clinton, and the 1990s, and the '69ers were in power in Washington and entering their prime earning years everywhere else, and suddenly—at Harvard and across the country—most of the students who had come of age with Vietnam and rock 'n' roll woke up and realized that yes, they believed in premarital sex and homosexual rights and abortion on demand, and yes, they still listened to *Rubber Soul* and sometimes, when the mood took them, even Hendrix, but in everything else, they were parlor liberals, they were the powers-that-be, they were their parents, they were the Man.

They were James Fallows, president of the *Crimson* during that fateful year and would-be Conspirator Against a Harvard Education, who is now a dignified and cheerful pillar of establishment journalism—a former Carter speechwriter, former editor of *U.S. News & World Report*, and, at present, an *Atlantic Monthly* national correspondent.

They were Nicholas Lemann, who succeeded Fallows in the *Crimson* president's chair, from which eminence he agonized, as the first reports of Pol Pot's killing fields trickled in, over whether to "look at events in Indochina as Americans with liberal values or as the Indochinese must look at them. . . . The Khmer Rouge can certainly no longer meet with our approval on our own terms," and yet "on their own terms they continue to be most of what we supported them for—staunch nationalists, socialists, remakers of their own society."

Quoth Lemann in 1975: "It is a conflict that I am not ready to resolve. . . . I continue to support the Khmer Rouge in its principles and goals but I have to admit that I deplore the way they are going about it." He resolved it eventually, one presumes. Twenty years later, in the roaring nineties, Lemann was *The New Yorker*'s main political reporter, and today he is dean of the Columbia School of Journalism.

They were Marty Peretz, then a long-haired assistant professor and a darling of the radicals, now part owner of *The New Republic*, which has, under his leadership, drifted away from its socialist roots and is now the organ of the Democratic Party's right wing, the intellectual nerve center of parlor liberalism. "I think that the sight of the takeover," he said later, "was the beginning of my turn politically, from left to right."

They were Miles Rappaport, a member of Harvard SDS in 1969 and Connecticut's secretary of state three decades later; Jamie Gorelick, gassed by police on the steps of University Hall, who rose to be deputy attorney general in the Clinton administration and later a member of the 9/11 Commission. They were even Bill Clinton himself—a Georgetown, Yale, and Oxford man, not a Harvardian, but a gleeful, bearded participant in the almost-revolution, and then the embodiment of the revolution's concessions and compromises, its transformation from a bohemian revolt into what David Brooks has brilliantly termed "bourgeois bohemianism," in which the rhetoric of revolution was co-opted by corporate America, by Nike and Apple and all the young Turks of the tech boom, and the incidentals of the 1960s protests—the Birkenstocks, the organic foods, the comfortable clothes and achingly authentic furniture—became the essentials of a new, self-congratulatory upper-class zeitgeist.

But this transformation didn't happen to everyone. Not everyone became a parlor liberal, not everyone became a Bobo, not everyone made the Clinton compromise, in which the sexual revolution was accomplished (in the Oval Office, no less) and the other revolutions were put off indefinitely, placed somewhere out there, just beyond the bridge to the twenty-first century. A few kept the radical faith—support for the Khmer Rouge's principles and goals, let's say, if not their methods—and if they didn't end up running seedy bookstores (like Revolution Books, a Cambridge shop just down the street from Quincy House, where Mao's face looms from the window), most of these diehards went into academia, where tenure softened the temptations of the market, and where the constant influx of young people kept the flame of radicalism flickering, albeit faintly.

So the modern university was born—a place where the professors are to the left of most students, and the students themselves are divided between those who follow in their parents' post-1960s footsteps, believing in free love *and* free trade, and those who read Noam Chomsky and Howard Zinn and *Mother Jones* and believe in freedom, period; freedom from every structure of oppression, every arch and wall and flying buttress of the vast military-industrial-patriarchal complex, which they believe to have been barely dented by their forefathers' noble efforts.

The first group—the parlor liberals, the New Democrats—are larger by far, forming the political mainstream at elite colleges. They sit comfortably on the left of the American political spectrum, believing in gun control and gay rights, in affirmative action and abortion, in a multilateral foreign policy and a significant social safety net, and they will likely vote Democratic until they die. Yet there is still something conservative about them. They are creatures of their class, not would-be traitors to it, and they are deeply uncomfortable with radicalism in any form. This discomfort usually targets bogeymen like the Christian right, but it extends easily to anyone who displays too much self-righteousness and zeal, too much anger at institutions and leaders and structures of powers—to the Chomskys as well as the Kenneth Starrs, and to the Sean Penns and Michael Moores on Oscar night. Parlor liberals are ultimately well disposed to the world and to their privileged place in it, believing that what injustices there are can be righted without too much upheaval and unrest, and perhaps even without raising taxes.

The 1990s were golden years for the parlor liberals, young and old alike—broad sunlit uplands in which it seemed possible that the ruling class of a globalized world could do good by doing well, that a consultant in Boston and an Internet prince in Silicon Valley might participate in the spread of democracy and capitalism and the glorious, Internet-fueled end of history to the farthest corners of the globe. The younger members of this ruling class, my classmates and my friends, were almost throwbacks to the late-Victorian liberals, believing once again in the inevitable triumph of Progress, which throughout the nineties went by various shorthands: the Information Revolution, the New World Order, Globalization, the Third Way, and all the other phrases that tested well in focus groups.

But these years were also good to Harvard's minority—the street liberals, that is, who rejected their fellow elites' comfort with the world order in favor of a fervent belief that the whole damn mess is corrupt, all the institutions and the governments and the schools and certainly the authority figures, those white males and the others they've co-opted or bought or fooled. While the parlor liberals basked in the rising Dow and the wiring of the world, the street liberals pointed to the misery of migrant workers and sweatshop slaves, and argued that dark forces everywhere—the CIA and the IMF, the Christian Coalition and Big Oil, the World Bank and the Harvard administration—are still conspiring against anyone who dares to be different or rebellious or Other. The world, they insisted, remains the prison it has always been, with the only difference being that now the oppression is invisible, enshrined in custom rather than law, or worse, banished to the third world.

Like most paranoiacs, street liberals are flush with facts. You will never meet anyone so well informed, so well read, as a campus protestor, so long as you stay on his or her chosen ground of labor relations, or World Bank malfeasance, or police brutality, or U.S. perfidy in East Timor and Latin America. Yet they have a deep aversion to argument, by which I mean argument on a higher level than a simple marshaling of statistics. Street liberals like to keep things simple: If people are badly paid, then they should be given raises; if workers suffer after a round of IMF-ordered budget cuts, then spending should be increased and the IMF abolished. Arguments that complicate these easy answers—that bring in economic theory, political trade-offs, and ultimate questions about the nature of justice and the role of government—are deeply suspect, since logic and philosophy are themselves ideologically tainted, having been long used by the ruling class to justify their privileged position.

Between this paranoia and the breezy optimism of parlor liberalism yawns a vast philosophical divide. The divide fuels the modern university's ongoing liberal civil war, and it effectively guarantees that even when the two branches of the campus left agree on the surface, you can be sure that there are deeper waters swirling below.

For instance, street liberals and parlor liberals are officially united in their staunch opposition to the deadly trio of racism, sexism, and homophobia. But the parlor liberals believe in a world where racism can be conquered—indeed, where it *will* be conquered, if we can just keep affirmative action in place long enough—while street liberals often insinuate that parlor liberals are themselves subconsciously racist. Or parlor liberals think the major battles against sexism have been won, and that what we need to do is close up the wage gap, crack the glass ceiling, and keep abortion legal. Whereas street liberals have been known to locate sexual oppression in the marriage contract, or in the pains of childbirth, or even in heterosexual sex, with its inevitable overtones of rape.

As for homophobia—admittedly, parlor liberals are somewhat less sanguine, acknowledging that there is considerable work to do, especially in the Midwest and South. But eventually (and sooner rather than later) there will be gay marriage, they assume, and then things will fall into place. Whereas street liberals see unconquerable homophobia and heterosexism *everywhere,* in religion and politics and the military, but also in romantic comedies, in college formals, in beer ads and baby photos and the English language itself.

This gulf naturally extends to the role of the university and the purpose of a college education. The parlor liberal, if he stops to think about it, probably views college principally as a training ground for his career, a place of preparation for the success that awaits him. If he is particularly idealistic, he may regard the school as a temple of sorts, dedicated to learning and perhaps even Veritas, which has been stripped of its religious meaning but not its religious overtones. But whatever his cast of mind, the parlor liberal believes that college should be largely detached from politics, or at least from trendy causes that might interfere with the business of résumé-building.

Not so the street liberal. For him, not only is the university an inherently political institution, it is often *the* political institution of the modern age, the source of radical movements, protest politics, and insurgent presidential candidacies from Eugene McCarthy down to Howard Dean. Were it not for the university, the New Left wouldn't have existed, and the 1960s wouldn't have taken place. No Port Huron in '62, no Berkeley in '64, no Wisconsin in '67, and no Chicago and Paris and Berkeley again in 1968, the high-water mark of the whole business. In the mythology of neo-Marxism, the student holds a mythical place alongside the worker and the peasant—the holy trinity of protest, you might say.

Thus, for street liberals, campus activism often seems to be the point of going to college, as if the whole setup of dorm rooms and public spaces and sympathetic professors exists principally as a stage for political drama, for activism of all stripes. The classroom is strictly secondary. As one fatuous profile of Harvardian student-activists put it, "Because these causes impart more emotional importance than, say, the implications of Kantian thought, student protestors can encounter difficulties focusing primarily on academics." Or as an earlier generation had it: *Teacher, leave them kids alone.*

There is something self-indulgent in this, something philistine in the activist student's fuck-you to all that a college education has to offer. Such self-indulgence is exacerbated by the too often accurate stereotype of the student radical who graduates into corporate America, telling himself lies about effecting change from within. Many of the Living Wage Movement's hangers-on were like this — kids who were in it for the thrill, the frisson of protest, the chance to inject a little drama into their high-stress, high-achieving lives.

But the charge of self-indulgence doesn't fit the hard-cores, the leaders, the people who chanted the chant and walked the walk, the ones who ended up sleeping, unshowered and unkempt, on the floor of Massachusetts Hall that spring. They didn't sell out, at least the ones I watched: They graduated and joined the Peace Corps, or Teach for America, or went to law school to become activist lawyers and fight the Man on his own home turf. *I'm traveling the country, coordinating national students-against-sweatshops groups,* Ben McKean, one of the PSLM's leaders, told me a year after graduation, when I bumped into him on the Washington Mall during D.C.'s annual day of anti–World Bank fervor. Protests and activism aren't just hobbies for these students, or a chance to go slumming with the working class — they're a way of life. Call them fools, if you will, but not hypocrites.

❖

But what to protest? This is the street liberal's dilemma, for in theory the answer could be everything. In practice, there isn't enough time in the day, so the various issues tend to be divided up among the campus's various identity groups. The feminists protest patriarchal oppression, the gays homophobic oppression, the minorities racist oppression, the labor activists capitalist oppression, and so on down the list. As a result, the political life of a campus like Harvard moves in predictable cycles, as one issue after another takes center stage, and one interest group after another rises to protest the injustice of it all, while the others provide moral support from the sidelines and wait patiently for their turn in the sun.

Some of these cloudbursts of protest are scheduled well in advance. National Coming Out Day, for instance, is sponsored each fall under the aegis of the Harvard Bisexual, Gay, Lesbian, Transgender and Supporters Alliance, or BGLTSA. (Gay groups inevitably have the worst acronyms on campus, reflecting the need to keep tacking on additional letters as each new orientation emerges from the closet of oppression.) For the most part, Harvard's Coming Out Day is a fairly tame affair—stickers are handed out, banners waved, protests scheduled, and a good time had by all. The spirit is often more celebratory than angry, and why not? There are few places where it is easier to be openly gay than within the confines of an elite American university.

I say "for the most part," though, because in my sophomore year, the institutional BGLTSA decided to hand out blank posters to all its members, and instructed them to go forth and spread the transgressive word in venerable Harvard Yard. The slogans that adorned some of those posters offer a pretty good sense of what my more radical classmates thought about sex. SOCRATES FUCKED BOYS; U CAN 2, read the first one I saw as I walked to class; it was the only one I had the balls to tear down. Later on, I passed I WORSHIP THE LORD WITH MY WET QUIVERING CLITORIS (there was a picture, too, if memory serves), and then, just to hammer the anti-religious point home, SAINT SEBASTIAN: THE FIRST FAG IN THE MILITARY. The Yard was blanketed with them—TASTE MENSES on one kiosk, ENJOY COCK on another, HAVE A GOLDEN SHOWER adorning a third.

Writing in response to the ensuing outcry—some of it from gay students who disavowed the stunt and founded, in protest, a group called BOND (Beyond Our Natural Differences)—one of the BGLTSA's leaders offered the street-liberal sexual credo: "As a co-chair committed to recuperating pathologized sexualities and gender identities, I am not willing to re-closet those of us who fall outside monogamy. . . . One person's 'sensationalism' is often another's way of desiring and living."

This was the All Sex Is Good side of street-liberal ideology—the gay side, in both senses of the word. The All Sex Is Dangerous side also scheduled its protests in advance, in the form of Take Back the Night week, a springtime festival of feminism whose principal goal—stopping rape—annually metastasized into a series of rallies, study groups, and workshops in which upper-middle-class women learned how to face down the various forces conspiring against their happiness and safety. There were "eat-ins" to protest the male-dominated advertising world's objectification of women; judo classes where co-eds learned how to cripple; Take Back the Arts events to confront gender bias in the American art community. One year there was a strategy meeting devoted to "strengthening the pro-choice side," where it was explained that abortion is really a matter of defending women's bodies from the "aggressive fetus," which one panelist compared to "a Central Park rapist."

If the organizers did their job properly, by the end of Take Back the Night week, every facet of female life would have been examined, dissected, and shown to be (even now) firmly in thrall to the patriarchy. The proof, as one harangue-happy professor told a candlelight vigil for rape victims, was right in front of their eyes. *Why aren't there*

209

more ads for birth control on television? she wondered. Undoubtedly the patriarchy's fault. *Why does my spell-checker have no word for matriarchy?* Yep, the patriarchy again.

So street liberals emerged from the closet each fall and took back the night each spring. As for the protests that weren't scheduled, that bubbled up naturally from the wells of radical discontent, they were nearly always the result of some perceived slight against ethnic minorities. The Black Students Association's silent protest of Harvey Mansfield's class, following his comments about the link between grade inflation and the influx of black students in the 1970s, was one example, but more typical were the various bursts of outrage from Harvard's easily offended Asian-American activists. One month it was the supposed racism of the waiters at Cambridge's popular Temple Bar, who waited too long to seat a group of Asian-American law students and nearly reaped a boycott. Another month it was the sins of a *Crimson* comic strip entitled *The Misanthropic Mr. Chu,* whose title character's salient characteristics—he was short, beardless, antisocial, and fond of physics—sparked complaints that the paper was perpetuating negative stereotypes about male Asian students. (The latter controversy reached such a fever pitch that the strip's creator— a short, beardless physics student named Haiwen Chu—decided to change his main character to a WASP and the strip's title to *The Misanthropic Mr. Whitman.*)

Such touchiness is perhaps best understood as a reflection of the peculiar place that Asian-Americans occupy on the street-liberal spectrum of victimhood. Like most minority groups, Asians have their history of persecution and prejudice, but lately their high grades and test scores have left them "overrepresented" in higher education, which tends to make them victims, rather than beneficiaries, of collegiate diversity programs. For Asian-American street liberals, then, fighting back against perceived slights may be a way of distancing themselves from their own success, and establishing credibility in a movement where a minority group is often judged on how down-trodden it can claim to be.

The high point of their outrage occurred in my junior year, when a student named Justin Fong—nicknamed Juice—wrote an essay for *FM* decrying the cliques and self-segregating behavior of Harvard's Asian community. The piece was inflammatory, to say the least. "Your common Asian at Harvard," he wrote, is "an economics or computer science concentrator (also pre-med and advanced standing); spends his or her time at some exclusively Korean club in Boston that none of us would ever hear of . . . hangs out with Asians; hangs out only with Asians; walks to class with Asians; plays a stringed instrument in addition to the piano; eats dinner at a table full of Asians; talks on his or her cell phone (made in Asia), in an Asian language with Asians; has Asian parents; eats Asian food preferably in Asian restaurants in Asian districts of Asian Boston; complains that General Wong's Chicken is not sufficiently 'authentic.'"

Over the top as it was, Juice Fong's essay was at heart an earnest lament over how self-segregation "perpetuates the stereotypes and racial divisions that we already have," complete with an appeal for everyone to "just get along." Alas, this Rodney King conclusion was lost on Harvard's street liberals, who first attacked Fong for racial insensitivity, then trained their guns on the paper that had dared to print his piece.

The *Crimson* was often a target of street-liberal venom, not only because it declined to back every left-wing cause célèbre that came down the pike, but also because it suffered—in spite of rather pathetic attempts at encouraging diversity—from a long-running dearth of minority writers. But the Juice Fong scandal was the only instance in which Harvard's street liberals actually marched on the building, banners waving and slogans flying. "Journalism, not racism," they chanted, and it didn't take long for the *Crimson* to cave.

To be fair, there was a brief attempt at standing up for free speech and all that. The paper editorialized that there was nothing to apologize for, since they did not edit opinion pieces for content, and the views expressed were clearly Fong's alone. This admirable resolve lasted for precisely one day (the day of the protest). The next morning the paper's president penned a statement in which he declared that while "the *Crimson* does not shy away from publishing material that is controversial or that some may find offensive," Fong's piece made "unsupported generalizations" and therefore did not meet the paper's "standard of argument." Since adhering to these standards is especially important "on an issue known to be sensitive . . . the *Crimson* apologizes for publishing a piece that did not adhere to its standards."

The decision to buckle on the Fong issue was sadly typical; parlor liberals (who were thick on the ground at the *Crimson*) generally lacked the energy to fight their more radical classmates, particularly when the issues involved seemed trivial at best. But there were exceptions, and a reliably amusing one during my four years was Harvard's Undergraduate Council, a student government organization that most students never gave a damn about, making it an ideal forum for strident street-liberal activism. The UC, as we called it, had only one real power—it disbursed funds to student groups—but it offered a student bully pulpit, and in the years before I arrived on campus, this pulpit was used with a vengeance by the student body's elected representatives, who passed resolution after resolution decrying everything from Burmese tyranny to the treatment of migrant workers on American farms.

This last issue proved their undoing. In a bid for solidarity with poverty-stricken fruit pickers, the UC succeeded in banning grapes from Harvard's dining halls. Harvard's slumbering majority, who had been too busy to care about the sloganeering of student politicians, awoke and found that activism had consequences—unpleasant, grape-stripping consequences.

The Great Grape Debate that followed was a disaster for the street liberals, not merely because it culminated in a referendum that restored the fruit to dining halls, but because it ushered in a revolution in UC politics. As part of the backlash against overzealous activism, the campus elected, shockingly, two consecutive Republicans as UC president—not because of their conservatism but because each promised to focus on student services, rather than passing fruitless revolutionary edicts. Instead of combating heterosexism, freeing Tibet, and pushing for faculty diversity (but never ideological diversity), the Undergraduate Council began to focus on issues where it could actually effect change, like creating "Fly-By" lunches for students on the run between classes, or installing frozen-yogurt machines in the dining halls, or allowing universal keycard access to the thirteen upperclass houses. Small goals, yes, but also realistic ones: All three were accomplished by the time I graduated.

But political life moves in cycles, in small ponds like Harvard as much as in the United States as a whole. So it was that after two years of student services and bland Young Republican leadership, the street liberals stopped feuding, motivated their constituents, and united around a girl named Fentrice Driskell and her running mate, John Burton, an all-black ticket. Driskell was a typical would-be council president, blustery and gung-ho, but Burton was a more unusual figure. In addition to his student government activities, he wrote for *The Harvard Advocate*—the literary magazine that once nurtured T. S. Eliot, e. e. cummings, and others of similar eminence— and he had won various prizes for his writing. Perhaps because of this literary commitment, the veep-elect was known for his spotty council attendance, a habit many of his fellow UC representatives found less than endearing.

The student-services candidate in that election was Sterling Price Adams Darling, who was fond of suspenders and bow ties and carried himself with all the dignity expected of a young person with four last names. A born parliamentarian, Sterling practically knew Robert's Rules of Order by heart. As UC secretary, he was brilliant, wielding bylaws and parliamentary procedure like rapiers; as a candidate for the UC presidency, he was a failure. The Driskell-Burton ticket won the election in a landslide.

Then the comedy began. Harvard Undergraduate Council elections are governed by stringent, John McCain–style campaign-finance laws that forbid any candidate from spending more than a council-allotted sum of fifty dollars on the campaign. Candidates are also banned from using materials (buttons, signs, placards, and so forth) borrowed from other student groups, unless those materials are available to everyone—a "freely available resource," to use the technical language of the law. It was this last point that was apparently lost on John Burton, who pilfered around a hundred blank buttons from the offices of the BGLTSA in the waning days of the campaign, transformed them into Driskell-Burton pins, and passed them out to various friends and supporters.

From this mildly sleazy beginning, the UC quickly created its own version of the just-ended Clinton scandal—a case of history repeating itself, first as farce and then as farce again. There was even a Bob Woodward figure to throw into the mix: the *Crimson*'s UC reporter, Parker Conrad, a redheaded Park Avenuer with a nose for scandal. It was Conrad who, in the aftermath of the Driskell-Burton victory, induced BGLTSA co-chair Michael Hill to complain, on the record, about Burton's thievery; from this pebble came the avalanche. No sooner had Burton taken office than two articles of impeachment were put forward, charging him first with stealing the buttons, and second with lying to the Election Commission about whether the buttons were a freely available resource.

His supporters fought back. Driskell claimed that officers elected in campus-wide votes could be impeached only by referendum, while Hill and the BGLTSA (who had endorsed Burton) hastily disavowed their complaints about the purloined buttons and urged the council to withdraw the articles of impeachment. The council ignored both objections and scheduled a trial.

By then it was apparent that no one would emerge from this scandal looking clean. Burton was a petty thief and probably a liar; Parker Conrad's *Crimson*, which called for Burton to resign, was obviously hungry for scandal; Mike Hill's BGLTSA was just as obviously desperate to save a gay-supporting, street-liberal vice president, however slimy his behavior. Meanwhile, three of the ten sponsors of the impeachment bill were defeated presidential candidates, and seven of the ten were Republicans, which made their collective motives seem slightly less than driven-snow pure. As for Fentrice—well, her claims to the moral high ground pretty much vanished when she told *The Boston Globe* that "racism at Harvard is a very subtle thing. . . . It's not a thing to toss around lightly, but we're beginning to wonder."

We're beginning to wonder. With that, Fentrice ensured that the scandal wouldn't be about buttons or lies or payback for a lost election. No, it would be about race and racism, about *a bunch of conservative white males impeaching a black vice president,* as one Burton backer told the *Crimson*. So it was that the Harvard chapter of the NAACP, the Black Men's Forum, and the Black Students Association descended on the UC's usually sparsely attended meetings. So it was, too, that Burton—tweedy and bespectacled and faintly pompous—became an unlikely martyr figure, an avatar of street liberalism's persecution complex.

The impeachment vote, complete with student attorneys, endless parliamentary wrangling, and grandstanding speeches, was supposed to take twenty minutes; it was eventually extended to nearly three hours. The hapless Michael Hill ("Harvard's Kato Kaelin," someone whispered to me) served as the star witness, stumbling and backpedaling through his testimony, disavowing his earlier complaints about the button thefts, and insisting unconvincingly that all of the candidates were free to "come in and take one" of the BGLTSA's buttons. ("But what about a hundred?" someone shouted in the gallery.) The prosecution, having failed to realize that Hill might not deliver, came across as sadly incompetent, while the defense wore power suits, tossed around strident objections, and seemed to have confused Sever Hall with an actual courtroom.

Burton himself was silent, but his crowd of supporters sported yellow ribbons, waved signs and banners (DOWN WITH BUTTONGATE, read one), and booed whenever someone cited the *Crimson*. (In the back row, a laptop-wielding Parker Conrad just smiled and went on typing.) Sterling Price Adams Darling gave an impassioned speech in which he proposed, with wild implausibility, that those extra buttons might have tipped the tide for Driskell-Burton; he was booed and heckled. Fentrice Driskell, placed in the unlikely position of presiding over her own vice president's trial, governed the chaos with all the grace and dignity of an Ivy League Lance Ito.

In the end, the council voted forty-one to thirty-eight to impeach Burton, meaning that he escaped the ax, since passage required a two-thirds majority. Though not a vote of confidence, the outcome did allow Driskell and Burton to soldier on with their term and eventually pass resolutions on labor and the environment, police brutality and sexual violence. They also attempted a UC Census, a comprehensive and wildly intrusive poll of Harvardians that was supposed to help the council better understand the concerns of its constituents, or some such rot. The student body, perhaps less than thrilled by questions like *Since the beginning of the school year, have you had sexual intercourse when you were so intoxicated that you were unable to consent?*, ignored the census in droves. When it came time for another election, they ignored Driskell-Burton's handpicked successor and voted in a glad-hander named Paul Gusmorino.

His platform? Student services, of course.

. . .

But neither Coming Out Day, nor the Fong affair, nor even Buttongate could compare to the living-wage movement. It's remarkable, in a way, that the issue wasn't seized on sooner. When I arrived at Harvard, raising the wages for the dining hall workers, janitors, and security guards who toiled in our houses and lecture halls seemed to be a lower priority for campus activists than the longer-running student campaign to force Harvard to sever ties with sweatshop-exploiting apparel giants such as Nike and Adidas. True, stopping sweatshops might be laudable, but those exploited workers were far away, sweating out their days in dismal, distant Jakarta or Bangkok or Kuala Lumpur, out of sight and therefore largely out of mind. Whereas Harvard's employees were *right here*, mopping our floors and cleaning our toilets, earning what the Living Wagers called "poverty wages" while we lived off parental cash and plotted our six-figure futures. If they were oppressed, then we were among their oppressors.

Harvard kids have always been waited upon: When the student body was entirely white and male, richer in blue-blood heirs than National Merit Scholars, students often came to campus trailed by their family servants. And there were a few of my classmates who seemed to believe that the year was still 1895, and that the harried men and women who work for Harvard were liveried servants, standing at our constant beck and call. These were the students who thought nothing of defacing university property; who waltzed into dining halls drunk and belligerent and dressed down the staff when their cheeseburger wasn't cooked to perfection, or their vegetarian lasagna was befouled by a stray bit of meat.

But such students were rare. Most of my classmates were polite and even friendly, and we made an effort to know the names of the dining hall staff and the security guards whom we passed two or three times every day. Yet our conversations with them rarely went beyond the superficial, as if both sides were too well aware of the gulf between their lives and ours. There were exceptions: Nick, my long-running roommate, was great friends with a Quincy House dining hall checker (they shared Greek ancestry and exchanged Christmas presents our senior year), and Sally Maddox's parents took a Winthrop security guard out to dinner annually, to thank him for looking out for their daughter. For the most part, though, students and Harvard employees passed like ships in the night.

Then came the Living Wage Movement, with its tales of Harvard lives lived on the edge of ruin, of dining hall workers holding down three jobs, of the university outsourcing its security guards to avoid the costs of negotiating with unions. The activists' tactics were tiresome: They invaded university offices and staged teach-ins for bemused secretaries; they held noisy protests that were inevitably overrun by Cambridge's radical fringe; they dragged celebrity alums like Matt Damon to campus (he spoke alongside Ben Affleck, and both departed in a limo that allegedly contained a bashful Gwyneth Paltrow). And there was a tendency, among the unradical parlor-liberal set, to dismiss the living-wage activists the way they dismissed the people who marched against Juice Fong, and the racism criers, and the animal-rights kids who locked themselves in cages across from Au Bon Pain one sunny spring day.

But alongside that temptation were the workers themselves— mopping the floors at five A.M., cleaning our bathrooms at midday (and those bathrooms were *dirty*, as we knew all too well), serving our dinners at five P.M. and then washing our dishes a few hours later, all for wages we would have disdained in a summer job. Sure, the parlor liberals believed in capitalism, and in the wisdom of the market and the importance of efficiency in the New Economy, and they knew, as many people seemed not to, that much of Harvard's nineteen-billion-dollar endowment was earmarked by the donors for academic purposes and couldn't be tapped into whenever a janitor needed a raise. God knows they hated the noisy tactics of the protestors, and the vast penumbra of progressive causes that surrounded the Living Wage Movement, the "Free Mumia" nonsense and the Ralph Nader temptation and the Chomskyan belief that U.S. foreign policy was best understood as a series of increasingly fascist power grabs. But even so, watching the workers toil and suffer, and listening to the administration's endlessly repeated claims that they had "studied the matter," and that "most" employees made ten bucks an hour (never mind the ones who were outsourced and thus weren't counted as Harvard employees), many parlor liberals found it hard to escape the conclusion that maybe, just maybe, the protestors had it right.

It was hard for me to escape that conclusion, and I wasn't a liberal at all.

❖

It's worth saying a few words at this juncture about that rarest of breeds, the college conservative, who serves for the most part as a bemused bystander to the ongoing liberal civil war. Young conservatives at elite schools tend to fall into two camps. There are the born-and-raised Republicans, sturdy corn-fed kids from southern and western states, whose conservatism is a bred-in-the-bone matter of lower taxes, good business sense, and (usually Protestant, sometimes Mormon) family values. If these kids aren't dragged leftward by the prevailing winds of college life, they will likely end up getting involved with local party politics and maybe running the school's Republican Club, where they will boast of their commitment to *raising the Republican presence on campus* and maybe *getting George W. Bush reelected in 2004!!!* At Harvard, these lifelong Republicans tended to filter into either the Undergraduate Council, as we have seen, or the Institute of Politics, where they curried favor and dropped résumés with the various Republican semi-bigwigs—Bill Bennett, maybe, or Lamar Alexander—who came to preach the Grand Old Party's gospel in the alien soil of the Ivy League.

Then there are the converts, mostly wonkish kids who have rebelled—as I did during my teenage years—against the environment of reflexive liberalism that swaddles an overclass childhood, and immersed themselves in right-wing ideology much as other, similarly geekish teenagers might lose themselves in computer programming, or alternative rock, or Dungeons & Dragons. This sort of Republican is likely to be a zealous proselytizer, interested less in winning elections than in winning converts, and convinced that all his liberal friends require to see the light is a dose of Milton Friedman, Charles Murray, Norman Podhoretz—or even Evelyn Waugh, since a subset become faux-Tory snobs, fond of brandy and bow ties and *Brideshead Revisited*. Perhaps because of this passion for the war of ideas, the convert can usually be found at his campus's conservative newspaper, penning diatribes against the bevy of easy targets an elite university provides. *The Harvard Salient*, where I eventually became editor, was such a paper.

Both breeds of conservatives are viewed with deep disdain by parlor liberals and street liberals alike. (*You're not a bad guy for a Republican*, people were fond of saying to me, and my friends often suggested, sotto voce, that *Ross doesn't really believe all the things he writes*.) The disdain of the street liberals, good Marxists that they are, is understandable, but the contempt that parlor liberals bear for their conservative classmates is, I think, a more irrational matter, borne less of real ideological differences and more of cultural prejudices. Republicans are associated, in the parlor-liberal mind, with the South, with open religiosity and forthright patriotism, and with a va-

THE LIBERAL CIVIL WAR

riety of cultural signifiers (NASCAR, televangelists, John Ashcroft, guns). They are feared, in the end, less for what they propose in public debate than for who they are and how they live.

The truth is that if you set aside the abortion issue (a major sticking point, to be sure), the actual gap on matters of policy between the mainstream left and the mainstream right is remarkably small—a matter of emphases and percentage points and modest shifts. For the past thirty years, conservatives have given ground on moral and cultural issues (cohabitation, divorce, gays, pornography), and liberals have made social and economic concessions (on tax rates, welfare policy, prisons and crime and guns and even the environment), to the point where the gulf between, say, the Clinton and the George W. Bush administration is far less significant than the angry voices at either end of the spectrum would have one believe. Mind you, this is not to say that the debates over whether the upper class should be taxed at 39 percent or 34 percent, whether we should allow snowmobiles in Yellowstone or drill for oil in a wilderness that few Americans will visit, and whether we should invade Iraq without UN approval or merely *bomb* Iraq (and Serbia, of course) without UN approval, are unimportant or not worth having. But neither do they reflect a vast philosophical chasm in American political life.

Indeed, if Harvard's parlor liberals had spent a little more time swapping ideas and engaging in debates with the Main Street conservatives in the Republican Club, or with the neocon types who were running the *Salient* when I arrived on campus, they would have found that while campus conservatives are more religious than campus liberals, and a tad more suspicious of government power, both share a staunch commitment to free enterprise, to free speech, to freedom of sexual choice, and to the whole capitalist-meritocratic project that provides the closest thing there is to a Harvardian public philosophy. There are differences of emphasis—parlor liberals support affirmative action for now, and with misgivings, while campus conservatives oppose it; parlor liberals support at least civil unions and often full-fledged gay marriage, while campus conservatives oppose the latter and are only gradually accustoming themselves to the former. But in their overall optimism—about democracy, about capitalism, about progress, about America—parlor liberals and campus conservatives have far more in common with each other than either has with street liberalism.

And why not? If Marxists are, as was once suggested, just socialists in a hurry, then American conservatives are for the most part just American liberals with lead feet.

It was this realization that eventually forged my own sneaking sympathy with Harvard's street liberals, for all that I abhorred most of their ideas and nearly all their tactics. They at least shared my sense that there was something *wrong* with Harvard, and with the entire culture of meritocracy and achievement and cheerful capitalism— something that had to do with greed and ambition and corruption, with the lavish spreads that awaited us at McKinsey and Bain recruiting sessions and the hollow-eyed weariness of the immigrant women who cleaned up the mess afterward, long after we had sought out the bars and then our beds.

The Living Wage Movement's answer to this wrongness was a sit-in, and wage floors, and better health benefits. I agreed with them, about the higher wages if not the appropriateness of civil disobedience, but it often felt like they were trying to put a Band-Aid on a machete wound—a wound that wasn't Harvard's bottom-line mentality but an entire system of selfishness in which our university was just a small wheel turning within larger ones. Of course, the rule of self-interest, which stretches back to John Locke's insistence that God gave the world "to the use of the industrious and rational" (and not to the fanatics and troublemakers who had made such a mess of human affairs), has made for a wildly comfortable world—a world in which a simple New England university might be worth nineteen billion dollars and its students might count on earning millions of their own. Even many of this selfish world's apparent victims, its janitors and food servers and security guards, are victims with color televisions, with stereos and CD players and video games, with riches beyond the ken of an earlier age's servile classes.

But somewhere in the middle of my college years, lost in the dark woods of Harvard, I decided that I wished for a different world. I had no revolutionary program, none of the rage for equality that makes for a modern Marxist. I called myself a conservative still, but I was different from the Republican I had been in high school, when the GOP had seemed to offer the answers to my discontent. I wanted something higher and more romantic than American politics could offer, I decided: something nobler than the Heritage Foundation, more ancient than FOX News. A new form of chivalry, perhaps—but no, I had read Edmund Burke's *Reflections on the Revolution in France*, like any good conservative, and I knew that the age of chivalry was dead and gone. We were doomed, Burke lamented, to inhabit instead the age of "sophisters and economists and calculators," which was as neat a description of 1990s Harvard as you were likely to find.

Of Burke, Thomas Paine once wrote sneeringly that "he laments the plumage, but ignores the dying bird." The remark is telling, a reminder that the world of chivalry was really a world of misery, of disease and death for the countless thousands unlucky in their birth or biology. A skinny commoner like myself would have been lucky to survive infancy in the ancien régime, as one of my professors pointed out early in a class on medieval history. (*Look around you*, he said to the twenty-odd students, *and know this: Maybe four of you would have reached your current age in 1300.*) My desire, in the end, was for something as unreal and self-indulgent in its own way as the street-liberal vision of revolution and utopia: a return to the past, but a past stripped of its squalor and brutality, with only the finer, higher things remaining. Perhaps even those things were no more real then than now, and the only difference between past and present was the priests and the poets and the historians, who had invented saints and heroes, martyrs and conquerors—until time passed, and the world put away the priests and debunked the historians and invented *The New Yorker* to keep the poets quiet.

But in the latter 1990s, when Internet hucksters were lauded as the colossi of our age, it was hard to believe something finer and more heroic had not once existed and been lost somewhere on the way to our present meritocratic idyll. I wasn't the only one at Harvard who thought so. There was a social circle of sorts, forged largely by Tim Wallach, a Floridian who served as the *Salient*'s publisher during my sophomore year, and then as its social chair. Tim lived in a large room in Eliot House, with wood floors and high ceilings and a charming fireplace, and he began hosting gatherings on weekend nights. A collection of *Salient* types, friends and hangers-on, could gather there, drink obscure Germanic beers, and argue endlessly and drunkenly about philosophy and politics, literature and art and sex and God and everything else, until we staggered home to an early-morning bed, having discussed everything and settled nothing.

The regulars at Tim's were a motley crew. There was Colleen McGraw, a rosy-cheeked Irish Catholic girl and a rare Harvardian with working-class parents: Her father was a New York steamfitter, and her older brother was a West Pointer, which went a long way toward explaining the good-natured distance she kept from Harvard liberalism. Jake Culhane, a Minnesota Lutheran, had been an applied-math major and a rock-ribbed Reaganite before being dragged into our stranger, more alienated realm. Ladislaw Kowalski, a prep school boy and the son of Polish immigrants, was a former Ayn Rand devotee who wanted to like religion but had fallen under Nietzsche's spell; he wore his shirts unbuttoned halfway to the navel even on the coldest Cambridge days. (*Be a MAN, Ross,* he would bellow as I swaddled up in scarves and mittens.) Rounding out the regulars (though other guests abounded, including some "intelligent liberals," as we deigned to call them) was my old friend Forth Shelby, of Straus B and the Porcellian, still as steeped in history as when he had debated Nick and Damian in that long-ago of freshman year.

Tim was the north star of these evenings—these Symposiums, as we half jokingly dubbed them, after Socrates' famous drinking party. He was prodigiously well read, defiantly undogmatic, ready to consider any argument under the sun. *I could never take him seriously,* a more hardheaded friend told me years later, *after the night when he proposed that Sicily in the eighteen hundreds might have been the ideal human society.* But that was the beauty of those nights, and of Tim's sternly philosophic cast of mind. It was not that he believed that clan and vendetta, when mixed with Catholicism and the hot Mediterranean sun, were necessarily the finest things this world had to offer, any more than he necessarily believed that *homosexual love is the highest form of eros*, as he suggested one night, or that *in the nineteen thirties, we would have all joined the Communist Party.* No, it was that he was willing to ask the question, to make the argument, and to let us wrangle over it long into the night.

The Symposiums did not survive Tim's graduation at the end of my junior year. I meant to host similar gatherings myself the following fall, but amid the hubbub and pressure of a Harvard senior year, they never materialized. It was probably for the best, since it was Tim who had provided the spark; and Tim's room, fireplaced and wood-floored, with its Jazz Age posters, overstuffed bookshelves, and well-stocked bar, had been the perfect setting for our antimodern malcontent. My own 1960s-issue carpet and cinder-block suite would have sullied the experience and the memories.

No, better to leave the Symposium as it should be remembered, with the clock on Tim's mantel showing long past midnight, a heap of empty bottles and red-rimmed wineglasses on the table, and someone talking passionately and tipsily, holding the rest of us rapt. Let it be Forth, and let him be describing his hero Regulus, the Roman general taken prisoner by Carthage and released to negotiate a treaty, who urged his countrymen against making peace and then honorably returned to Carthage, knowing he would be tortured to death. Let the past become the present, the mythic become the real, and the meretriciousness of modern collegiate life fall away—and let us not think of how fleeting the moment is, how briefly conjured and how quickly gone . . .

The left is lucky, in a sense. It has revolution. All the right has is nostalgia.

❖

A successful revolution, however, is a difficult thing to pull off, as Harvard's living wagers learned when their sit-in limped through its first week—ignored by the administration, attacked by the *Crimson,* denounced by the Undergraduate Council. But they stuck it out, and eventually the whole business caught fire. This was thanks in part to a burst of endorsements: There was Robert Reich, who was in Cambridge to address the Harvard Democrats, and AFL-CIO honcho John Sweeney, who phoned in a message of support, and then Teddy Kennedy appeared on campus, pinned a living-wage button to his lapel, and tried to enter Mass Hall to encourage the protestors. (He was turned away by Harvard's cops.) But the real boost came, necessarily, from the national media. With the exception of the Boston papers, the press had largely ignored the sit-in during its first week. But as the days dragged on and the tent city swelled, they began to pick up the story and then to run with it.

They wouldn't have had the chance, if the Living Wage Movement hadn't been fortunate in its chief antagonist. The office where they sat and slept and yapped on cell phones belonged not to Josiah Quincy or Nathan Pusey but to Neil L. Rudenstine, a craggy scholar of English literature who occupied his grand, centuries-old post with an almost defiant modesty. Rudenstine was a vanishing figure, a stooped presence in the wintry yard, a halting speechmaker who tended Harvard's fund-raising fires and seldom raised his voice on any other issue of note. Even if the protestors could have been evicted, it was painfully clear that he was not the man to do the job.

I met Rudenstine just once, and then only in passing, as a freshman at the President's Barbecue, which he co-hosted with the president of Radcliffe College, whose anachronistic office would be phased out that spring. Rudenstine was courtly and smiling, even after having pumped the hands of a thousand-odd Harvardians that day, but I remember thinking how unassuming he seemed, how craggy and tired-looking, even as he flashed his beaming, skeletal grin at yet another National Merit Scholar or high school valedictorian.

He was a tragic figure, in a way. The son of a Danbury, Connecticut, prison guard father and a mother who worked her whole life as a waitress, he climbed into the rarefied air of academia as a scholar of English literature, an expert on the obscure and charming verse of Sir Philip Sydney. His mind was razor-sharp, apparently—a friend of mine worked the presidential beat for the *Crimson* for two years and later wrote that Rudenstine "stays up-to-date on the latest developments in nearly every academic field . . . he reads not only the latest in Shakespeare scholarship but also genetics. He reads in some eclectic discipline for at least an hour every day, he says." When Rudenstine was chosen by the secretive suits of the Harvard Corporation to steer the ship of Harvard, Inc., into the twenty-first century, there was hope that he might bring the gifts of a brilliant humanist to bear on the university's undergraduate education, which was agreed to be in need of a strong dose of what the then-president of the United States liked to call "the vision thing."

But all that Rudenstine seemed to do—all that he was allowed to do, perhaps, by the strictures of the age—was raise money, and more money, and still more, until the university's deficits melted away and the endowment grew and grew, leapfrogging from billion to billion, leaving our rivals in the dust. By the late 1990s, that most magical of times for investment portfolios, Harvard's endowment had grown to such staggering levels that it became a running joke among undergraduates and an object of wonder and puzzlement to the outside world. *How did Harvard get so much money?* they asked.

And then—*What do they need it for?*

Perhaps Rudenstine could have offered an answer before the job wore him out, before the glad-handing and the fund-raising and the burdens of Harvard's Byzantine bureaucracy took their toll. I like to think so: I like to think that he had a vision for the university as a school, rather than as a business enterprise, and that he once wanted to do more than please the men who picked him, and massage the egos of the would-be donors who filled his barbecues and teas and receptions. But there was never any evidence to support this hope; indeed, his non-fund-raising initiatives were so sparse that the long send-offs, in the *Crimson* and elsewhere, were reduced to citing a bureaucratic innovation—Rudenstine's creation of a provost's office—as a signal achievement of his decade in office.

RUDENSTINE'S ROLE WAS SUBTLE, one of these valedictories was headlined. Which is one way of putting it.

There was no question of confrontation, then, from the sit-in's bold beginning to its triumphant end. Rudenstine was a man of suasion, not force, and I suppose he thought he had learned the lesson of 1969, which was that dragging kicking and screaming radicals from a Harvard building would inevitably backfire on any president foolish enough to try it. Perhaps that was even the proper lesson to learn. True, tear gas and truncheons might not have been necessary this time around; I can't imagine that the living-wage protestors would have put up the kind of fight that the SDSers did. But when Nathan Pusey called in the cops, he was doing so to defend (in some shaky sense, admittedly, since ROTC was probably on its way out anyway) the ideal of patriotism, and the notion that Harvard's history and destiny were intertwined, in some important sense, with the history and destiny of America as a whole. Whereas what possible principle could Rudenstine have invoked to justify summoning the police? The utility of cheap labor, perhaps?

This was the difficulty for a conservative like me, wandering past the tent city every day and listening as leather-lunged Marxists shouted, *No justice, no peace*, deep into the springtime night. I wanted to root against them; I wanted to side with Rudenstine and Harvard's administrators against the self-righteousness and incivility of their opponents. Yet how could I be on the side of authority, of age and wisdom and hierarchy, when the authority in question seemed to be guided by no principle higher than the bottom line? How could I even *be* a conservative when there was nothing being conserved except Harvard's precious multibillion nest egg? Yes, part of me wanted Rudenstine to expel the protestors from the building, to have them severely disciplined (and shaved and bathed, for that matter). But a larger part wanted him to raise worker wages, to better the lives of the women who cleaned our bathrooms, whispering to one another in Spanish as they mopped the tiles and scrubbed the toilets.

Rudenstine did neither, trusting that time would do his work for him. He may have underestimated the protestors, who rose before seven every day to hold planning sessions, endured weeks of rising temperatures without air-conditioning, washed first their hair and then their clothes in the bathroom sink, and took turns hanging out of windows to catch a glimpse of the sun and chat with supporters and the press. (They were always careful to keep someone in the bathroom, knowing that the sit-in would be crippled if the cops ever managed to lock them out of it.) He certainly underestimated the sit-in's appeal, which extended beyond the tent city of hangers-on to sympathetic dining hall workers who brought food and drink to their would-be saviors, sympathetic TFs who held classes outside Mass Hall, sympathetic professors who forgave missed lectures and assignments, and sympathetic priests and ministers who held various services, including a Catholic mass, on the greensward beside the president's office.

Worse, having ruled out both confrontation and capitulation, Harvard lacked an obvious exit strategy save the hope that exams, or perhaps summer vacation, would eventually force the protestors out. And just because the administration had decided to ignore the protestors didn't mean that the world would.

It took a week before *The New York Times* picked up the story, but once they did, the rest of the national media quickly followed suit: CNN, *The Washington Post*, the *L.A. Times*, and on down the list, even around the world. (In early May, when the *Post* reporter got there, one of the protestors had just been on the phone with Italian national radio.) Once the press smelled Harvard blood, it didn't matter how many times the university issued some variation on *We believe in the same principles as the students, we just disagree on the solution*; nor did it matter how many times they insisted that *very, very few* workers earned less than a living wage. All it took was one such worker willing to talk to a reporter—like Frank Morley, say, a sixty-year-old contract custodian who made ten dollars an hour while commuting an hour to work every day and dipping into his retirement account to make ends meet. Morley had just quit a second job bagging groceries because he was getting only four hours of sleep a night. When asked about the living wagers, he happily told the *Post,* "We'd be dead without them."

Couple this kind of story with the inevitable reference to the university's vast resources: *Harvard's predicament appears particularly awkward, with the sit-in coming not long after the university announced a highly successful conclusion to its $2 billion capital campaign,* the *Post* noted dryly. Then throw in the bleeding-heart columnists, nostalgic for their own days of protest, who made the pilgrimage to Cambridge and churned out essays with titles like "Harvard's Brightest Minds Put Spotlight on Hypocrisy" or "Harvard Students Showing Compassion." (*You want heroes?* Bob Herbert of the *Times* wrote in a typically over-the-top effort. *Take a peek inside Massachusetts Hall.*) Stir it all together, and there was no way that Harvard—the filthy-rich corporate university that wouldn't even pay its security guards $10.25 an hour—was going to come out looking like the good guy.

What Rudenstine and company had, in the end, were economic arguments. The protestors had moral ones. Even in an age when people seemed to confuse the two, the fight wasn't a fair one.

The AFL-CIO brokered the deal in the end, a sign of just how big (or at least big for their britches) the protestors had become. Though not the sweeping victory that the Living Wage Movement had wanted, the deal was a victory nonetheless: While Harvard didn't acquiesce to a formal living wage, the university promised to convene a committee of faculty, students, administrators, and workers to reevaluate Harvard's labor policies. In addition, a moratorium on outsourcing was announced, pending the committee's report, and the university promised an early renegotiation of the contract with its custodians' union. Not bad, all in all, for a protest that had begun three weeks before with a university spokesman insisting, *We're not going to speak to them while they're occupying a building.*

The committee convened the following fall, with the PSLM's own Ben McKean as one of the two student representatives. It released its findings in December, calling for an immediate wage hike for service workers, equal pay for directly hired and outsourced workers, an increase in benefits, and a "fair bargaining clause" that would require that wages keep up with inflation. The report didn't demand an official living wage, but it recommended that Harvard pay its workers in the range of $10.83 to $11.30 an hour—numbers that seemed to validate the contention that the university was behaving in a miserly fashion to some of its employees. So did the first major contract negotiation of the post-sit-in era, in which Harvard's janitors saw their wages rise to $11.35 an hour, above both the Cambridge living wage and the committee's recommendations.

The Living Wage Movement's response to this apparent victory was deeply telling. No sooner had the janitors' union voted 270–8 to accept the new pay scale than the protestors announced that not only was $11.35 unsatisfactory, but nothing short of fourteen dollars an hour would be acceptable. By way of explanation, one of the movement's student leaders wrote in the *Crimson* that "as the living wage campaign has progressed, it has become increasingly apparent through conversations with workers that the Cambridge wage figure is inadequate . . . it was meant to serve only as a base from which to move up." Which is to say, the Progressive Student Labor Movement was committed not to a living wage but to higher wages period, with no ceiling in sight. More to the point, the writer went on, the "PSLM has never just been about achieving a living wage. . . . [It] is an organization dedicated to the principle of solidarity between workers and students as we struggle for a more just and democratic university and society."

Here was street liberalism in a nutshell—a legitimate thirst for a better world joined to grandiose rhetoric, constantly shifting objectives, and strong-arm tactics. Let others celebrate $11.35 as a victory for Harvard workers. Its student architects saw it for what it really was, what they had always intended it to be: a stepping-stone on the way to utopia.

We're a campaign, Ben McKean had said before the sit-in began, *and campaigns end*. But like any good street liberal, he didn't say when.

All of this unpleasantness was still in the future, though, on the sit-in's last day, when hundreds of well-wishers thronged the Yard to watch the remaining sitters-in emerge, unshowered but unbowed, from the ancient doors of Massachusetts Hall. There was no question of their going quietly: A two-hour rally preceded the triumphant exit, with speeches from faculty and workers lauding the protestors, rafts of balloons floating and popping in the spring air, and even a congratulatory phone call from Teddy Kennedy, broadcast over the PA system. Inside Mass Hall, the occupiers swept and filled trash bags and tried to make the place pristine. ("They even vacuumed," the police chief said wonderingly.) Outside, the crowd sent up rousing cheers for the Harvard cops, who had pulled fifteen-hour shifts monitoring the sit-in and its accompanying tent city. Nineteen sixty-nine was a distant memory.

Eventually, their vacuuming done, the day's heroes appeared, filing out between two rows of well-wishers like stars on the red carpet, or astronauts emerging from a successful shuttle mission. There were hugs and tears and a chorus of *We shall not be moved*, and red roses for each of the twenty-three students who had stuck it out for the entire sit-in. They had been inside for twenty-one days, three hours, and fifty-two minutes, and in that time had been endorsed by four senators, four hundred faculty members, and nearly every local politician worth mentioning. They looked very pale and very happy. For a moment I envied them.

Rudenstine's staff did some celebrating of their own. Once the protestors had departed, the secretaries and assistants held hands and fairly pranced back into their offices. Inside, they tore aside sun-burned signs urging justice for janitors and threw open the windows to the spring air. As the scent of protest wafted away, they broke out the champagne. "To young America!" one staffer cried, raising his glass.

Outside, the party broke up eventually, and on the Yard's long lawn, dozens of shaggy-haired campers folded tents and rolled up their sleeping bags. The victorious students filed home to sleep in Harvard-issue beds again; the professors returned to their offices; the workers to their mops and kitchens; the reporters to their news-rooms. After weeks of drums and chants and ruckus, the Yard was strangely silent, the only sound the low, droning gabble of tourists and the whip-whip of Frisbees. The dozing heat of the New England spring settled in around Mass Hall, and you could feel the more sedate rhythm of campus life reasserting itself—just in time for exams, as it happened.

That evening, for the first time in nearly a month, the sprinklers came on, washing Harvard Yard clean.

CHAPTER EIGHT

The Last Summer

E VERY THURSDAY NIGHT THROUGHOUT the sum-
mer, the Yale Club of New York holds a well-attended happy
hour for youngish Elis and other Ivy types working and living in Manhattan. The event is not advertised, as far as I know; no invitations are sent, and there are no signs in the club lobby, no WELCOME
YOUNG IVY LEAGUERS or DRINKS AND EATS: THIRD FLOOR placards beside the doorman's post or near the bank of golden elevator doors.
There is nothing officially exclusive about it, and anyone in suitable
clothes could theoretically come in off the street, pay the five-dollar
cover charge, and wander amid the heaped hors d'oeuvres and flitting waiters. But in practice, only certain people—*our kind of people,*
an earlier generation might have said—appear at the club each Thursday, filling the long, wide-open room with the smell of midsummer
sweat, held at bay but not defeated by an endless array of colognes
and perfumes and body washes.

There are brawny young men in jackets and loosened ties, with
pin-striped shirts and blond hair cut to sweep across their foreheads:
the would-be investment bankers taking a brief siesta from round-
the-clock internships at Goldman Sachs and J. P. Morgan. They crowd

and jostle against artsier males in sleek shirts and designer jeans—unshaved cinephiles taking film classes at NYU or Hunter, snobby artistes working somewhere in the Village, Eurotrash stopping off between Frankfurt and Nassau—while in and around the clumps of laughing, cursing men, the women swirl, shouting into cell phones to make plans for *later on, when we'll meet up at this bar, I forget what it's called, but Spencer will be there, you know Spencer, don't you?* These are auction-house girls, summering at Christie's and Sotheby's, and eager interns at glossy magazines, with their health-club legs and orthodontured smiles. Or they are the strivers: the future law students with their pantsuits and PalmPilots, chattering away with the more rumpled network-news interns, unpaid and overworked, floated on parental money or spunk.

I was with one of these in the summer before my senior year, on my first Thursday in New York: Rachel Lowenstein, a pretty, hard-charging Californian who was interning at ABC and hated it. *My boss is so weird and mean,* she had told me earlier, over drinks at the Harvard Club a few blocks away, where another friend of hers held a cheap summer membership, the kind reserved for current students. The Harvard Club was cool and ossified, with antlers on the walls and crimson drapes and deep carpets, and there was no one our age there, only decrepit alums clutching Rob Roys, so we bolted for the Yale Club, because it was more *happening,* to mingle with Yalies we'd never met.

But there were some Harvardians, like Lucianne Roth, tall and buxom in tight pants, smiling and waving her cell phone at us. Lucianne had the hair of a Chandra Levy, whose summer it was—the summer of Levy and Gary Condit, Lizzie Grubman in the Hamptons and shark attacks on the cover of *Time*—and with her was Matilda Catesby, a friend of Sally Maddox's, strangely thin in her designer clothes. She worked at Sotheby's, which would be embroiled in scandal soon enough, though no one would care, not about rich people fleecing other rich people, not in the age of Enron, when there would be worse sins to dwell on, poorer victims to pity.

But all of that was yet to come. Matilda was telling us about a cocktail party she had attended the previous night, a dress-up affair organized by the auction house for its young employees.

"So we all showed up there," she said, "expecting just drinks and food, you know, and we were all having a good time when they opened the doors and this whole bunch of guys came in, all swaggering, in suits and ties . . . like something out of *Wall Street* or something, very eighties."

The latest group of new arrivals, of interns and students and summer analysts, swept in around us, chorusing the usual questions . . . *So where are you working again? When did you start? Do you like it? Are they paying you? That little, huh?*

"So who were they?" Rachel asked.

"That's the thing—they were all I-bankers. Sotheby's had invited them; we have some kind of mixer arrangement with a couple of the investment banks, I guess, where we throw parties and the firms send over all their summer people."

So where are you living? Really? What's the rent? That much? Wow!

"Anyway," Matilda went on, "so I'm talking to a couple of them, and I ask one of them, 'What are you guys doing here?' And he says to me, like it's the most obvious thing in the world: 'We're your future.'"

I laughed. We all laughed. "I mean, the nerve of saying something like that," she said. *"We're your future."*

Are you writing a thesis? Are you going anywhere for August? Do you realize that we're graduating next year? I know, it's just horrible!

The night rushed on. Outside, dusk was falling—no, it *had* fallen, and Matilda was talking to someone else, and Lucianne had disappeared. We used up the drink tickets that came free with the cover charge, and began paying the high prices that define New

York—seven dollars for a beer, ten for a mixed drink. The hors d'oeuvres diminished, too, and at first waiters darted to replenish them, but not for long, and around me people began to murmur—loudly, because it was still too noisy for anything else—about leaving, about going elsewhere, about going to Brooklyn, to the Village, to uptown, to downtown, to anywhere but here.

I found myself with Matilda again. "Have you talked to Sally?" she asked me, rummaging impatiently in her handbag. "She's coming up here at some point, right?"

Sally Maddox was in Kentucky for the summer, but she would be in the Hamptons in late July for a monthlong stay with her roommate, Alice Triller, who was working for the *Southampton Press* and living with her younger sister in a rambling house that belonged to one of the paper's editors. I knew Alice only a little, but I was at least slightly infatuated with her that summer—infatuated without hope, because she had a boyfriend.

"I'm going out to visit them in August for a weekend," I told Matilda. "Once my job's done here, I mean."

"Yeah? I went out there with some people a couple of weeks ago . . . lay on the beach, you know the drill. It's so nice out there, don't you think?"

"Oh, absolutely," I replied with all the false conviction of someone who had never set foot on Long Island.

Now plastic cups, sticky with alcohol, lined the tables and windowsill; the waiters smoked in the corridors and glanced significantly at the clocks. Yet the end felt sudden anyway: One moment the party was in full swing, and then we were gathering ourselves up and making our way down, in the gleaming elevators that carried us into the gleaming lobby, where revolving doors spun us out into the darkness and the dying Manhattan heat.

People pawed at their cell phones and said their goodbyes, and there was some last, faintly desperate talk of hitting a few bars, of extending the night and the Ivy League camaraderie a little further. But everyone was just drunk enough to be sleepy, so the idea died, the chatter waned, and our little group broke apart and scattered, toward cabs and subways and another day of summer jobs.

"See you next Thursday!" someone shouted as I turned away and began trekking north, through midtown's empty canyons, the distinct and cloying Yale Club scent fading quickly into the acrid smell of the city.

The last thing I heard was the distant sound of Rachel Lowenstein talking into her cell phone, loud enough to be heard blocks away, though only because the streets were empty, the day's noise finished.

"No, no . . . I'm going *home*." Her voice faded, falling away from me. "No, I would, you know I would, but I have to *work* tomorrow. . . ."

❖

Yes, *work*—the summer job, that brief taste of the post-college life to come. Such summer experience is a crucial part of a Harvard education. For hard-charging young elites, there are no lazy days of June and July, no beachfront relaxation, no familiar, comforting work at some hometown job. The Harvard summer is no time for having fun; it's a time for "building contacts" and "making connections," a time when every choice, from sophomore year on, is freighted with career-altering consequences. Let's say you want to work for Mercer or Bain, Bear Stearns or J. P. Morgan after graduation. Then you'd better work for them the summer before, or better yet, the summer before *that*, as my friend Nick found out in the spring of his junior year, when firm after firm asked him, somewhat snidely, why he'd interned in Washington, for the *UN* of all places, the previous summer, instead of working for *them*? Was he really *committed* to business? Was he really *sure* he wanted to be an investment banker?

But the summer job is about more than the future. It's also about keeping up with your classmates, who are all doing something fabulous with their summer, something that either takes them to New York or Washington (the safe choices, for the future politicians, lawyers, and businessmen), to California (the bold choice, for the future entertainment mogul or screenwriter), or to Guatemala to build low-cost housing (the politically conscious choice, for the street liberal). Getting a good internship is thus a signifier of your elite status. *What are you doing with your summer?* everyone asks, and nobody wants to be caught going home to lifeguard.

My job in the long summer of 2001 was perfect in that regard, as long as nobody looked too closely at the details. It took me to Manhattan, first of all, which was still bathed in the late-1990s glow; there was no Osama to darken its glittering skyline, and though the Dow had already peaked, nobody was ready to admit that the age of giddiness was over. Even better, I worked at *National Review,* a major political magazine, which was a splendid new paragraph atop my résumé and a nice name to drop when people asked about my summer plans. It was unquestionably a step up from my first two college summers, when I lived at home in Connecticut and wrote up online study guides, condensing Shakespeare and Aeschylus for lazy high schoolers.

So life was good—but only up to a point. I was in Manhattan, yes, but I rented a room in the least bright-lights-big-city place imaginable: the priory attached to Saint Vincent Ferrer, a Gothic church set amid the brownstones of the Upper East Side. Cheaper than most Manhattan housing, my room—which I had found through the priest at my family's church in New Haven—was a lucky break, in a sense. But the priory was strange and lonely, a labyrinth of carpeted corridors and empty rooms, a relic staffed by the aged and suspicious, and pervaded by a mood of gloom and decay. For any Catholic, it would have been a dispiriting place to live, with its hushed halls and faded priests, its intimations of the Church's crisis; for a college kid of twenty-one, it felt like a tomb.

As for *National Review*—it was a major magazine, certainly, but it was wonkish and political, with nothing glamorous about it: no celebrities flocking in for cover shoots, not even a stray senator or undersecretary stopping by. And it was a conservative magazine, which reduced its cachet considerably among my friends and neighbors. *Somewhere in Montana, there's a kid who would crawl on broken glass to intern at* NR, one of my co-workers rightly pointed out, but few of my classmates would have shared the sentiment.

There was, however, one great perk to the job, which was the chance to meet William F. Buckley, Jr., the great man, the right's godfather, the urbane and wicked prince of the conservatives. He no longer edited in any official capacity, having retired in the late 1980s, but his influence endured. The magazine reprinted his syndicated columns in every issue, and he also kept up a "Notes and Asides," where he corresponded faithfully with readers on obscure lexical and grammatical points. Occasionally he would drop a longer article into the magazine—a remembrance of Whittaker Chambers in one issue, a breezy tour through Abercrombie & Fitch's soft-core porn in another. He still kept an office, too, and an assistant, in the Lexington Avenue building, halfway between the editorial and business departments. Everywhere were the shelves of his books, a march of familiar titles (*God and Man at Yale, McCarthy and His Enemies, Up from Liberalism*) that evoked the right's long half-century rise from ash to power.

The current editors, his chosen heirs, dined with him every second Monday, and as a special treat I was asked to dinner on my first day, along with my fellow intern, Jaime Sneider, a Columbia conservative. I had only just met Jaime, but he and I sealed our friendship that night, gawking together at Buckley's fantastic uptown lair—the gimlet-eyed butler; the cooks and maids murmuring in Spanish; the dinner table with glasses of cigarettes by each place setting; the luxurious sitting room with its lush tapestries and lacquered tables. We gawked, too, at Buckley himself, who swept down to greet us, his eyes bright and curious, his wit languid but mischievous, and his flesh slacking a bit with age but still held together by a lurking energy, a sense of coiled potency. His wife, Pat, was with him, a thin, imperious figure, gracious but cutting, with an anglicized drawl to match her husband's. Buckley was simply gracious, and masterful at handling his celebrity, which he somehow acknowledged and set aside at the same time, disarming us with his good cheer and his famous blade-thin smile.

That night, which passed in a blur of wine and delicate meats and leisurely conversation, would be our only up-close glimpse of Buckley, or so we assumed at the time. A month and a half at the job did nothing to dent this impression. Then, in the middle of July, there was a phone call for me. The clipped voice at the other end belonged to Buckley's personal assistant.

"Bill would like to invite you and Jaime to go sailing with him this Friday," she said. "You can? Splendid. You'll be picked up at Stamford at six, then. At the train station, yes. Excellent. Have a nice day."

So Jaime and I rode the train along the Connecticut coast to Stamford, where Buckley picked us up, wearing a jaunty cap and driving a Land Cruiser. "We'll stop off at my house first," he told us as we pulled away from the station. We were spirited off to his summertime cottage, which waited for us at the end of a long gravel drive, beside

a long lawn that drowsed, green and new-mown, in the shade of occasional trees. It was a big place, with an attached carriage house—
"my study," Buckley told us as he parked the car in front—and a
porch running down the side. Beyond the house, the lawn sloped
down through gardens and past a small swimming pool, its water a
pale blue against the white tile, and beyond this, rocks and then the
Long Island Sound, drenched that day in a shimmering haze.

Inside, we were introduced to Buckley's "boat boy," Ben, a
bearded Yale student hired for the summer to help out on the sailboat. Drinks with Pat followed, in a sea-facing room with deep armchairs and a huge tiger-skin rug dominating the floor, and while we
chatted, a small dog leaped into her lap.

"He's new," she declared as the dog, an adorable King Charles
spaniel, nuzzled at her long fingers. "His name is Sebastian, but we
call him Sebby."

There was general agreement on Sebby's excellence, and then
Pat announced grandly that it was time for the news. A switch was
pressed, a screen was lowered from the ceiling, and a projector
whirred while Buckley fumbled with the remote, settling on NBC. It
was a slow news day, as I recall, but it hardly mattered; news-
watching with the Buckleys consisted mainly of them bantering for a
half hour, which in turn consisted largely of him offering various as-
sertions and her dismissing them airily, with a pull of her cigarette
and a wave of her hand.

"No, no, duckie, you've got it all wrong as usual," she would
say, and Buckley would shrug and flash us the famous smile, the long
expanse of teeth slashing his face, reaching for his ears.

Afterward, we went to the docks, where the boat boy awaited
us, and Buckley's vessel *Patito*. It was the first large sailboat I had
been on, and the only one yet on which I have been asked to take the
helm—an experiment that came about once we had motored out of

the harbor, leaving behind Stamford's swarm of yachts and sailboats and motorboats, and Buckley and the boat boy had set the sails in order, the young man springing nimbly around the boat while the older man shouted orders, knotted ropes, and steered.

"Do you do this every summer?" I asked the Yalie a little later, after wrestling with the wheel for a time and then turning it over, with some relief, to Jaime.

"No, no," he said. "He"—a nod to Buckley—"takes out an ad in *The Yale Daily News* every spring, for someone to crew his boat during the summer, and I answered it."

"He didn't know quite as much about sailing as I'd like," Buckley confided to us a moment later, as his first mate scrambled to fix a rope near the bow. "But he does as he's told well enough, and he has other duties . . . Speaking of which"—he raised his voice—"how about those hors d'oeuvres, Ben?"

So Ben went belowdecks and emerged with champagne and salmon-spread crackers, prepared by the cook back on land. Sometime later he mixed martinis, which was where his real skill lay, Buckley said loudly—*in martinis, Ben, not sailing!*

We drank them as the sun swept lower, and eventually Jaime and I fell into some kind of interminable argument—about religion or politics, I can't remember which, save that we were jockeying to sound intellectual and earnest, to impress our host with the range and depth of our young minds. Buckley seemed to be paying close attention, cocking his head to one side as we went back and forth, until finally he stirred from his position at the wheel, reached for his martini, and cleared his throat.

"It's a fascinating argument you're having," he said, "but perhaps I can impart a trace of my wisdom here?"

"Of course," we said hastily, bracing ourselves for a bon mot, or perhaps some stunning profundity. "Please do."

"Well, gentlemen"—his sudden grin seemed to swallow his

cheeks—"it seems to me that you should probably put those sweaters on now. The sun's going down, you know, and once you get cold out on the water, you're not likely to warm up."

We anchored in Oyster Bay, in a narrow inlet where a number of other sailboats were bobbing, while behind the sheltering arm of land the sun disappeared, and the trees along the shore flailed the bay with shadow. The cook had prepared steaks, which Ben warmed for us somehow, and there were salad and baked potatoes, and then pie à la mode, all eaten on a table that folded down in the main cabin, in the middle of a wraparound couch. It could have passed for a dinner at a four-star restaurant, I thought at the time, though my experience of such establishments was limited to a few meals with Sally Maddox. My appreciation of the meal was also probably influenced by the vast on-boat bar, which was full enough to be the envy of a final club.

Buckley drank the most, but if it affected him, I never noticed, whereas Jaime and I fell into a drunkenness so deep I can barely remember our conversation. We talked about the Red Sox, I think—our host was writing a book set around 1946, the year that Pesky held the ball—and Ayn Rand, with Jaime asking Buckley if he had been there on the night when Ludwig von Mises had famously reduced her to tears by calling her a "little Jew girl." (Buckley hadn't, to everyone's regret.) We talked about Hamden, where I had gone to high school, and where Buckley had lived as a young man after graduating from Yale. *I wrote* God and Man at Yale *there*, he told me, and I sloshed my wine and felt myself swell up, the suburban dullness of Hamden Hall suddenly transformed by this historical coincidence.

After dessert had been set aside and Ben had gone to clean up, Buckley gathered himself up from his seat and peered down at us. "I generally take a swim after eating," he said. "You're all welcome to swim as well, of course."

Now that he mentioned it, a swim seemed *just* the thing. (I imagine practically anything would have sounded like just the thing at that point in the evening.) But then I considered the matter more deeply and heaved a deep and regretful sigh.

"I'd swim, sir," I said. "I *would* swim, I really would like to. But I'm afraid I didn't bring a bathing suit."

It had taken me so long to reach this conclusion that Buckley had already begun to climb the ladder, and now he regarded me with unconcealed amusement. "Well, neither did I. After all, it's quite dark out there. And we're all men here, you know."

When he was gone, Jaime and I sat for a moment in silence, the dinner settling in our stomachs and the wine rising to our eyes.

"You aren't actually going to go swimming, are you?" he asked me.

"Aren't *you*?" I demanded.

"Well . . ."

"Well what?"

"I don't really like to swim very much in general."

"Well, Jaime," I said grandly, "neither do I, honestly. But you know, I think there comes a time in a man's life when he has a chance to say to his grandchildren, *I once went skinny-dipping with William F. Buckley, Jr.* And this, Jaime, *this* is that chance."

Somehow that settled it. We downed the dregs of our wine and went topside, where Buckley was just leaping from the bow, a flash of plummeting white flesh in the darkness. Jaime and I undressed quickly, then shouted and leaped in after him. In midflight, I saw Buckley already climbing the ladder, reaching for his towel—and then, as the cold water shocked me sober, I remembered how poor a swimmer I really was.

"I'm drowning, Douthat!" someone shouted nearby, as I surfaced, spitting salt and floundering. It sounded vaguely like Jaime, but I had troubles of my own.

"Swim for the ladder," I managed to shout, pawing jellyfish

aside, dog-paddling frantically, wondering if sharks frequented Oyster Bay. "For the *ladder*, Jaime!"

Afterward, Buckley went below to his berth, apparently to retire for the night, and Jaime and I sat on the boat's bow with Ben, watching the lights on shore dim and the stars brighten.

"So how often do you do this?" I asked Ben after a while.

"How often?" he said. "I only started in June, and I have to go home for a while in August, so basically every weekend for two months, I'd say. It's a good deal: I get to be outside all the time on the weekends, and then I can work on my thesis research during the week."

"Is it usually just you and him?"

"Oh no, no—I mean, once or twice, but he has guests out on the boat almost every weekend. Usually it's old friends from Skull and Bones, ex-ambassadors, people like that . . . I've heard sometimes you get European nobility, deposed Romanovs and stuff."

"He writes books about sailing," Jaime said. "Some of them are down below, I think, in the cabin. My father used to read them."

"Yeah," Ben said. "He had a bigger boat once, I think. He'd sail it to the Caribbean, to Europe, around the world, I don't know where. Not anymore, or not the way he did once. But he isn't close to quitting or anything. He still sails every weekend, March to September or October. He'll still be taking the boat out when I've gone back to school, almost every Friday night."

I leaned back, feeling the craft sway, the ocean stir. "Who can blame him?"

Just then there was a sound of clattering bottles from below. A moment later, Buckley emerged into the night air, dressed for sleep in boxers and a T-shirt, his hair a little tousled. He had a bottle and three plastic cups in his hands.

"Just a nightcap," he said cheerfully. "Would anyone fancy some brandy?"

We slept on the cabin's couch, Jaime and I, and woke with the dawn, having had very little sleep. The morning light felt refreshing nonetheless, and there were English muffins and jam for breakfast, and then we raised the anchor and turned north, for Stamford and home. It was a brilliant day, the Sound glittering, and we played Ghost, a word game—which Buckley won, naturally, with some high-vocabulary skulduggery at the end—and then he sent Ben to fish out his cell phone and dial up the number for his house.

"We're on our way home now, duckie!" he shouted into the phone when Pat came on the line, while the wind caught his white hair and the boat knifed the water. "Yes, we'll be back for lunch!"

And we were. We docked the boat, piled into the Land Cruiser, drove back, and cleaned up in the cottage's grotto-like basement, which was complete with a changing room, a sunken bath, and a warm-water pool where Buckley swam laps while Jaime and I showered and changed. There was an hour or so that we spent sprawled on the lawn near the ocean, while bees droned in the gardens nearby, and then we ate lunch on the wraparound porch, with a portly priest whom Buckley called Padre, while Pat smoked beneath a vast black sun hat and talked about seeing *The Producers,* and about dinner with the Kissingers and the Limbaughs at Le Cirque.

Afterward, Buckley took us into the carriage house to see his study, a vast space hung with endless bookshelves beneath which were scattered little easels and tables and piles of magazines. (One, I noticed, had a younger Pat Buckley gracing the cover, draped in designer clothes.) Some of the shelves were entirely filled with Buckley books—the political volumes, the sailing books, the Blackford Oakes spy novels. "Take any of my books you like," he said, so we each grabbed a handful and he autographed them, then drove us back through the Saturday glare to the Stamford station, where we thanked him (maybe too profusely, but he was gracious anyway) and boarded the train back to New York.

"So tell me, did that *really* all just happen?" I asked as we collapsed into our seats and the train began to move.

"I still can't believe you made us go swimming," Jaime said, and then our giggles carried us off, and so did the train, running west toward the city, leaving Buckley and Pat, Ben the boat boy and Stamford behind.

❖

So it was a strange summer, with long lulls and bursts of the surreal. My job was dull in the way of all internships, full of menial tasks—photocopying and faxing, transcribing and archiving, fetching and distributing. Eventually I graduated from errands to gossip. Amid the white heat of that summer's Gary Condit imbroglio, I was tapped to write a daily digest of the scandal for the website. "Condit Watch," they called my roundup, and in my Lexington Avenue cubicle, I pored over the minutiae of mistresses and gifts, suspicious denials and rumors of kinkiness, the public shame of the Condits, the public agony of the Levys, while the city baked beneath me.

Outside of work, I was alone much of the time, my closest friends having scattered to White House jobs or thesis research in Paris. Manhattan was filled with potential new friends, but the only one I made was Jaime. We took long lunches together, arguing about movies and sharing right-wing gossip—who had been fired from *National Review* for anti-Semitism, who was a recovering drug addict, who had slept with Ann Coulter, and so forth. Like many young conservatives, Jaime was a former Objectivist, and sometimes, as we walked up Third Avenue to lunch, he would growl fiercely at the sky-scrapers, like a pagan swept up by a Dionysian madness. Then he would laugh and say, *Sorry, you know how excited Ayn Rand was about skyscrapers, don't you?*

Usually I was alone with my thoughts, and with the city. I went to mass some mornings, sitting in the dusty shadows with old women and a few stray businessmen, big and potent men in their suits and wing tips, out of their element in a place where priests shuffled on the altar, making blood out of wine, flesh from bread. I wandered through Central Park at dusk, reading by the cement basin of a skating rink—sometimes D. H. Lawrence, more often Stephen King—and watching the pigeons swirl and dive from apartment buildings. In the twilight at the Central Park Zoo, I found partygo-ers in formal wear circulating amid barking seals; on the lawns where people flew kites, I listened to seven-year-old girls shriek, with awful sophistication, about who among them looked more like Britney Spears.

There were moments in that summer when I felt that I stood at the very center of the world, the fixed point around which all else moved. At such times I was swollen with epiphany, and I understood the secret of Harvard's success—which is that it doesn't end with col-lege, that it still exists out in the wider world, and that all of my adult life, all the people I would know, the jobs I might have, and the worlds I would conquer, would be nothing more than an extension of my four years in Cambridge, a lifelong river flowing from college springs.

At other times, walking alone on the Upper East Side at twi-light, I wondered if this was what I really wanted for myself. Har-vard had made me yearn to be elite and connected and successful, to be *inside,* you might say, and here I was in Manhattan, at a national magazine, dining and boating with WFB, with my senior year just around the corner and a broad sweep of success awaiting me beyond that. But all my fears remained, all my doubts about my place in the world, and as I stared up at the frowning apartments ringing Central Park like battlements, it seemed that their doors were shut and locked against me, and that I was outside still. I wondered, then, if this was the other secret of Harvard, that no matter how far you go toward the center of the world, there is always another door, another *inside*—a place you cannot go, a prize that is denied you, and a hunger that isn't satisfied.

I did a lot of walking that summer. Most mornings I walked to work, thirty blocks down Lexington Avenue, past the Chrysler Building and the General Electric Building and Grand Central Station, noting the little details on the older skyscrapers, the filigree and flourishes, the gargoyles and stone faces leering from fifty stories up. I went north toward Harlem and had my hair cut in a slumping barbershop where old men spoke Spanish and carved at my neck with a gleaming razor blade. I went east to the river and strolled along the jogging paths or sat on the benches, staring out across Roosevelt Island, across Queens.

And I walked south once or twice, all the way to Greenwich Village and the tangled streets below—to the once hip bars of Bleecker Street and the street markets of Chinatown, to City Hall and Battery Park. To Little Italy and Canal Street. To the Brooklyn Bridge. To the World Trade Center.

❖

Early in August, I left my job and New York and went east through a dismal rain to the Hamptons, where Sally Maddox was visiting her roommate Alice—Alice who had strayed through my thoughts often that summer, Alice who was brilliant and beautiful and considerably out of my league.

I had met her the previous fall, in John Picker's harshly graded Gothic literature class (where Alice earned the only A). I'd even taken her to a dance while she and her boyfriend were enduring a temporary breakup—but as a stopgap date only, a warm body volunteered by Sally. I had a marvelous time (Alice was the most beautiful girl I had ever taken to anything), but I'm not sure she enjoyed herself, since my combination of euphoria and anxiety ("He's so *nervous,*" her room-mates told her after meeting me that night) sent me racing repeatedly to the bar, whereas she, with an exam the next day, barely touched a drop. By the end of the night, we were seated at a table overlooking the dance floor, and I was slopping wine on my shirtfront and bab-bling inanely about love, or the existence of God, or some other topic one should never broach on a date. She listened patiently and never, to my knowledge, was so ill mannered as to glance at her watch.

Shortly after that formal, Alice and her boyfriend reconciled, but we had coffee once or twice during the spring, mainly to talk about literature. She was already at work on what would become her senior thesis, and she showed me one of the chapters, a haunting, memory-rich essay about mortality and her childhood goldfish. I re-turned the favor, letting her look at a melodramatic short story I had written that fall, about a vaguely Ross-like Harvard freshman who finds himself allergic to computers and televisions and technology in general, then falls in with a group of Nietzschean romantics with a taste for violence, and then—well, I hadn't gotten that far quite yet.

Alice lived only forty minutes from New Haven, and after school let out Sally and I went down to celebrate her birthday before our summer jobs began. Over drinks in a Norwalk bar, she and Sally agreed that I should visit them in the Hamptons that summer, and of course I said I would, entertaining visions of beachfront parties and sprawling cottages, sparkling sand and skimpy bikinis, with nary a spoilsport boyfriend in sight.

The reality proved damper and more dreary. Fog ran up the beaches and hid the mansions; there were sweaters instead of bikinis and hot cocoa instead of beer. On my only full day there, it poured all morning and afternoon, so we drove into East Hampton and went shopping, an exercise that consisted of my carrying Alice and Sally's purses as they darted from shop to shop, and offering hopelessly gauche advice when they called me in to consider various outfits.

"Don't you think the neckline is a little, um, floppy?" I said to Sally as she held up a particularly expensive dress.

"Floppy?" she said, raising an incredulous eyebrow, while Alice and a passing salesclerk giggled. "Did you say *floppy?*"

I admitted that I had.

"Ross, that's how the dress is *made*. That's the whole *point*."

At nightfall the weather cleared a little, and we drove to dinner at the home of a friend of theirs. It was a weathered cottage that sat on the fringes of an expansive lawn, with fields and woods and apple trees behind. Beach Andy, they called our host, apparently to distinguish him from a variety of other Hamptons Andys. He was a Cornell student, and he had gone to high school with Donovan Foxx, a classmate of ours and a friend of Alice's, who was lifeguarding in the Hamptons that summer.

Andy, I quickly realized, regarded Sally and Alice as *his* girls and was displeased to be entertaining a Harvard interloper. He had two other friends to dinner, young men with biblical names—Isaac or Ishmael, I can't remember which—who ignored me while complimenting Andy's cooking in a weird and wooden fashion that bespoke some careful plan aimed at impressing the female guests.

After dinner we filled Jeremiah or Ezekiel's truck with firewood and then went out to the beach, where there were rumors of thunderstorms but no rain, only webs of mist and a bank of fog out in the darkness beyond the breakers. As we dragged the logs from the bed of the truck, our eyes grew accustomed to the blackness, and about a hundred yards down the beach, we saw a spread of blankets and a pile of damp driftwood that some of Beach Andy's friends had gathered and were now fruitlessly trying to light.

Donovan Foxx was there, and I suddenly remembered that I despised him. He was tall and strapping, with tight-curled dark hair crowning a face that was long and strong and horsey, and he spoke in the raspy, affected voice of a would-be hipster. His friends all talked the same way, barking at one another and into their cell phones in a strange argot—a mélange of slang from various eras, calculated for what they probably thought was maximum cool, if they thought about it at all.

"Yo, where my peeps at, yo?" Donovan asked loudly when people didn't show up at the appointed hour.

"They'll get here. Those cats are mad ill, yo," his dreadlocked white companion said as we piled the logs high and fished for tinder.

Eventually the fire crackled, the beer was broken into, and one of the would-be beatniks hauled out his guitar. He sang Dylan and Hendrix, badly, while I made useless small talk with Donovan and then sprawled with the girls, drinking and watching the fire and shivering a little.

"This is awful," Sally muttered after an hour or so had passed. "Isn't it?"

"It's not so bad," Alice said. "If the weather were better, we could go swimming, like we did the other night . . ."

"Well, we can't," Sally snapped, her pretty nose twitching violently.

There was a long silence that wasn't silent at all, what with the chatter of the hipsters, the crash of the waves, and our troubadour crooning "All Along the Watchtower." I glanced at Alice, who was staring out to sea.

Beside her, Sally sighed ostentatiously. "How can you guys *stand* it?"

I had downed three beers at that point. "It's better when you're drunk," I told her with a hint of condescension.

Sally didn't drink. "I think I might go back to the house," she said. "We've got the DVDs of *Sex and the City.*"

So she left, but Alice stayed and so did I, because I had a vague fantasy that something would happen between us, though of course it wouldn't. Beach Andy came over after a while and hit on her—a fruitless effort, but still I envied him for having the guts to try. I sat silently or made occasional pointless remarks as I downed another beer, then another.

The would-be Dylan groaned on, launching into "Tangled Up in Blue," and I watched Alice watch the sea, her eyes luminous and lovely in the firelight. People wandered off to piss into the darkness and then wandered back to cluster around the fire, chattering and drinking. A Jeep was stuck, far down the beach, spinning its wheels while a crowd of men laughed and shouted and tried to shove it loose. Some people went to help, kicking up sand as they left the campsite, and when they came back, Donovan couldn't find his cell phone. We dug around for it while he borrowed the guitar player's phone and called his phone, trying to make out the ring, telling us to be quiet and cursing the waves and the distant shouts from the now-freed Jeep, which was being driven in circles and figure eights.

"Can anyone hear it?" he said, his ear to the sand, the hipster affectation slipping away. "Can anyone hear it? I have to find it—I can't lose my *phone,* you guys!"

So it was a miserable night, with bad beer and a guttering fire and a collection of people I didn't like, and a girl I wanted but couldn't have. In memory, though, I sometimes manage to twist it into something else—something at once idyllic and melancholy, because none of us realized that amid the crashing waves and bonfire smoke an age was ending, that the darkness beyond our firelight was creeping in and bringing with it falling towers, falling stocks, falling bombs. . . .

But it wasn't at all like that. I was cold and drunk and tired, and eventually we left the beach and went back, with Beach Andy and his cronies as company, and made pancakes and talked drunkishly until they reluctantly allowed us to shoo them out of the house. Sally was asleep on the sofa, and Alice in her bed, and I staggered into the guest room and fell asleep as well.

Then morning came with a damp breeze and drizzle, and there was sand in my bed and stale pancakes for breakfast. They drove me to the train station and sent me back to New York and then to New Haven—and then, two weeks later, to Cambridge, where our last collegiate year was about to begin.

The summer was over.

CHAPTER NINE

The Days After

I WATCHED THE TOWERS of the World Trade Center fall in the common room of Quincy 616, our eight-man senior-year suite, sitting on a ratty wraparound couch that we had bought at the Salvation Army the previous day and dragged home triumphantly, like a trophy buck, in the back of Nick's ancient station wagon. There was drinking that night, the night of September 10, after we hauled the sofa inside, and the new television, and arrayed them alongside our built-in bar beneath posters of the Simpsons and Indiana Jones, the Godfather and Guinness. We took shots at the bar, christening our new room with ouzo, and then we went out to wander the campus. The weather was warm, and classes hadn't yet begun, and people milled around outside until all hours. Camp Harvard, we called this opening week, with the year's pressures still distant, when people could pretend that Harvard was a place where parties mattered more than résumés, and kegs were as important as careers.

Sometime before midnight, we hiked up to the Yard, where the freshman class was having one of its endless orientation activities. We wandered through the crowd posing as freshmen, pretending to have just met one another — *Where are you from again? What dorm did you say you were in?*—and striking up conversations with first-year girls, aping their mix of eagerness and terror, which we remembered so well and were almost nostalgic for, now that we could feel the end of our own college years creeping in. When we told them that we were seniors, they first gaped at us and then feigned sophistication, claiming to have seen through us all along.

Later, we returned to the river carrying pizza, and sat in the shadow of Quincy House, smoking strawberry tobacco from a hookah that Nick had picked up, along with the ouzo, on a trip to the Levant the previous year. A Harvard cop wandered by and sniffed at us, looking for marijuana, and growled that he wanted us *gone by the time I get back here*. We thought this was hilarious, but we dutifully packed up the hookah and went upstairs to our sixth-floor suite, a vast spread that was our reward for three years of cramped quarters. There we sprawled on the couch, tipsy and contented, as we watched Camp Harvard fall asleep below us—the lights going out in Lowell House and Winthrop House, in the Spee and Phoenix club-houses, in the Hillel and the *Lampoon*'s castle, until only the street-lamps on Mount Auburn still burned yellow, showing the night's stragglers the way home.

❖

It was Nick who woke me the next morning, sometime before ten, pounding on my door, dragging me downstairs bathrobed and bleary into our common room, where the sun was pouring in and the TV was on, showing the towers burning and a red bar of stunning news scrolling underneath.

I took it in slowly: the hysteria edging into the newscaster's voice, the references to "more planes in the air," and the quick cuts to billows of smoke rising from the Pentagon; the absence of the president, the absence of authority figures in general, and the numb silence that enveloped us, the watchers, broken only by the sound of Nick on his cell phone, frantically trying to reach his brother, who worked in the financial district—far enough away to be safe, as it turned out, but nobody knew that then, any more than we knew anything about what was happening in Lower Manhattan. Or what was about to happen.

Given enough time, I suppose the initial shock would have faded, and my still-sleepy mind would have been able to internalize everything that I was seeing, to accept the burning towers and the panicked announcers and fit them into some reassuring schema, some ordered world in which *the buildings are on fire, and a lot of people have died, but everyone on the floors below the fire is probably on the way down, and maybe they can send helicopters to the roof to get the people on the top floors, and then figure out some way to put the fires out . . .*

But then the first tower fell.

Every attempt to describe the horror has only succeeded in diminishing it. September 11 didn't kill irony, as was famously and fatuously suggested, but it defied literary art and broke metaphor and simile. In those terrible moments, whether you were in Manhattan or Brooklyn or a Harvard dorm, everything looked and sounded like itself.

The planes crashing into buildings—glimpsed in that famous handheld shot where the man in the foreground looks up a moment too late, missing the plunge and seeing only the impossible fireballs—looked like planes crashing into buildings.

The people jumping to their death, an image of horror so palpable that it was rarely shown again after that morning, looked like people jumping to their death.

As for the flames, the smoke, and the final fall, all that can be said of them is this: Before that morning we didn't know that such a thing could be.

Afterward, we did.

Around midday Siddarth appeared—the last of my roommates to arrive, having driven with his father up from Washington, where he had spent the summer working for the White House's Environmental Policy office, worrying about global warming. Later, it occurred to us that he had cleaned out his desk on the evening of September 10, meaning that perhaps only a single day, and the bravery of the passengers on United Airlines Flight 93, had come between him and death.

"I saw them," he told us while his father dragged a lamp and a laundry basket upstairs, pushing on while Siddarth stood numb amid his heaped suitcases and garbage bags of clothes. "We left D.C. at four A.M., and we went through New York at around eight . . . and I saw the skyline, in the distance, from the highway. I saw *them*.

"I saw them," he said again, more in wonder than in sorrow, "and they were still standing."

September 11 was Harvard's registration day, as it happened, when we were expected to troop to the Yard and pick up our study cards, which would be filled out, after shopping period, with the fall semester's classes. Somewhere in the lofty reaches of the administration, it was decided that registration would not be canceled—*If the semester doesn't start on time, then the terrorists have won* was presumably the thought—so we dutifully left our televisions and made our way through the September light to the crouching red-brick bulk of Sever Hall. It could have been any other registration, except for the fighter jets bursting and soaring overhead, and the people gathered in anxious clumps to stare at the sky.

The day itself was impossibly beautiful: a brazen blue sky, a bright sun scorching the red brick, the foliage a rich green just beginning to be flecked with crimson. There was a strong wind, too, sweeping through campus that morning, raking the trees outside our windows, churning the Charles into froth, and billowing the banners in Harvard Yard. These were remnants of the previous day's freshman activity fair: JOIN HARVARD KENDO, they cried pathetically, or RULE THE WORLD: DO MODEL UN.

Within Sever, behind the usual folding tables piled with the usual packets and envelopes, waited the ancient men and women who served Harvard twice a semester: once to register students and once to proctor their exams. Usually we hated them: they were petty tyrants, smugly bureaucratic at registration and crotchety in the exam room, screeching at us to *remain seated until the booklets are collected* as if their protocols were the last defense against barbarism. But on this day they seemed to have a special wisdom. They had seen a shuttle explode and a president die; they had lived through a cold war and a world war, and some of them had fought; and now they were old and whispering bits of news to one another in the dusty classrooms, their bright eyes wreathed in shadows, watching another generation learn truths that they already knew.

Back in Quincy House, we ate dinner while twilight crept in, then we went back to our rooms, where we alternated between the television and the Internet, between wounding images and useless words. The news from rural Pennsylvania, where the fourth flight had gone down, was trickling in, and there was still on-air talk of missing planes and rumors of further attacks. The perpetrators were unknown, despite much chatter about al-Qaeda, and the president was silent. He had promised a speech that night, but his whereabouts were still a mystery. At Ground Zero, another building had collapsed—World Trade Seven, which had been burning steadily since that morning. A cloud still enveloped lower Manhattan; the dead were estimated in the tens of thousands.

Before nightfall Sally and Alice came over to Quincy House and sat silently with us on the couch. Alice later said she was comforted by our room's knowledge of politics, our ability to identify the various cabinet officials appearing on our television screens. Donald Rumsfeld was the most memorable of these: As I watched him strut and jockey with reporters, projecting a machismo that was calming in those confused hours, it occurred to me that alone of all Americans, he had probably been waiting his whole career for a day like this.

Certainly the same could not be said of Bush, who spoke around eight-thirty that night, fresh from Air Force One's panicked leap-frogging across the country. I wanted him to do well (there were eight people in our room, and I was the only one who had voted for him), but his text felt hastily written, and he stumbled through it, looking rabbity and out of his depth. That was how we all felt—he was feeling our pain, you might say—but the age of empathy was over, or at least temporarily suspended. We weren't looking for a president to share our anxiety; we wanted one who would rise above it, offer us his blood and sweat and tears, and tell us that we had nothing to fear save fear itself.

Bush would do better later, at the National Cathedral, and speaking to Congress, and especially at Ground Zero. For good or ill, September 11 would remake his presidency. But nobody sensed it that night—all we saw was an accidental president, a wastrel eldest son turned Texas governor turned commander in chief. We saw a man who had spent the day on the run—and who now saw the future no more clearly than we did.

❖

The day passed, and then more days, but the fear remained. It was a fear of tall buildings and public spaces for some, of air travel and mass transit for others, of plagues and radiation and mushroom clouds for the well read and overly imaginative. The fear assumed that there would be more attacks, and soon. After all, if al-Qaeda could do this great and terrible thing, surely they could perform a raft of other, smaller acts to keep their dark ball rolling, to feed our paranoia and our dread.

I expected car bombs, or maybe even suicide bombers. I pictured an explosion every time I walked through Harvard Square, imagining the newsstand shattered, the street musicians and goth kids ripped apart, the red brick stained redder, a scream of sirens amid the smoke and broken glass and shredded newsprint. It would have taken just a few such attacks to terrorize us all, to strip away the last of our American confidence and expose whatever lay beneath, and in a way I am still surprised that the attacks didn't come—that al-Qaeda allowed us to regroup, patch together our shattered nerves, and regain a sense of normalcy. A sign, perhaps, that they were not so strong as our fears imagined them to be.

But even without another attack, normalcy was slow in coming. My bedroom in Quincy House overlooked a busy street, and every day I could hear ambulances and fire trucks and police cars wailing past, cutting down from Mount Auburn Street to Memorial Drive. I had never really noticed them before, except as part of the background noise of a busy college town across the river from an even busier city. But that fall, when the sirens rose and fell outside, I felt a trace of dread, and sometimes I went to the window and stared out across the Cambridge rooftops toward where Boston's skyscrapers, the Prudential and the Hancock buildings, could barely be seen. I suppose I was making sure they were still there.

There was a good-sized terrorism scare in Boston a week after September 11. It started with John Ashcroft warning officials that the Hub might be a target, and quickly metastasized to embrace rumors of nerve gas on the subways, toxins in the water, and God knows what else. My mother called up to urge me to drink bottled water—a conversation, I realized later, that was repeated between countless anxious mothers and their Harvard offspring over the course of the weekend. People fled town; I skipped out on a Friday-night trip to Fenway Park. (*It's a high-risk target,* people told me, in the newfound jargon of that autumn.) In the end, the whole scare turned out to be the result of some mistranslated Arabic, but nobody laughed at those students who disappeared for the weekend and returned sheepishly in time for Monday class.

Then there were the envelopes of anthrax, which have almost been forgotten now, and whose source remains a mystery, but that autumn seemed an inevitable escalation by al-Qaeda. Rubber gloves sprouted in the post office; sneezes and fevers were scrutinized suspiciously; people researched gas masks. In Quincy House, one of the stranger kids—an unshaved white boy with vast Rastafarian hair—took to wearing a surgical mask in the dining hall. White powder was mailed to the Harvard Hillel, and though it turned out to be harmless, from then on there was always a policeman on the Hillel steps, blowing on his hands and watching passersby suspiciously.

Now we know how the Israelis feel, people said. It wasn't true, or even nearly true, but it was the best analogy anyone could find for our newfound fear, our sense of being poised on the lip of an unexpected abyss.

I would be lying, though, if I didn't admit that there was also something terribly exciting, even exhilarating, about that autumn. There was fear in the air, but there was hope as well, and a sense that the pointlessness of the last decade was on the way out, that something new and finer was being born. The attacks gave us the gift of knowledge: the knowledge that history hadn't ended yet, that everything taken for granted was in fact vulnerable. Even here, even in America. Even at Harvard.

Much of my own ennui, my desire for vanished honor and lost piety, melted away in those months. After witnessing the fruits of al-Qaeda's medieval zeal, my nostalgia seemed at best self-indulgent, at worst perverse—and more to the point, I was reminded of how much good remained in our own society, in deep wells that the September massacre had tapped. Partisanship dissipated: Our politicians linked hands and sang "God Bless America"; they prayed together in the National Cathedral and embraced in the Senate chamber. The fourth estate seemed to rediscover idealism and soaring rhetoric, shaking off the venom and pointless scandals of the 1990s like sleepers awakening from a lotus-drugged dream. And our president, gaining his war legs, began to speak of sacrifice and struggle, of good and evil—a language that hadn't been heard in generations, but that rang sweetly in our ears, at least for a time.

At Harvard, people read poetry—Auden here, Housman there—and sang patriotic songs; flags sprouted everywhere, on cars and rooftops, lapels and dormitory balconies. Later, various commentators would trivialize this phenomenon: *Buy a flag*, Bill Maher had snarked, *it's literally the least you can do*. But it wasn't trivial at Harvard, a campus that had banished the U.S. military years before, a campus whose students had long passed fading monuments and patriotic exhortations without a second glance. The flags that we hung out symbolized a sea change, or so I thought for a while—a departure both from the achievement-obsessed 1980s and '90s and from the radical decades that preceded them. They illustrated our sudden sense that great things were about to be asked of our generation, that September 11 would be our defining moment, our coming of age, and that we might yet have a chance to become the men and women that our grandparents had been, the heroes of an epoch.

In our grief and anger, we have found our mission and our moment,

George Bush proclaimed two weeks after the day, addressing a joint session of Congress. *Our nation, this generation, will lift the dark threat of violence from our people and our future. We will rally the world to this cause by our efforts, by our courage. We will not tire, we will not falter, and we will not fail.*

Our nation, this generation. Few at Harvard bore the president any love, but I think souls were stirred by his rhetoric nonetheless. *Do you think there'll be a draft?* people asked, and if there was worry in their voices, there was also a trace of excitement, a sense that we now knew how Harvard men must have felt in 1860 and 1917 and 1942, when dread coexisted with enthusiasm, and uncertainty with the desire for action. I was at a party that fall with my roommate Nate, now an ROTC officer, and I watched the girls pepper him with questions, like antebellum women flirting with a boy in blue or gray. *Do you think you'll be shipped overseas when you graduate?* Matilda Catesby demanded breathlessly—she who had been courted by investment bankers just that summer, in Manhattan before the fall.

Yes, the age of the I-banker seemed to be passing away. People talked about government service, they talked about the military, they deluged the CIA table at October's job fair, and they chattered about learning Arabic. Some of this patriotic job searching wasn't entirely disinterested; the stock market, which had been sinking slowly for months, was now in free fall, and while the recruiters descending on campus still put on a good show, it was clear that the boom was over, at least for now. English concentrators with two semesters of economics would no longer waltz to Wall Street, as they had in previous years, and the job market would be distinctly chilly that year—even at Harvard.

But wasn't this providential? It was, I thought that fall, as if the gods of history were closing off those older, softer options, as if they were telling us gently that the time for selling out was done, and a new and sterner age had dawned.

. . .

Not everyone shared this sentiment, even in those first bracing weeks, but there, too, the post–September 11 age seemed to offer a tremendous dose of moral clarity. I had sympathized with Harvard's street liberals for a time, but no longer—not when cries of *No justice, no peace* gave way to calls for peace at any price; not when the Living Wage Campaign happily folded itself into a progressive meta-movement known as the Harvard Initiative for Peace and Justice, whose principal purpose seemed to be protesting a war not yet begun. I attended one of these protests, a dreary affair thick with green peace ribbons and fatuous placards, where a Quincy House tutor bellowed to wild applause that yes, the Taliban might be harboring al-Qaeda, but didn't the United States itself harbor militia groups? Indeed, hadn't we once harbored none other than Timothy McVeigh? So who were we, in the end, to go abroad in search of enemies, when we tolerated so much evil here at home?

For such fools, their eyes bright with the flame of impassioned idiocy, September 11 seemed to be just another stage for histrionics and paranoia; a chance not to mourn but to march and grandstand; to quote Gandhi (AN EYE FOR AN EYE MAKES THE WHOLE WORLD BLIND, read a Quincy House banner), as if the words of the Mahatma were enough to settle any debate; to send out the long, poisonous e-mails that clotted Quincy House's open e-mail list, likening the outburst of patriotism to a fascist takeover, or worse, suggesting that we somehow had this coming—because of our refusal to ratify the Kyoto Protocol, or support the International Criminal Court, or any one of a hundred one-worlder pet issues, as if the terrorists were a collection of outraged UN bureaucrats instead of murderous fanatics intent on tearing up the liberal political order, root and branch.

Yes, moral clarity—that was what best characterized those days. And it wasn't just conservatives who felt it. All across elite America, from Harvard to Hollywood, parlor liberals shook themselves awake, looked anew at the radical nonsense that was being spouted by America's far left, and reacted with appropriate dismay and distaste. For a brief and hopeful moment, the American left and right seemed to speak with one voice, a voice that defied barbarians abroad and disdained barbarians at home, whether they were troglodytes like Jerry Falwell, blaming gays for the wreckage of Manhattan, or decaying monuments like Susan Sontag and Gore Vidal, clutching their ancient grudges and spouting their *Yes it's a tragedy, but* line to a world that seemed to have passed them by.

So it was a bad autumn for street liberals, indeed for tenured radicals of all stripes, and for the pernicious academic notions that they had cultivated for so many years. The market for Edward Said's litany of Palestinian grievances shrank dramatically, and the Islamic scholar of the moment was the unreconstructed Orientalist Bernard Lewis, Said's longtime foe. The "blame America first" school of foreign policy analysis endured an emperor-has-no-clothes moment, and while the Noam Chomskys and Howard Zinns were hardly beaten, they were temporarily driven to the margins of polite society (though their book sales boomed among the anti-American fringe, hinting at the radical renaissance to come). Indeed, postmodernism itself was widely seen as having been discredited and perhaps even killed off by September 11, to the point where Stanley Fish himself felt compelled to commandeer *The New York Times* op-ed page and defend its continued relevance—a sign of slippage if there ever was one.

There was even a new seriousness at the highest reaches of Harvard, where the age of Rudenstine limped to an end in October, and a new president took the reins—or seized them, more like it, and set the horses to a startled gallop. This was Lawrence Summers, once Clinton's treasury secretary, whose appointment the previous year had been greeted by a collective yawn. He was an economist, after all, and a centrist, budget-balancing type, whose chief qualifications for the job were presumed to be managerial—and whose imposing corpulence seemed to make him the embodiment of the last decade's incurious capitalism. He had been selected, we assumed, to stay the course, tend the machinery, and keep the cash flowing.

The real Larry Summers was nothing like the man we anticipated. He was a free-marketeer, yes, a Clinton Democrat who had little patience for student radicalism and the demands of social justice. But he was also loud and active and curious, bustling about campus with questions and demands and displaying what we came to realize—to the dismay of the professoriate and the delight of just about everyone else—was a strong desire to shake things up. He ate in campus dining halls on occasion, spilling sauce and crumbs on his shirt as he chatted with students, probing and debating and behaving in ways that would have been unimaginable during the excruciatingly polite presidency of Neil Rudenstine. Even his bulk was less a mark of sedentary self-satisfaction than an expression of his boundless appetite—for knowledge, for understanding, for activity and change and, yes, for pizza. His flesh spilled out, but so did his personality, and beneath lay the sharp beak and glittering, intelligent eyes of a velociraptor.

He set a new tone early, in speeches given in the shadow of September 11, which were bold enough to broach the topic of the moral responsibility that the university bore to the United States—a responsibility, Summers insisted, that was similar to that borne by any American citizen. In the reflexively anti-American world of academe, this sentiment was radical enough; more radical still was his emphatic praise for the U.S. military, and for undergraduate military service. Students serving in ROTC had long been exiled to MIT, originally for the Vietnam-related reasons that had so enraged SDS in 1969, but lately because of the military's "don't ask, don't tell" policy toward gay soldiers, which was held to violate Harvard's nondiscrimination policy. Alumni and campus conservatives had protested for years to no avail; whatever administrators thought of the matter, it was a faculty decision, and everyone knew where Harvard's faculty stood when it came to deciding the competing claims of patriotism and sexual identity.

But now here was Summers, throwing down the gauntlet, lauding military service, demanding that ROTC grads be allowed to list the program in their yearbook pages, and addressing their commissioning ceremony at year's end, something no president had done in a generation. "Every Harvard student should be proud that we have in our midst students who make the commitment to ROTC," he declared in one speech; in another, he pointedly bemoaned the "post-Vietnam cleavage between coastal elites and certain mainstream values," and expressed his hope that the war on terror, lacking the "moral ambiguity of Vietnam," might serve to accomplish a "reconciliation of values" between the academy and the country at large.

This style of rhetoric earned Summers praise from the political right. Campus conservatives lapped up his speeches, *The Weekly Standard* and *The Wall Street Journal* lauded him effusively, and for a time rumor even linked him to right-wing bombshell Laura Ingraham. But Summers was far from a conservative; he was, if anything, the perfect parlor liberal, and thus the ideal figure for an autumn when America's liberal mainstream seemed to regain its faith in itself; an autumn when decadence and radicalism alike seemed poised for banishment, and when the future seemed to belong to serious ideas and to courageous men and women willing to stand up for them.

One of Summers's serious ideas was a reform of Harvard's curriculum. Whispers of change were heard in the corridors and dungeons of the college's curricular Gormenghast. Summers was meeting with "top University deans," the *Crimson* reported that fall, to discuss "major changes" in undergraduate education. There were hints that the number of freshman seminars (small classes taught by senior faculty) would be expanded, mutters about making study abroad a more realistic possibility, and discussions about engineering broad increases in the number of professors. Summers was interested in hiring younger faculty, professors whose best days were still in front of them, not tenured has-beens coasting on achievements decades old. He also wanted more of an emphasis on academics among undergraduates, and less of a focus on extracurriculars, and he hinted that we should be learning a few facts amid the endless "approaches to knowledge," which we knew could mean only one thing: a reform of the dreaded morass of the Core.

I found all of this tremendously cheering, but more than a few faculty members were less than pleased with their new president's attitudes, not to mention his shake-things-up style. Their sentiments were best expressed by Summers in a commencement speech given after I graduated. As an illustrative anecdote, the president recounted asking an art historian about the disappearance of the old Fine Arts 13 elective, the art survey course taught at Harvard for generations. The historian, he recalled, "reacted with a mix of condescension and hilarity," and wondered how Summers "could possibly expect any self-respecting scholar to propel our students—like a cannonball—from 'Caves to Picasso' in one academic year."

I imagine this was a common response to Summers in the overspecialized world in which most professors moved—a world where research was king, generalism was disdained, and the notion of survey courses smacked of canons and dead white males and other relics of an antediluvian academy. Unlike, say, the resistance of an administrator—like Dean Harry Lewis, a Harvard lifer who made little secret of his disdain for the new president, and who was gone within a year—the professoriate's entrenched biases could not be overcome easily. In an important sense, they *were* the university, at once its only permanent members and its vital resources, and this made ruffling their feathers a dangerous business at best.

. . .

The most famous ruffled plumage that fall belonged to Cornel West, then one of Harvard's seventeen university professors, a lofty rank of scholars who were above the usual bureaucracies, answering to the president alone and allowed to teach in any department they pleased. West was a flamboyant character with his three-piece suits, flaring Afro, and soaring rhetoric—usually employed in the service of whatever radical cause happened down the pike. He taught African-American Studies 10, a literature survey and one of the college's most popular courses, and he was part of the dream team of black academic superstars who had been wooed to Harvard by the largesse of Neil Rudenstine and the persuasive power of Henry Louis Gates, Jr., the politically nimble Af-Am Studies department head. In the late 1990s, West had become the most public of Harvard's public intellectuals, shuttling easily between projects as disparate as Bill Bradley's presidential campaign, cop killer Mumia Abu-Jamal's prison meditations, and a rap CD (though West preferred the Nietzschean term "danceable education") that his personal website modestly called "a watershed moment in musical history."

In this time, his literary output hadn't exactly flagged, but his books were increasingly either compilations of previously published materials or transcripts of meandering, earnest conversations with like-minded intellectuals such as bell hooks and Michael Lerner. The last book that Brother West, as he liked to be called, had published through a university press was *The American Evasion of Philosophy,* way back in 1989.

To some people, this only increased his iconic status. Instead of producing dry-as-dust tomes, they argued, West was exploring the boundaries of academic discourse, bringing what he termed a "prophetic Christian perspective" to a wider audience than the university could afford him. To others, it confirmed West's status as a campus joke: a colorful affirmative-action appointee with a flair for self-dramatization whose actual intellectual output was, as Leon Wieseltier wrote in a scathing mid-1990s review, "almost completely worthless . . . noisy, tedious, slippery, sectarian, humorless, pedantic, and self-endeared."

Whether he was an icon or a fraud, the grades in West's class were notoriously high, even by the inflated standards of Harvard's humanities, and there were rumors that he had skipped out on some of his academic duties during the Bradley campaign. This notion was scoffed at by nearly everyone who knew him, but it reached the ears of Larry Summers, who apparently raised it—along with the issues of grade inflation and academic output—during an October meeting with West. To this day, nobody knows what happened in that interview, save that Summers left thinking all was well, and West left in a fury. Later, he would claim that Summers had questioned his supposed absences from class, attacked him for recording his CD, and—worst of all—insisted on monitoring West's academic work over the coming months.

Summers angrily denied the last point, but only after West had bolted to Princeton's greener pastures. At first, when reports of his star professor's anger began showing up in the press, Summers issued a public "no comment" and maintained that stance even when the usual street-liberal circus came rolling into town. Jesse Jackson swept through Harvard, his eyes peeled for microphones; Al Sharpton threatened to boycott the university if West was kept from working on his presidential campaign; rumors arose that most of the Af-Am faculty were planning to jump ship. Signs sprouted on campus: GET UPPITY ON MASSA SUMMERS'S PLANTATION, read one; STUCK-UP PEOPLE LOVE LARRY SUMMERS, sneered another.

So a debate that probably began with innocent mixed signals— Summers was fresh from a government job where subordinates jumped at his orders, while West was the pampered star of a pampered department, accustomed to being treated as a pearl of great price—became complicated by racial and academic politics. Summers had determined that the Af-Am department would no longer have the special treatment it had enjoyed under Rudenstine, a stance that had earned him few allies among West's colleagues, and the disastrous interview was interpreted as a salvo in this battle. Worse, in a summer meeting with the department's faculty, Summers had expressed skepticism about affirmative action—"The jury's still out," one professor claimed the new president had said. If true, this remark was folly: a touch of campus politics' third rail that won Summers no friends and left him scrambling, once the West affair brought these issues seething to the surface, to mend fences and reclaim his liberal bona fides.

That January, while West pouted, Summers publicly affirmed his commitment to affirmative action, to diversity in higher ed, and to the African-American studies department. Then he met with West shortly after the New Year and apologized repeatedly for his conduct. At the time, West seemed mollified, and the talk of his departure subsided. But the progress made by the apology was quickly undone, or so West claimed later, by unconciliatory comments Summers made to *The New York Times*, and by the president's subsequent failure to call while West was convalescing from prostate cancer surgery. (By contrast, West said, Princeton's president and provost called him weekly.)

In April, after rebuffing Summers's too-little-too-late effort to reopen the lines of communication, West formally announced that he was jumping ship. Another Af-Am star, K. Anthony Appiah, was also going to Princeton (though Appiah said he was making the move for personal reasons), and in a mid-May interview with NPR's Tavis Smiley, West hinted broadly that Henry Louis Gates, Jr., was likely to join them. West also took the interview as an opportunity to complain that Larry Summers was "hanging with the wrong crowd," and to call Harvard's new president "the Ariel Sharon of American higher education. . . . He acts like a bull in a china shop; he acts like a bully in a very delicate and dangerous situation."

The Ariel Sharon of American higher education. Was this comment—dropped at the height of that spring's intifada, when Sharon was being fitted out for devil's horns by street liberals the world over—thinly veiled anti-Semitism? Or was it just "childish" and "patently ridiculous," which was the verdict of the heretofore pro-West *Crimson*, whose editorial added that "after the disgraceful way he has acted over the last week, the Harvard community will not miss Cornel West."

Either way, at the moment when Larry Summers lost a great name to a rival school, it was West, not the president, who looked childish and intemperate, even to many of his defenders. Everything that followed from this was predictable: Gates stayed at his post, and the bulk of the dream team remained with him; the fracas over affirmative action died down; and West vanished into whatever well-cushioned spot Princeton had prepared for him.

The important thing is that the precious Harvard tradition is bigger than Summers, myself, or any of us, West had said in January, one of his few public statements during the controversy. But by the time we graduated, only Summers remained to shape that tradition, bloodied by the controversy but unbowed, still clutching his big ideas and bull-in-a-china-shop methods. West had taken his prophetic voice into the wilderness of New Jersey, and it seemed at the time that he carried an entire decade with him, a decade that had been as swank and gaudy and well tailored as his three-piece suits, but ultimately just as empty.

❖

So the world of Harvard felt renewed—and my own private world, too, felt rich that year with a sense of new possibilities, new beginnings. Alice Triller and I took a linguistics class together that fall, to satisfy the Core's dreary "Social Analysis" requirement; we did problem sets together on weekends, and we sat high up in the lecture hall passing notes and laughing at the strangeness of the class. I was falling in love with her, though it was October before I admitted that it was more than a crush, and months more before anything came of it. But in the meantime, I felt a sense of cresting ardor that spilled over to embrace my classmates and the university as a whole. The shadows of freshman- and sophomore-year failure, of Rachel Polley and the Porcellian, seemed to fall away, and my affection for Harvard—given grudgingly for so long—felt purified and made new, just as the looming sting of graduation tinged it with melancholy.

Even my politics, long a factor in alienating me from the wider sweep of college life, seemed to bring me closer to my college classmates, to raise me higher in their estimation. It wasn't that people decided conservatives were right, exactly, in the shattered, fearful months after September 11, but there was a sense that perhaps we ought to at least be listened to, which at Harvard was no small thing. Indeed, for my right-wing writings, I was even named one of *FM*'s Fifteen Intriguing Seniors, alongside poor doomed Suzanne Pomey, whose charmed life had only weeks left to run.

FM gave the fifteen a dinner at Harvard Square's fanciest French bistro, where we were each expected to perform a composition that expressed something intimate about ourselves. I sang "Part of Your World" from *The Little Mermaid,* belting out the lyrics *I want to be where the people are,* coaxing my fellow intriguing people to sing along. *Bright young women,* we warbled, *sick of swimmin', ready to STAND* . . .

There were other small victories that autumn: a grand and gripping World Series, with bald eagles and "God Bless America" and a shocking Yankees loss to warm my vindictive New England heart. In the winter we had the Patriots, an unlikely team with an unlikely quarterback who brought happiness to the Quincy suite where my roommates and I watched the season's every snap, all the way to the gripping blizzard game against Oakland. After it was over and the Pats had won, we all ran outside, hurling ourselves into the drifts, shouting and throwing snowballs and making snow angels, just as the Patriots themselves were doing only fifty miles away.

Two weeks later, they were Super Bowl champions. *This year, we are all patriots,* the team's owner proclaimed that night, which could have been offensive but instead seemed perfectly appropriate— though perhaps not to Rams fans.

That same month, the first *Lord of the Rings* movie was released, and I dragged Alice to see it, despite her avowed dislike of fantasy. There in the darkened theater, wondering if she would like the movie (she would), wondering if I would ever muster the nerve to tell her I loved her (I would, but not till spring, after she had broken up with her boyfriend, and after some anguish, she would become my first and thus far only girlfriend, my first and thus far only love, which is an important story but a different one from this), I heard Cate Blanchett's Galadriel breathe the movie's opening line.

The world has changed, she said. *I feel it in the water. I feel it in the earth. I smell it in the air.*

The world has changed.

❖

I don't want to say, looking back, that this was all an illusion. The world did change that fall, our nation did go to war, the boom did come to end, Harvard did gain a new and vigorous president. Even at this early date, it's clear that the autumn's ripples will still be spreading years and decades hence.

But somehow I expected those ripples to affect Harvard, its students and recent graduates, and the larger elite culture in which we moved, far more than they did. I thought for a time that the spirit of 1990s Harvard—the spirit of the overstuffed résumé, of privilege without sacrifice, of ambition without ideals—might have been dealt a mortal wound, and that my generation's future would be sterner and brighter, like steel in winter's light. My classmates and I had always been successful, at least as our world defined success, but it seemed fleetingly that we might be offered a chance to be great.

Disillusionment came rapidly enough. It seeped in first with the realization, gained as graduation gave way to the beginning of real life, that we Harvardians would not be going to war. There was no call from Washington, no draft, not even an appeal for volunteers; we were told to resume our normal lives, not asked to take up arms. And so we did. In spite of the long nights spent researching the CIA and the chatter about the draft, there was no rush to join the military or the intelligence services, or even the government. Larry Summers could give as many speeches as he wanted, but ROTC wasn't coming back to campus even without the stumbling block of homosexuality. There simply weren't enough cadets to fill a Harvard brigade, both before September 11 and after.

A few of my friends did volunteer to serve, but they were people who would have anyway, with or without September 11—like Nate, who went into the air force; or Forth Shelby, who joined the State Department and as of this writing is in Iraq, trying to bring order to a Baghdad slum. Forth was not alone: Several of his Groton and Porcellian friends went into various branches of the service, as if some residue of the older world of noblesse oblige remained in those institutions and had rubbed off on them.

For the rest of us, though, joining the military or the CIA or the foreign service involved risking too much—not only our lives but our private ambitions, our dreams of fame or wealth or power. Throughout our youth, we had been encouraged to look out for ourselves, to compete ferociously for the prizes and honors and scores that marked success in the meritocratic world. We had been bred into a striving selfishness, and after such an education, I wonder if even a presidential call to arms would have convinced us to subordinate our own ends to those of the nation, to lose our egos and our résumés in the anonymity of the platoon or the embassy, Langley or Paris Island.

Maybe a real world war would have done it, but what came instead were fits and starts of conflict, quick military victories and muddy, bloody aftermaths. These wars, the wars of September 11, may well be remembered as a defining moment for my generation, but not for my generation of elites. Young Americans are fighting and dying in distant lands, but we are not among them; they are, for the most part, from middle-class and working-class families, groups decidedly underrepresented at Harvard. If, as Larry Summers suggested early that fall, September 11 offered a chance for reconciliation between America's elites and America's military, then that chance was rapidly squandered—much like the unity and moral clarity of that autumn, which collapsed so quickly into a feast of partisanship and recrimination, of neoconservative zeal and Deaniac rage.

Instead of going to war, we went out into the paths that had been prepared for us, and as the bracing shock faded, the attitudes that our education had instilled in us came rushing back. You could observe these attitudes on graduation day—in the rain-drenched Quincy House courtyard where our diplomas were officially handed out, after the larger Yard ceremony was over. One by one, in dripping mortarboards, we mounted the stage as a Quincy tutor reeled off our awards, offices, honors, and GPAs, and noted where each of us was going next—to Oxford! to Yale Law! to Mercer Management

Consulting!—while our parents cheered and eyed one another with ill-disguised competitiveness. (*Yes, that's ours—Harvard Med School, you know!*) For those students who hadn't yet found employment or chosen a career path, the tutor was left to trail off apologetically, as if in faint embarrassment. Mounting the platform, I was thankful that I had stumbled into a job late in May, in the most privileged way possible, when the new owner of *The Atlantic Monthly* decided to staff a Washington office and came hiring at the *Crimson*, because where else would you hire young talent but the most talented school in the world. . . .

You could see such pre–September 11 attitudes in Larry Summers as well, once the initial excitement surrounding his presidency faded, and he settled into the business of running Harvard. He liked to say in those early days that while most Harvard students would be embarrassed to admit never having read a Shakespeare play, few would be similarly ashamed to admit knowing nothing of the difference between a gene and a chromosome, or the definition of exponential growth. It was a nice thought, and one that segued neatly into Summers's long-term plan for expanded science and math requirements, for a focus on genomics research, for a vast new science campus across the Charles in Allston, where Neil Rudenstine had spent years buying up the city's land.

But it was also dead wrong. Nobody is required to read Shakespeare at Harvard (and few do), and it's not in the sciences where Harvard's educational mission is suffering, where rigor has waned, grade inflation expanded, and general drift taken hold. The sciences, broadly defined, dominate today's Harvard, and it's the conquering, calculating spirit of science that has driven the humanities into the shadows of theory, of postmodernism, of irrelevance. The fact that someone as brilliant as Summers could believe the opposite speaks volumes, I fear, about his prejudices and priorities.

I imagine that Summers will at least make a start at solving Harvard's superficial problems: the inflated grades, the lousy student-teacher ratio, the "approaches-to-knowledge" nonsense of the Core. Indeed, the Core has already been recommended for elimination, by a yearlong curricular review conducted after my graduation.

But the review also concluded, with painful obtuseness, that the main challenge facing Harvard undergraduate education is to ensure that every student be "educated in the sciences in a manner that is as deep and as broadly shared, as has traditionally been the case in the humanities and the social sciences." This is the vision of Summers, I fear, the vision of an economist and a man of the technocratic '90s who shares the prejudices of that age: toward the rule of the market, the importance of the quantifiable and the profitable, the ascendancy of science and technology. Prejudices that cripple liberal arts education.

To see the attitudes of pre–September 11 Harvard distilled to their unpleasant essence, though, you had to sift through the mass e-mails that circulated after graduation, after we had left the comforts of college and gone out to seek our fortunes in the wider meritocratic world. There was a formula to such messages—they were transparently designed to strut and preen, to parade accomplishments, to show that college was over but your rise had only just begun. *Hi all*, they would begin, *I just wanted to let you know that I've arrived in X* (usually New York or Washington, sometimes L.A. or London) *after an exhilarating summer spent doing Y* (working for NASA, assisting a fashion designer, helping to fix Argentina's currency). *I'll be here for a year doing Z* (a Gates Fellowship, an I-banking job, a gig with the White House speechwriting office) *and then it's off to a quick vacation in P* (Belize, Europe, Rio) *before I start at Q* (Morgan Stanley, Yale Law, Stanford Med). *Pretty crazy, huh? Oh, and check out the attached pictures!*

The worst of these e-mails strayed into my in-box two months after the start of the Iraq war, whose battles I watched in the bars of

Washington, D.C., surrounded by my fellow young American elites, all of us jawing about our jobs and our bosses, our summer plans and our long-term goals, while on the bank of televisions other young Americans fought and died far away, in Nasiriyah and Umm Qasr. The e-mail was sent by a girl named Alison Leary, another one of *FM*'s most intriguing seniors, now on a scholarship to England. She was writing to us ("to some of you for the first time in awhile," she allowed) because she felt compelled to "share the incredible experience" that she had just enjoyed at the Academy of Achievement's International Achievement Summit.

The Academy describes itself as a "non-profit organization dedicated to the education and inspiration of youth," and in the pursuit of this laudable goal it holds an annual conference at which overachieving graduate students—like the lucky Miss Leary—are feted, congratulated, and permitted to hobnob with the cream of the overclass elite. The list of dignitaries present that weekend in Washington included, by Alison's count, Colin Powell, Sandra Day O'Connor, Ruth Bader Ginsburg, "the incomparable Kathleen Battle," Bob Woodward, "Pulitzer Prize winner Herman Wouk," George Clooney, Steven Soderbergh, "another Pulitzer winner, Thomas Sheehan," Ben Bradlee, Hillary Clinton, John McCain, Trent Lott, Bill Frist, Tom Daschle— "the last 5 all speaking to us in the Senate Caucus Room"—Ralph Nader, Aretha Franklin, and "noted scientists." There was also Bill Clinton, who "molested" her hand; Shimon Peres, who kissed her cheek; Elie Wiesel, "a man of letters, a survivor, and a warrior for peace"; and "those pictured in my photo book, which I will send along."

Amid all this excitement—the dinner at the Naval Observatory, the speeches at the Lincoln Memorial and the Supreme Court, the Banquet of the Golden Plate on the final evening of the conference—it occurred to Alison that "since Commencement, I have been worried that while Harvard gave me so much awe, it also made me jaded about success and achievement." But "this event filled me with awe again—awe of what my peers have accomplished, awe for what the honorees have attained, and awe for what someone, even if it is only one person in this world, believes that I can achieve. My chest cavity swelled with pride to be dancing with such extraordinary people, in the room where the NATO treaty was signed, to live music. I had a feeling of being truly alive and I hope it stays with me for some time . . . as I stay in England this summer and work in Parliament . . . as I travel to the beaches of Normandy to honor those who gave their lives in WWII . . . as I travel back to the US and move to CA to start classes at Stanford in the fall . . . (which also provides you with a brief update on my life and plans!)."

It was all here, all that was loathsome about Harvard's culture—the frantic name-dropping, the boasting thinly disguised as bringing you up to date, even the bathetic nod to D-day and the Second World War. Most people weren't this smugly awful, of course, and Alison Leary's e-mail met with appropriate outrage among my friends. But mixed with our indignation was a none too subtle envy, a sense that her brazen darts had hit home, and that we despised her as much for being invited to this absurd gala as for writing about it so shamelessly. What was Harvard, after all, but the original Academy of Achievement? Hadn't we chosen it for the same sense of proximity to celebrity, of preordained success that swelled Alison Leary's chest as she danced "in the room where the NATO treaty was signed"? Didn't we share, in some sense, her obvious belief in worldly success—defined in terms of books published, riches earned, celebrity attained—as the sine qua non of human existence, the thing most deserving of "awe," the thing that we must never, ever become "jaded" about, the only thing that should make us feel "truly alive"?

Privilege, I have termed the sum of these poses and prejudices, though I don't mean the privilege of old—of social registers and massive Newport cottages, or farther back, of titles and family crests.

No, ours is the privilege that comes with belonging to an upper class grown large enough to fancy itself diverse; fluid and competitive enough to believe itself meritocratic; smart enough for intellectual snobbery but not for intellectual curiosity.

Such privilege is wonderfully self-sustaining. It brings just enough wealth and success and education to keep us floating safely above the "simple" idealisms of family, faith, and flag, yet not so much that we are tempted into the extremes of the older upper classes, with their taste for flagrant decadence or philosophic austerity. Not for us the zealous piety of the medievals, the enlightenment enthusiasms of the eighteenth century, or the imperialist adventures of the Victorians—and not for us the blowback that such enthusiasms risked, the religious wars and revolutions, the strife of decolonization. Our politics are moderate, our religious zeal nonexistent, our sex lives promiscuous but always safe. We are rich but not too rich, powerful but not too powerful, and there is no danger that we will succumb to sloth and excess—not when the cult of competition is so strong, the anxiety of affluence so sharp.

We have dropped the old ideals, but we still must believe in something, and so we believe in success. And God knows, nothing succeeds quite like it.

❖

On the last day of all, after the rains of commencement had passed and the campus lay steaming and empty in the sudden June sun, Nick and Nate and Siddarth and I drove west from Harvard along the same road that had carried me to college four years before, the Mass Pike and then I-91, going south toward the Connecticut border. We were in Nick's station wagon, headed for Six Flags New England and then back to campus for a final night of drinking, a last hurrah before we caught our early-morning trains and planes out of Boston, out of college, and into adult life.

It was just past noon and somewhere west of Worcester when the station wagon began to rattle and shake. We pulled over and discovered that the front tire was loose, shuddering on its axle as we drove. After some halfhearted attempts at fixing the problem, we swung into a nearby Jiffy Lube, whose manager suggested we try an auto shop in suburban Springfield, where we were dispatched to Sears to buy some indispensable part—and there was a brief trip to McDonald's because we were starving, and then a long stretch of waiting at the repair shop while the sun dropped and the day disappeared. It was nearly evening when we finally reached Six Flags, tired and carping at one another, and the parking attendant smiled and explained that the park was open for only another three hours, and it would cost us twenty-five dollars each, which was the reduced rate but seemed pretty unreasonable all the same.

"Why don't we go bowling instead?" someone suggested. So Nick threw the car in reverse and did a U-turn, ignoring the one-way sign and the squealing tires and the protests of the parking attendant, while we whooped and shouted, our good mood suddenly restored, our hopes for the day revived.

The first bowling alley we found was on a rise overlooking the Mass Pike, with an immense plaster statue looming over its deserted parking lot—a man in a white tuxedo and a white stovepipe hat, twenty feet tall and sporting a handlebar mustache. We cruised around his feet, searching in vain for some inscription or explanatory plaque, and then we gave up and went into a building that stank comfortably of beer and cigarettes and stale pizza. The proprietor took our money and handed out shoes without raising his eyes from a grainy black-and-white basketball game; a gang of strutting teenagers occupied the arcade, feeding quarters into Pac-Man and

Mortal Kombat and other relics of our childhood; at the far end of the alley, a group of fat old men smoked cigars in their undershirts. Otherwise we were alone, in a place where the ceiling leaked and the walls were stained and the carpets had turned brown with age, a place where our cell phones didn't work and there were no clocks to mark the hours. We drank pitchers of cheap beer and bowled for a long time and barely looked at our watches, and by the time we were finished, it was past twilight, past when we had planned to go.

Even then the others wanted to stay a little longer, to order another pitcher and play video games in the now empty arcade. But my head hurt and my cash had run out, and while they played, I wandered out into the parking lot, where night had fallen over the cracking pavement, the scattered cars, the looming statue.

It was one of those June evenings when the very darkness seems warm, the streetlamps out along I-90 pulsing humidly, the cars flashing down the highway in hot streaks of red and yellow light. I sat on the hood of Nick's car and waited for my friends, while the crickets stirred and the mosquitoes gathered and the last night of Harvard slipped away. Though people had been saying *College is over* with mordant satisfaction for months and months, practically since senior year began, this ending still felt sudden, unexpected, unfair.

Even so, college *was* over, because soon Nick and Siddarth and Nate would emerge from the bowling alley and realize, as I had already, that we had lingered here too long—that it was too late to go drinking in Cambridge, or to wander the campus a final time. Instead, we would sleep in the suburbs, at Nick's parents' house, and he would drive us into Boston early the following morning, and we might catch a glimpse of Harvard as we passed on Storrow Drive, a flash of brick and ivy, of blue and gold roofs glinting in the morning sun, but that would be all . . . and the next time we set foot on campus, it would be as alumni, as strangers, as trespassers in a world that had belonged to us once, but no longer and never again.

That was how college ended for me: waiting for my friends on the hood of a battered station wagon somewhere in the hills of Massachusetts, under the blank gaze of a top-hatted statue. Waiting to let go of Harvard; waiting for Harvard to let go of me.

Sometimes I think I am waiting still. Though three years have passed since then, there are times when I imagine myself still there, lingering in the darkness above the Mass Pike, expecting an end that doesn't come, a curtain that never falls. A Harvard education is not easily left behind, it turns out—the pull of privilege is too strong, my efforts to escape it too weak, too halfhearted. I have never braved danger, never feared for my life; the wars of my country are fought by other men. My Catholic faith is real, but so is my worldliness: I seek the approval of men far more than the favor of God. I chose journalism, with its traces of romance, over business, but I had no aptitude for the latter anyway, and my thirst for wealth and achievement is as great as any of my classmates. Even this book has been written as much in ambition as in idealism.

Yet I also wonder how much I really want to escape my education entirely, to shed my Harvard skin in favor of some purer, less polluted coat. This book has cast a cold eye upon my generation of elites—on our ambitions and our vices, our place in this country and in the world—but I hope the reader has also grasped how much I loved Harvard, my classmates and teachers but also the institution itself, the bricks and mortar and the traditions bound within them, tarnished though they might have been.

I love it, and I miss it even now—the lunatic schedules and sleepless nights, the angst and ambition, the protests and résumé-building. I miss slouching glum-faced to a lecture on a freezing February morning, and I miss stumbling home drunk at three on a warm spring night. I miss the few classes where I learned something worth knowing and the many classes where I didn't; I miss the hated final clubs, the cramped and squalid freshman-year rooms, the Living Wage Movement and the Symposium. I miss my friends—and I miss my enemies.

More than anything, I miss the place itself: the bustle and color of Harvard Square, swarming with tourists and gregarious bums; the cool green quiet that prevailed in odd corners of the Yard, in the shadow of fading Victorian inscriptions; the way the river looked in the snow, a white highway snaking west into New England. And the loveliness of Cambridge evenings: the spring nightfalls when the red-brick River Houses seemed to glow, faintly, in the slanting light; or the burned-out winter twilights, the dry grass and the slate-gray water and the sky darkening to a deep and wintry blue.

I hope, in the end, that I love Harvard as we should love the world: not because it is good (it is not) but because there is good in it, and things worth fighting for. Perhaps the rest will pass away, until in my memory and the memory of my classmates only the best remains, the beauty of the place and the promise of greatness, a promise that went unfulfilled in my four years but endures nonetheless—as if around another corner, through another ivied gate, there waits the university of our imagination, the Harvard of our unrequited dreams.